"The important news is that Mr. Lattimore has provided a generally self-consistent, personal, sanely literal version of the four texts most central to our tragic history. . . . It is an achievement that places us more deeply in his debt than any other in a long and diligent career."

—*The New York Times Book Review*

"It gives the reader an impression of these writings which is very close to that made by the original. . . . This is a valuable addition to existing translations." —*Library Journal*

"The importance of Lattimore's skilled and careful work and of his highly informed literary sense, is that you do indeed come away with a new and strong sense of who the reporters are. And when you know that, it expands the meaning of the story." —*The Boston Globe*

RICHMOND LATTIMORE, whose renderings of the *Iliad* and *Odyssey* of Homer, the odes of Pindar, and the plays of Aeschylus, Euripides and Aristophanes have set new standards for Greek translations, was for many years Professor of Greek at Bryn Mawr. He is also well known as a poet and as co-editor of *The Complete Greek Tragedies*. His honors include awards from the National Institute of Arts and Letters and the American Council of Learned Societies.

THE FOUR GOSPELS

AND THE
REVELATION

NEWLY TRANSLATED
FROM THE GREEK BY
Richmond Lattimore

WASHINGTON SQUARE PRESS
PUBLISHED BY POCKET BOOKS NEW YORK

A Washington Square Press Publication of
POCKET BOOKS, a Simon & Schuster division of
GULF & WESTERN CORPORATION
1230 Avenue of the Americas, New York, N.Y. 10020

Published by arrangement with Farrar, Straus & Giroux, Inc.
Library of Congress Catalog Card Number: 78-20880

ISBN: 0-671-41987-0

First Washington Square Press printing February, 1981

10 9 8 7 6 5 4 3 2 1

WASHINGTON SQUARE PRESS, WSP and colophon are
trademarks of Simon & Schuster.

Printed in the U.S.A.

CONTENTS

PREFACE

§ IT WAS WHILE I WAS TEACHING VARIOUS
Greek texts to beginning students that I was struck by
the natural ease with which *Revelation* turned itself into
English. I undertook the translation, and *The Revelation of John* appeared as a separate volume in 1962. I
have continued with the Four Gospels, but with many
interruptions for other tasks. *Revelation* went out of
print, and the publishers, Harcourt Brace Jovanovich,
kindly reverted the rights to me, so that we have been
able to add it, with some slight revision, to the Four
Gospels.

I have held throughout to the principle of keeping as
close to the Greek as possible, not only for sense and
for individual words, but in the belief that fidelity to the
original word order and syntax may yield an English
prose that to some extent reflects the style of the
original. The aim of at least some other contemporary
translators has been, avowedly, just the opposite: to be
faithful to the sense but to render it in contemporary
idiom. This is, of course, a perfectly legitimate aim, and
is part of the reason why there is room for a number of
modern translations.

Let me illustrate. I have translated *Mark* 10.27: "for
men it is impossible, but not for God, since for God all

things are possible." I could have written: "Men cannot do it, but God can do anything." That says the same thing, but does not reflect the way Mark wrote. At *John* 11.21 and 32, first Martha, then Mary say: "Lord, if you had been here, my brother would not have died." So I translated, and cannot claim originality, for the words are identical with those of the Revised Standard Version. I had thought that so simple a statement could be translated *only* in this one way. But I have not found it in any other translation that I have consulted.

Consider a more extended passage. For *Mark* 7.1-5 I have written: "Then the Pharisees gathered to him, and some of the scribes who had come from Jerusalem, seeing that some of the disciples were eating their bread with profane, that is, unwashed, hands: for the Pharisees, and all the Jews, will not eat unless they have washed hand against fist, thus keeping the tradition of their elders; and when they come from the marketplace they will not eat unless they have purified themselves, and there are many other observances that are traditional with them, the washing of cups and vessels both wooden and bronze: the Pharisees and the scribes asked him: Why do your disciples not walk according to the tradition of our elders, but eat their bread with profane hands?" Let me try to put this into what is more like a contemporary idiom: "The Pharisees, with some of the scribes, went out from Jerusalem to visit him. They noticed that some of his disciples ate without first washing their hands, which made their hands profane. The Pharisees and the Jews in general observe a tradition handed down from their ancestors not to eat without first washing their hands thoroughly. When they come in from the marketplace they will not eat until they have purified themselves. They have many other such traditions, like washing their cups, whether these are made of wood or bronze. Because of all this the Pharisees and the scribes asked Jesus: Why do your disciples disobey our ancestral tradition by eating with profane hands?"

Now, other modern translators have modernized this passage much more successfully than I have. My heart is not in this kind of rearrangement of the syntax. Still, all the essential meaning is there. But to me it reads much less like Mark than the version which stands in my translation.

It will follow, or should, that since each of the Gospels, and *Revelation*, is the work of a different author with a different style, they should read differently in English. I noted that *Revelation* seemed to translate itself, and my aim has been to let all of my texts translate themselves with as little interference as possible. But it is not always so easy. To go from *Revelation* to *Matthew* is like going from Ruskin to Carlyle. *Mark* in particular offers problems. Since Mark is, by general if not universal consent, the earliest evangelist, we start with his gospel. Matthew and Luke drew on him extensively, but constantly saw fit to rewrite him after their own manners. He can, as illustrated above, be abrupt and crabbed. Also, the nature of the language itself produces difficulties. There are some terms, such as the various forms of *skandalon* (see note on *Matthew*, page 269), which cannot always be translated in the same way, which really cannot be translated at all, but for which the translator will have to devise some kind of paraphrase which will convey the essential sense.

To this end also, I have written some simple notes, to explain my translations or give alternative interpretations. Without competence to comment on the manuscript tradition, I have simply followed the text of Westcott and Hort, *The New Testament in Greek* (New York: Macmillan, 1957). The rare exceptions have been noted. Words enclosed in square brackets are of doubtful authenticity. I have also regularly consulted *The Pelican Gospel Commentaries*, namely, D. E. Nineham, *Saint Mark;* J. C. Fenton, *Saint Matthew;* G. B. Caird, *Saint Luke;* and John Marsh, *Saint John.*

MARK

Mark is believed to have written his gospel after Peter's death in Rome, which is presumed to have been around A.D. 64. It is generally agreed that Mark's is the earliest of the four gospels.

§ THE BEGINNING OF THE GOSPEL OF JESUS Christ. As it is written in Isaiah the prophet: Behold, I send forth my messenger before your face, who will make ready your way. The voice of one crying in the desert: prepare the way of the Lord, make straight the roads before him. John the Baptist was in the desert preaching the baptism of repentance for the remission of sins. And all the land of Judaea came out to him and all the people of Jerusalem, and they were baptized by him in the river Jordan, confessing their sins. John was clothed in camel's hair, and a belt of hide around his waist, and he ate locusts and wild honey. And he preached, saying: He who is stronger than I is coming after me, and I am not fit to stoop down and untie the thong of his shoes. I baptized you with water, but he will baptize you with the Holy Spirit.

And it happened in those days that Jesus came from Nazareth in Galilee and was baptized in the Jordan by

3

John. And as soon as he came out of the water he saw the skies split and the Spirit like a dove descending upon him; and there came a voice from the skies, saying: You are my son whom I love, with you I am well pleased. And immediately the Spirit drove him out into the desert. And he was in the desert forty days, being tested by Satan, and he lived with the wild animals, and the angels served him.

After John was betrayed Jesus came into Galilee preaching the gospel of God, saying: The time is fulfilled and the Kingdom of God is near. Repent and believe in the gospel. And as he went along past the Sea of Galilee, he saw Simon and Andrew the brother of Simon casting their nets in the sea, for they were fishermen. And Jesus said to them: Come, follow me, and I will make you fishers of men. And at once they left their nets and followed him. And going on a little farther he saw James the son of Zebedee and John his brother, these also in their boat mending their nets. And at once he called them. And leaving their father Zebedee in the boat with the hired workers they went away, and followed him.

They came into Capernaum. And at once on the sabbath he went into the synagogue and taught; and they were astonished at his teaching, for he taught them as one who has authority and not like the scribes. And immediately in their synagogue there was a man possessed by an unclean spirit, and he cried out, saying: What is there between us and you, Jesus of Nazareth? Did you come to destroy us? I know you, who you are, God's holy one. Jesus reproved him, saying: Be silent and go out from him. And convulsing him and crying out in a great voice the unclean spirit went out of the man. All were amazed, so that they took counsel together, saying: What is this thing: a new kind of teaching? By his authority he gives orders even to unclean spirits, and they obey him. And immediately the rumor of him spread into the whole region about Galilee.

When they came out of the synagogue, they went
immediately to the house of Simon and Andrew, along
with James and John. And Simon's mother-in-law was
lying in a fever, and they told him about her forthwith.
He went over and took her by the hand and raised her;
and the fever left her, and she served them. When it
was evening, after the sun set, they brought to him all
those who were ill, and those afflicted with demons,
and the whole city was assembled before his door. And
he healed many who were ill with various diseases, and
he cast out many demons, and would not let them
speak, because they knew him. Then very early in the
morning he got up and went out to a lonely place, and
there he prayed. Simon and his companions went in
search of him, and found him, and said to him: All are
looking for you. He said to them: Let us go elsewhere,
to the neighboring communities, so that I may preach
there also; for that is what I set out to do. And he went
into all of Galilee preaching in the synagogues and
casting out demons.

A leper came to him and entreated him, saying: If
you wish, you can make me clean. He took pity on him,
and stretched out his hand and touched him, saying: I
wish it; be clean. And at once the leprosy went from
him, and he was made clean. Then he sent him away at
once with a stern order, saying: See that you tell no
one, but go and show yourself to the priest, and bring
him the gift for your purification that Moses ordained,
as a proof to them. But the man went out and began to
talk about it at length and spread the story about, so
that Jesus could no longer come openly into the city,
but must remain outside in unfrequented places. And
they came to him from every direction.

§ When he returned to Capernaum, it became known,
after a few days, that he was in a house there; and so
many gathered that there was no space before the door
and he preached the word to them. They came bringing

him a paralytic who was carried aloft by four men. When they could not reach him because of the crowd, they took away the roof from over the place where Jesus was, and when they had made an opening they lowered the bed where the paralytic lay. Jesus seeing their faith said to the paralytic: My child, your sins are forgiven. There were some of the scribes sitting by, and they said to themselves in their hearts: Why does this man talk this way? He blasphemes. Who can forgive sins, except God alone? Jesus knew at once in his mind what they were saying to themselves, and said: Why do you have such thoughts in your hearts? Which is easier, to say to the paralytic: Your sins are forgiven, or to say: Arise, take up your bed and walk about? But so that you may know that the son of man has authority to forgive sins upon earth—he said to the paralytic: I tell you, rise, take up your bed, and go to your house. And the man arose and took up his bed and went out, in the sight of all; so that all were astonished and glorified God, saying: We have never seen the like.

He went back to the seaside; and all the multitude came to him, and he taught them. As he went by, he saw Levi the son of Alphaeus sitting in the tollhouse, and said to him: Follow me. And he stood up and followed him. And it happened that he dined in his house, and many tax collectors and sinners dined with Jesus and his disciples; for there were many of them, and they followed him. The scribes of the Pharisees, seeing that he ate with sinners and tax collectors, said to his disciples: Why does he eat with tax collectors and sinners? Jesus heard them, and said to them: The strong do not need a physician, but those who are in poor health. I did not come to summon the just, but the sinners.

The disciples of John, and the Pharisees, were fasting. And they came and said to him: Why do the disciples of John and the disciples of the Pharisees fast, but your disciples do not fast? Jesus said to them: Surely the members of the wedding party cannot fast while the bridegroom is with them? For as long a time as they have the bridegroom with them they cannot fast. The days will come when the bridegroom is taken away from them; then on that day they will fast. No one sews a patch of unfulled cloth on an old coat; if he does, the new filling pulls from the old and makes the tear worse. And no one puts new wine into old skins; if he does, the wine will break the skins, and both wine and skins are lost.

It came about that on the sabbath he went walking through the sown fields, and his disciples began to pick the ears of grain as they went. And the Pharisees said to him: Why are your disciples doing what is forbidden on the sabbath? He said to them: Have you never read what David did when he was in need, and hungry, he himself and those with him? He went into the house of God when Abiathar was high priest, and ate the show bread, which none but the priests are permitted to eat, and gave it also to those who were with him. And he said to them: The sabbath was made for the sake of man, not man for the sake of the sabbath. Thus the son of man is lord even of the sabbath.

§ Once again he entered the synagogue, and there was a man there with an arm that was withered. They were watching him to see if he would heal him on the sabbath, so that they might bring a charge against him. Jesus said to the man with the withered arm: Come out into our midst. Then he said to them: Is it permitted to do good or evil on the sabbath, to save a life or destroy it? They were silent. He looked around at them in anger, exasperated at the hardness of their hearts, and said to the man: Stretch out your arm. And he stretched it out, and it became sound again. Then the Pharisees went out and immediately began plotting against him, together with the Herodians, to destroy him.

Then Jesus with his disciples withdrew to the seashores, and a great multitude followed from Galilee, and from Judaea and from Jerusalem and from Idumaea and from beyond the Jordan and the region of Tyre and Sidon; a great multitude came to him when they heard what he was doing. And he told his disciples that they should secure a boat for him, because of the crowd, so that they should not crush him; for he healed many, so that they thrust in upon him, to have those who were in torment touch him. And the unclean spirits when they saw him fell down before him and cried out, saying: You are the son of God. And he charged them many times not to divulge what he was doing.

Then he went up on the mountain and summoned to him those whom he had chosen; and they went forth and joined him. He made the number twelve, whom he named apostles, so that they might be with him, and so that he might send them forth to preach and to have authority to cast out demons. He established the twelve, Peter, the name he gave to Simon, and James the son of Zebedee and John the brother of James (and he gave them the name Boanerges, which means sons of thunder), and Andrew and Philip and Bartholomew and Matthew and Thomas and James the son of Alphaeus and Thaddeus and Simon the Cananaean and Judas Iscariot, who in fact betrayed him.

Then he went into a house; and the crowd gathered again, so that they could not even eat their bread. When his own people heard of this, they went forth to get control of him, for they said that he was out of his mind. And the scribes who had come down from Jerusalem said that Beelzebub had hold of him, and that it was through the prince of the demons that he drove out demons. He called them to him and said to them through parables: How can Satan drive out Satan? And if a kingdom is divided against itself, that kingdom cannot stand. And if a house is divided against itself, that house will not be able to stand. And if Satan rises up against himself and is divided, he cannot stand

but comes to an end. But no one can go into the house
of the strong man and seize his goods, unless first he
binds the strong man; then he can plunder his house.
Truly I tell you, all shall be forgiven the sons of men,
their sins and such blasphemies as they may speak; but
if one blasphemes against the Holy Spirit, he shall have
no forgiveness ever, but shall be guilty of everlasting
sin. This was because they said he had an unclean spirit.
Then his mother and his brothers came and stood
outside and sent one in to summon him. The crowd was
seated around him, and they said to him: See, your
mother and your brothers are outside looking for you.
He answered and said to them: Who is my mother and
who are my brothers? And looking about at those who
were sitting in a circle around him, he said: Here is my
mother, here are my brothers; whoever does the will of
God is my brother and sister and mother.

§ Once again he began to teach beside the seashore.
And the greatest multitude gathered to hear him, so
that he went aboard the ship and was seated out to sea,
and all the multitude was on shore facing the sea. He
taught them a great deal in parables, and said to them
in his discourse: Listen. Behold, a sower went out to
sow. And it happened as he sowed that some of the
grain fell beside the way, and birds came and ate it.
Some fell on stony ground where there was not much
soil, and it shot up quickly because there was no depth
of soil; and when the sun came up it was parched and
because it had no roots it dried away. Some fell among
thorns, and the thorns grew up and stifled it, and it bore
no fruit. But some fell upon the good soil, and it bore
fruit, and shot up and increased, and yielded thirtyfold
and sixtyfold and a hundredfold. And he said: He who
has ears, let him hear. When they were alone, his
followers along with the twelve asked him about the
parables. He said to them: To you are given the secrets
of the Kingdom of God; but to those who are outside

all comes through parables, so that they may have sight but not see, and hear but not understand, lest they be converted and forgiven. And he said to them: You did not read this parable? Then how shall you understand all the parables? The sower sows the word. And these are the ones beside the way where the word is sown, and as soon as they hear it Satan comes and snatches the word that has been sown among them. And there are some who are as if sown on stony ground, who when they hear the word accept it with joy; and they have no roots in themselves but are men of the moment, and when there comes affliction and persecution, because of the word, they do not stand fast. And others are those who were sown among thorns; these are the ones who hear the word, and concern for the world and the beguilement of riches and desires for other things come upon them and stifle the word, and it bears no fruit. And the others are those who were sown upon the good soil, who hear the word and accept it and bear fruit thirtyfold and sixtyfold and a hundredfold. Then he said to them: Surely the lamp is not brought in so as to be set under a basket or under the bed rather than to be set on a stand; for there is nothing hidden except to be shown, nor anything concealed except to be brought to light. He who has ears to hear, let him hear. And he said to them: Consider what you hear. Your measure will be made by the measure by which you measure, and more shall be added for you. When a man has, he shall be given; when one has not, even what he has shall be taken away from him. And he said: The Kingdom of God is as when a man sows his seed in the ground, and sleeps and wakes night and day, and the seed grows and increases without his knowing it; for of itself the earth bears fruit, first the blade, then the ear, then the full grain in the ear. But when the grain gives its yield, he puts forth the sickle, for the time of harvesting is come. And he said: To what shall we liken the Kingdom of God, and in what parable shall we place it? It is like the seed of mustard, which when it is sown in the ground is smaller than all the seeds on earth, but when it has been sown, it shoots up and becomes greater than all the other greens, and puts forth great branches, so that the birds of the air may nest in its shadow. With many such parables he spoke the word to them, according to what they could comprehend; but he did not talk with them except in parables; but privately with his own disciples he expounded all.

That same day when it was evening he said to them: Let us cross over to the other side. They sent away the multitude and took him along on the ship just as he was, and there were other ships with him. There came a sudden great storm of wind, and waves dashed against the ship so that it was beginning to fill. He was in the stern asleep with his head on his pillow; and they woke him and said: Master, do you not care whether we perish? He woke and scolded the wind and said to the sea: Silence, be still. And the sea subsided and there was a great calm. Then he said to them: Why are you frightened? Do you not yet have faith? And they were seized with a great fear and said to each other: Who is this, that the wind and sea obey him?

§ They reached the other side of the sea and the land of the Gerasenes. As Jesus stepped from the ship, a man possessed by an unclean spirit came out of the tombs and met him. He had made his dwelling among the tombs, and nobody could now bind him with chains; because he had often been bound with chains and fetters, and the chains had been torn apart by him and the fetters pounded to pieces, and no one was strong enough to subdue him. Day long and night long he was among the tombs and the hills, crying aloud and beating himself with stones. Seeing Jesus from afar he ran to him and bowed down before him and cried out in

a great voice, saying: What have I to do with you,
Jesus, son of the most high God? I adjure you before
God, do not torment me. For Jesus had been saying to
him: Go forth, unclean spirit, from the man. And he
asked him: What is your name? He answered: My
name is Legion, because we are many. And he
implored him at length not to send them out of the
country. By the hillside there was a great herd of swine
feeding; and the spirits implored him, saying: Send us
into the swine, so we may enter into them. He
consented. And the unclean spirits came forth and
entered into the swine, and the herd rushed over the
cliff into the sea, as many as two thousand, and were
drowned in the sea. Those who had been herding them
fled and carried the news to the city and the countryside; and people came to see what had happened. Then
they came up to Jesus, and they saw the man who had
been possessed by demons sitting clothed and in his
right mind, the man who had had the legion, and they
were frightened. Those who had seen told them how it
had happened with the man possessed by demons, and
about the swine. And they began to entreat him to
leave their territory. As he boarded the ship, the man
who had been afflicted by demons asked if he could go
along with him. Jesus refused him and said: Go home to
your people and tell them what your lord did for you
and how he took pity on you. And he went, and began
to report in the Decapolis what Jesus had done for him.
And all marveled.

After Jesus had crossed with his ship back to the
other side, a crowd gathered about him; and he was by
the sea. And there came to him one of the leaders of
the synagogue, Jairus by name, and when he saw him
he fell at his feet and implored him at length, saying:
My little daughter is at the point of death; so come and
lay your hands upon her, so that she may recover and
live. He went with him; and a great throng followed,
and they were crowded against him. There was a

woman who had been bleeding for twelve years, and had been treated in many ways by many physicians, and had spent all that she had, and got no benefit but rather got worse; she had heard about Jesus, and she came up behind him in the crowd and touched his mantle; for she said to herself: If I touch only his mantle I shall be healed. And immediately the source of her flow of blood dried up, and she knew in her body that she had been healed of her affliction. Immediately Jesus felt in himself that power had gone forth from him, and he turned about and said: Who touched my mantle? His disciples said to him: Do you see the throng that is crowding upon you, and yet do you ask: Who touched me? And he looked around to see who had done it. And the woman, in fear and trembling, knowing what had happened to her, threw herself down before him and told him the whole truth. He said to her: My daughter, your faith has saved you; go in peace and be healed of your affliction. While he was still talking, they came from the house of the leader of the synagogue saying: Your daughter has died; why do you continue to trouble the master? Jesus disregarded the talk that was going on and said to the leader of the synagogue: Have no fear, only have faith. And he would not let anyone follow him except Peter and James and John the brother of James. They entered the house of the leader of the synagogue, and he was aware of a great tumult, and people weeping and lamenting greatly, and going in he said to them: Why this tumult and weeping? The child has not died, she is asleep. They laughed at him. He drove out all the others, and took with him the father and mother of the child and those who were with him, and went in where the child was; and he took the child's hand, and said to her: Talitha cum; which is, translated: Little girl, I say to you: Awake. At once the little girl got up and walked about, for she was twelve years old. They were seized with great amazement. And he charged them at length that no one should be told

about this; and he said she should be given something
to eat.

§ He left that place and went to his own country, and
his disciples followed him. When it was the sabbath he
began to teach in the synagogue; and most of those who
heard him were astonished and said: From where does
the man derive all this, and what is this wisdom that has
been given to him, and what are these powers that are
fulfilled by his hands? Is not this the carpenter, the son
of Mary and the brother of James and Joseph and Judas
and Simon? And are not his sisters here among us?
And they made it difficult for him. Jesus said to them:
No prophet is rejected except in his own country, and
among his own kinsmen, and in his own house. And he
could not exercise any power there, except that he laid
his hands on a few who were sick and healed them; and
he marveled at their lack of faith.

He circulated among the villages, teaching. And he
summoned the twelve and began to send them out two
by two, and he gave them power over unclean spirits,
and he instructed them not to take anything with them
for the journey, except only a staff, no bread, no bag,
no coppers for the money belt, with sandals on their
feet, and no extra tunic. And he said to them: Once you
enter a house, remain there until you leave the district.
And when a place will not receive you and people will
not listen to you, as you leave it shake the dust from the
soles of your feet in witness against them. And they
went forth and preached the message of repentance,
and drove out many demons, and anointed with oil
many who were sick, and healed them.

Now King Herod heard of this, for the name of Jesus
had become well known to him; and they were saying
that John the Baptist had risen from the dead, and for
that reason the powers were working in him. But others
said that it was Elijah, and others that it was a prophet,
like one of the Prophets. But when Herod heard of it,

he said: This is John whom I beheaded. He has arisen. For Herod himself had sent men out and seized John and confined him in prison, on account of Herodias the wife of Philip his brother and his marriage to her. For John had said to Herod: It is not lawful for you to take the wife of your brother. Herodias held a grudge against him and wished to kill him, but she was not able to; for Herod was afraid of John, knowing that he was a just and holy man, and he kept him safe; and when he listened to him he was much perplexed, and yet he listened with pleasure. Then her opportunity came when Herod on his birthday gave a banquet for the nobles and captains and foremost people of Galilee; and the daughter of Herodias came before them and danced, and she pleased Herod and his guests. And the king said to the girl: Ask me what you wish and I will give it to you. And he swore to her: Whatever you ask me for I will give you, up to half of my kingdom. She went out and said to her mother: What shall I ask for? She said: The head of John the Baptist. So she hastened back to the king and made her request, saying: I wish you to give me forthwith the head of John the Baptist, on a platter. Though the king was grieved, because of the oaths and the guests he was unwilling to deny her; and immediately he sent a guardsman with orders to bring back his head. And the man went and beheaded him in the prison and brought his head on a platter and gave it to the girl, and the girl gave it to her mother. When his disciples heard of it they came and took up the body and laid it in a tomb.

The apostles rejoined Jesus and reported all they had done and all their teaching. He said to them: Come with me, you only, to a private place and rest a while. For there were many coming and going and they had no opportunity even to eat. And they went away on their ship, privately, to a deserted place. But many saw them going and were aware of them, and from all the cities they ran together on foot to that place, and arrived there before them. When he came ashore, he saw a great multitude, and he was sorry for them because they were like sheep without a shepherd, and he began to teach them at length. As it was growing very late, his disciples came to him and said: This is a lonely place and the time is late. Send them away so they may go to the farms and the villages round about and buy themselves something to eat. He answered and said to them: You give them something to eat. They said to him: Shall we go and buy two hundred denarii worth of loaves and give them to them to eat? But he said to them: How many loaves do you have? Go and see. When they had found out, they said: Five, and two fish. He gave them orders that all should be set down party by party on the green grass; and they took their places group by group, fifty and a hundred at a time. Then he took the five loaves and the two fish, and looked up into the sky, and gave a blessing, and broke the loaves and gave them to his disciples to set before them; and he divided the two fish among all. And all ate, and were fed; and they took up enough broken pieces of bread and fish to fill twelve baskets. Those who ate the loaves were five thousand men.

Immediately then he made his disciples board the ship and go on before him to the other side, to Bethsaida, while he was dismissing the multitude. When he had taken leave of them, he went off to the mountain to pray. When it was evening the ship was in the middle of the sea, and he was alone on the land. And seeing that they had to struggle to row, for the wind was against them, about the fourth watch of the night he came to them walking on the sea. He meant to pass by them. But when they saw him walking on the sea, they thought he was a phantom, and cried out; for they all saw him and they were shaken. At once he talked with them and said: Take heart, it is I. Do not fear. He went aboard the ship and was among them, and the wind fell. But they were still all too much disturbed, for they had not understood about the loaves, but their hearts had become impenetrable.

They crossed over to the other shore and came to Gennesaret and moored there. And when they disembarked, people at once recognized him, and overran that whole country and began to bring their afflicted out on litters wherever they heard that he was. And wherever he went, into villages and cities and farms, and in the public places, they set down their sick, and begged that these might only touch the hem of his mantle. And those who touched it were healed.

§ Then the Pharisees gathered to him, and some of the scribes who had come from Jerusalem, seeing that some of the disciples were eating their bread with profane, that is, unwashed, hands: for the Pharisees, and all the Jews, will not eat unless they have washed hand against fist, thus keeping the tradition of their elders; and when they come from the marketplace they will not eat unless they have purified themselves, and there are many other observances that are traditional with them, the washing of cups and vessels both wooden and bronze: the Pharisees and the scribes asked him: Why do your disciples not walk according to the tradition of our elders, but eat their bread with profane hands? He said to them: Well did Isaiah prophesy concerning you hypocrites, as it is written: This people honors me with the lips, but their heart is far away from me; they worship me vainly, teaching doctrines which are the precepts of men: relinquishing the commandment of God you cling to the tradition of men. And he said to them: You do well to reject the commandment of God so that you may keep your own tradition. For Moses said: Give due right to your father and mother; and: Let him who speaks rudely to his father or mother be put to death. But you say: If a man says to his father or his mother: Whatever I owe you is Corban, which means "gift to God," then you no longer let him do anything for his father or mother, making void the word of God through that tradition which you hand down. And you do many other things of such a nature as this.

Then he summoned the multitude once again and said to them: Listen to me and understand. There is nothing which can go into a man from the outside and defile him; but it is what comes out of a man that defiles him. And when he went indoors, away from the multitude, his disciples asked him about the parable. He said to them: Are even you so unable to understand? Do you not see that anything that goes into a man from the outside cannot defile him, because it passes not into the heart but into the belly, and thence goes into the privy? Thus he made all food clean. Then he said: What comes out of a man, that is what defiles him; for from inside the hearts of men proceed the vile thoughts, fornications, thefts, murders, adulteries, greedy dealings, vices, trickery, laxity, the vicious eye, blasphemy, pride, wildness. All these vicious things come from inside, and they defile a man.

He removed from there and went to the region around Tyre. There he entered a house and wished that no one should know him, but he could not remain hidden. Immediately a woman whose little daughter was possessed by an unclean spirit heard about him, and she came and threw herself at his feet. This was a Greek woman, by birth a Phoenician from Syria; and she asked him to drive out the demon from her daughter. He said to her: First let the children be fed; for it is not good to take the bread of the children and throw it to the dogs. But she answered him and said: Yes, Lord, even the dogs under the table eat of the children's crumbs. He said to her: Because of this saying, go; the demon has left your daughter. And she went back to her house and found the child lying on her bed, and the demon was gone.

Returning again from the region of Tyre, he went by way of Sidon to the Sea of Galilee through the middle of the Decapolis territory. They brought him a man who was deaf and could barely speak, and entreated him to lay his hand upon him. Then taking him away from the throng by himself, he put his fingers into the man's ears, and spat, and touched his tongue, and looked up into the sky and groaned and said to him: Ephphatha, which means: Be opened. And his ears were opened, and the binding of his tongue was dissolved, and he spoke normally. He charged them to tell no one but the more he charged them the more they spread the news. And they were very much astonished, saying: He has done everything well, and he makes the deaf hear and the speechless speak.

§ In those days, when there was once again a great multitude and they did not have anything to eat, Jesus called his disciples to him and said to them: I have pity for the multitude, because it is now three days they have stayed with me, and they have nothing to eat; and if I send them home hungry they will give out on the way. And some of them come from far away. His disciples answered him, saying: How shall we have enough bread in the desert to be able to feed these people? He asked them: How many loaves do you have? They said: Seven. Then he gave the word to the people to settle on the ground, and he took the seven loaves and gave thanks and broke them and gave them to his disciples to set before the people; and they set them before the multitude. And they had a few small fish; and he blessed them and told them to serve these also. And they ate and were fed, and they picked up what was left over from the broken pieces, seven baskets full. There were about four thousand people. Then he sent them away; and immediately embarking on the ship with his disciples he made for Dalmanutha and those parts.

Then the Pharisees came forth and began to argue with him, demanding that he give them a sign from the sky, making trial of him. He groaned in his spirit and

said: Why does this generation ask for a sign? Truly I
tell you, no sign shall be given to this generation. Then
he left them, and going on board once more he crossed
over to the other side. They had forgotten to take bread
and except for one loaf they had nothing with them on
the ship. He enjoined them, saying: Look to it, beware
of the leaven of the Pharisees and the leaven of Herod.
They were talking among themselves about not having
bread. And he was aware of it and said to them: Why
do you talk about not having bread? Do you not yet
see, do you not understand? Are your hearts impenetrable? Do you have eyes, but do not see, and ears, but
do not hear? And do you not remember when I broke
the five loaves for the five thousand, how many baskets
full of fragments you picked up? And they told him:
Twelve. And when it was seven for the four thousand,
how many basketfuls of fragments did you pick up?
And they told him: Seven. And he said to them: Do
you still not understand?

They came to Bethsaida. And they brought him a
blind man and entreated him to touch him. And he
took the blind man's hand and brought him away
outside the village, and spat in his eyes, and laid his
hands on him, and asked him: Do you see anything? He
looked again and said: I see people, like seeing trees
walking about. Then again he put his hands over his
eyes, and the man looked hard, and recovered, and saw
all things clearly. And Jesus sent him home, saying: Do
not even go into the village.

Then Jesus and his disciples went forth to the villages
of Caesarea Philippi; and on the way he questioned his
disciples, asking them: Who do people say that I am?
They answered and said: John the Baptist; and others
say Elijah, and others one of the prophets. Then he
asked them: And you, who do you say I am? Peter
answered and said to him: You are the Christ. Then he
warned them to tell no one about him.

Then he began to explain to them that the son of man
must suffer much and be rejected by the elders and the

high priests and the scribes, and be killed, and rise up after three days. He was telling them frankly. And Peter laid his hand upon him and tried to warn him, and he turned about and looked at his disciples and reproved Peter and said: Go behind me, Satan; because you do not think the thoughts of God, but of men.

Then summoning the multitude together with his disciples, he said to them: If anyone wishes to go after me, let him deny himself and take up his cross and follow me. For he who wishes to save his life shall lose it; and he who loses his life for the sake of me and the gospel shall save it. For what does it advantage a man to gain the whole world and pay for it with his life? What can a man give that is worth as much as his life? He who is ashamed of me and my words in this adulterous and sinful generation, of him will the son of man be ashamed when he comes in the glory of his father with the holy angels.

§ And he said to them: Truly I tell you that there are some of those who stand here who will not taste of death until they see the Kingdom of God arrived in power.

Then after six days Jesus took with him Peter and James and John, and led them up on a high mountain, alone, by themselves. And he was transfigured before them, and his clothing turned very white, gleaming with a whiteness no fuller on earth could give. And Elijah was seen by them, with Moses, and they were talking with Jesus. And Peter spoke forth and said to Jesus: Master, it is good for us to be here; and let us make three shelters, one for you and one for Moses and one for Elijah. For he did not know what to say, for they were very frightened. And there came a cloud that covered them, and there came a voice from the cloud: This is my son whom I love; listen to him. And suddenly looking around they could no longer see anyone with them, except Jesus alone. As they came

down from the mountain he charged them that they
should tell no one what they had seen, except when the
son of man should rise up from the dead. And they kept
his commandment, while questioning among themselves what it might mean to rise from the dead. And
they questioned him, saying: What do the scribes mean
that first Elijah must come? He said to them: Elijah
shall come first and restore all things. And how is it
written about the son of man, that he must suffer much
and be set at nought? But I say to you that Elijah came
and they did with him as they wished, as it is written
about him.

As they returned to the disciples, they saw a great
crowd about them, and scribes arguing with them. And
as soon as they saw him all the multitude were greatly
amazed, and at once they ran up to him and greeted
him. And he asked them: What are you discussing with
them? A man in the crowd answered him: Master, I
have brought my son to you. He has a speechless spirit.
And when this seizes upon him, it batters him, and he
foams and his teeth chatter, and he wastes away. I told
your disciples to drive it out, and they were not able to.
He answered and said to them: O generation without
faith, how long shall I be with you? How long shall I
endure you? Bring him to me. And they brought him to
him. When he saw Jesus, the spirit at once convulsed
the boy, and he fell on the ground and rolled about,
foaming. Then Jesus asked the father: How long has
this been happening to him? He said: Since he was
little; and many times it has thrown him into fire and
into water, to destroy him. But if you can, take pity on
us and help us. Jesus said to him: If you can? All things
are possible to him who believes. At once the father of
the boy cried out and said: I believe. Help my unbelief.
Jesus seeing that the crowd was growing around him
admonished the unclean spirit, saying to it: You
speechless deaf spirit, I command you, go forth from
him, and never enter him again. And the spirit, with
much screaming and struggling, went out of the boy;

and he became like a corpse, so that most of the people
said he had died. But Jesus took him by the hand and
raised him up, and he stood. When he had gone
indoors, his disciples asked him privately: Why were we
not able to drive it out? He said to them: This kind
cannot be made to go forth except by prayer.

Going from there they proceeded through Galilee,
and he did not want anyone to be aware of them; for he
was teaching his disciples, and telling them: The son of
man will be turned over into the hands of men, and
they will kill him; and three days after being killed he
will rise up. But they did not understand what he said,
and they were afraid to ask him.

They came to Capernaum; and when he was indoors,
he asked them: What were you talking about on the
way? They were silent, for they had been talking on the
way about who was the greatest. He sat down and
called the twelve and said to them: Whoever wishes to
be first must be last of all and servant of all. And taking
a child he set him in the midst of them, and embraced
him, and said: Whoever accepts a child like one of
these in my name, accepts me; and he who accepts me
accepts not me but him who sent me.

John said to him: Master, we saw a man driving out
demons in your name, and we tried to stop him,
because he was not one of our following. But Jesus
said: Do not stop him; for there is no one who will
exercise power in my name and then will be able to
speak ill of me. For he who is not against us is for us.
For if anyone gives you a cup of water to drink because
you are named as being Christ's, truly I tell you he shall
not lose his reward. And if anyone misleads one of
these little ones who have faith, it were better for him
to have a millstone hung about his neck and be thrown
into the sea. And if your hand makes you go amiss, cut
it off; it is better for you to go into life one-handed than
with both hands to wander off into Gehenna, into the
quenchless fire. And if your foot makes you go amiss,
cut it off; it is better for you to go into life lame than

with both feet to be thrown into Gehenna. And if your
eye makes you go amiss, pluck it out; it is better for you
to go one-eyed into the Kingdom of God than with both
eyes to be thrown into Gehenna, where their worm
does not die and the fire is not quenched. For everyone
will be salted with fire. Salt is good; but if the salt is salt
no more, with what will you season it? Keep the salt in
yourselves, and be at peace with each other.

§ Removing from there, he went into the territory of
Judea and beyond the Jordan, and again crowds
gathered about him, and again he taught them as he
was accustomed to do. And Pharisees came to him and
asked him whether it were lawful for a man to divorce
his wife, making trial of him. He answered and said to
them: What did Moses decree for you? They said:
Moses permitted a man to write a note of divorce, and
so divorce her. But Jesus said to them: It was for your
hardness of heart that he wrote you this commandment. But from the beginning of creation God made
them male and female. Because of this a man will leave
his father and his mother, and they will be two in one
flesh. So that they are no longer two but one flesh.
Then what God has joined together let man not
separate. At the house his disciples questioned him
again about this. And he told them: He who divorces
his wife and marries another is committing adultery
against her, and if she has divorced her husband and
marries another she is committing adultery.

And they brought children to him, so that he might
lay his hands on them. And his disciples scolded them.
But seeing this, Jesus was vexed and said to them: Let
the children come to me and do not prevent them; for
of such is the Kingdom of God. Truly I tell you, he who
does not receive the Kingdom of God like a child may
not enter into it. And he embraced them and blessed
them, laying his hands upon them.

As he set forth on his way, a man ran up and knelt

before him and asked him: Good master, what must I
do to inherit life everlasting? Jesus answered: Why do
you call me good? No one is good but God alone. You
know the commandments: Do not murder, do not
commit adultery, do not steal, do not bear false
witness, do not defraud; honor your father and your
mother. He said to him: Master, I have kept all these
commandments from my youth. Jesus looked at him
with affection and said: One thing you lack: go sell all
you have and give it to the poor, and you shall have a
treasury in heaven; and come and follow me. He was
downcast at that saying and went sadly away; for he was
one who had many possessions. Jesus looked around at
his disciples and said: How hard it will be for those with
money to enter the Kingdom of God. His disciples were
astonished at his words. But Jesus spoke forth again
and said to them: My children, how hard it is to enter
the Kingdom of God; it is easier for a camel to pass
through the eye of a needle than for a rich man to enter
the Kingdom of God. They were very much astonished
and asked him: Who then can be saved? Jesus looked at
them and said: For men it is impossible, but not for
God, since for God all things are possible. Peter began
to say to him: See, we have given up everything and
followed you. And Jesus said: Truly I tell you, there is
no one who has given up house or brothers or sisters or
mother or father or children or lands for the sake of me
and the gospel who will not receive a hundredfold [now
in this time, houses and brothers and sisters and
mothers and children and lands, with persecutions],
and in the time to come life everlasting. And many who
are first shall be last, and many who are last shall be
first.

They were on the road going up to Jerusalem, and
Jesus was leading the way, and they were amazed, and
those who followed were afraid. And taking the twelve
again, he began to tell them what was going to happen
to him: Behold, we are going up to Jerusalem, and the
son of man will be given over to the high priests and the

scribes, and they will condemn him to death, and give him over to the Gentiles, and they will mock him and spit upon him and flog him, and kill him, and after three days he will rise.

Then James and John, the sons of Zebedee, came up to him and said: Master, we wish you to do for us whatever we ask you to. He said to them: What do you wish me to do for you? They said to him: Grant us that in your glory we may sit one on your right and one on your left. Jesus said to them: You do not know what you are asking. Can you drink the cup which I drink, or be baptized with the baptism with which I am baptized? They said to him: We can. Jesus said to them: You shall drink the cup which I drink, and be baptized with the baptism with which I am baptized; but to sit on my right or on my left, that is not mine to give, but it is theirs for whom it has been made ready. When the other ten heard about it, they began to be indignant over James and John. And Jesus called them to him and said: You know that those who are supposed to rule over the Gentiles act as lords over them and their great men exercise power over them. It is not thus with you; but he who wishes to be great among you shall be your servant, and he who wishes to be first among you shall be the slave of all; for the son of man came not to be served but to serve, and to give his own life for the redemption of many.

And they came to Jericho. And as he was on his way out of Jericho with his disciples and a considerable multitude, Bartimaeus the son of Timaeus, a blind beggar, was sitting by the road. And hearing that it was Jesus of Nazareth, he began to cry aloud and say: Jesus, son of David, have pity on me. And many people told him angrily to be quiet, but he cried out all the more: Son of David, have pity on me. And Jesus stopped and said: Call him. And they called the blind man, saying to him: Take heart, rise up, he is calling you. He threw off his mantle and sprang to his feet and went to Jesus.

Jesus spoke forth and said: What do you wish me to do for you? The blind man said to him: Master, let me see again. And Jesus said to him: Go; your faith has healed you. And at once he could see again, and he followed him on his way.

§ When they came near Jerusalem, to Bethphage and Bethany, at the Mount of Olives, he sent two of his disciples ahead and told them: Go into the village that lies before you, and presently as you go in you will find a colt, tethered, on which no man has ever ridden. Untie him and bring him. And if anyone says to you: Why are you doing this? say: His master needs him; and he will return him to this place at once. And they went and found a colt tethered by the door, outside in the street, and they untied him. And some of those who were standing there said to them: What are you doing, untying the colt? They answered as Jesus had told them; and they let them be. And they brought the colt to Jesus, and they piled their clothing upon the colt, and he sat on him. And many strewed their clothing in the road, and others strewed branches they had cut in the countryside. And those who went before him and who came after him cried aloud: Hosanna. Blessed is he who comes in the name of the Lord. Blessed is the kingdom of our father David that is coming. Hosanna in the highest! And he entered into Jerusalem, into the temple; and after looking about at everything, since the time was now late, he went out to Bethany with the twelve.

On the next day as they went out from Bethany, he was hungry; and seeing in the distance a fig tree which had leaves, he went to see if he could find anything on it; and when he reached it he found nothing but the leaves, for it was not the season for figs. Then he spoke forth and said to it: May no one eat fruit from you any more, forever. And his disciples heard him.

They came to Jerusalem. And he went into the temple and began to drive out those who sold and bought in the temple, and he overturned the tables of the money changers and the stalls of the sellers of doves, and he would not let anyone carry any vessel through the temple, and he taught them and said: Is it not written that: My house shall be called a house of prayer for all the nations? But you have made it into a den of robbers. And the high priests and the scribes heard him, and looked for a way to destroy him; for they feared him, for all the populace was smitten with his teaching.

When it was late, they went forth from the city.

As they passed by in the morning they saw the fig tree dried up, from the roots; and Peter remembered and said to him: Master, see, the fig tree which you cursed is dried up. Jesus answered and said to them: Have faith in God. Truly I tell you, if one says to this mountain: Rise up and throw yourself into the sea, and does not deliberate in his heart but believes that what he talks about is happening, it shall be his. Therefore I tell you, all that you pray for and ask for, believe that you get it, and it shall be yours. And when you stand praying, forget anything you have against anyone, so that your father in heaven may forgive your transgressions.

They returned to Jerusalem. And as he walked about in the temple, the high priests and the scribes and the elders came to him and said: By what authority do you do this? Or who gave you this authority, to do these things? Jesus said to them: I will ask you one thing, and you answer me, and I will tell you by what authority I do this. Was the baptism of John from heaven or from men? Answer me. They discussed this among themselves, saying: If we say: From heaven, he will say: Then why did you not believe him? But if we say: From men—They were afraid of the people, for these all held John to be truly a prophet. And they answered Jesus and said: We do not know. And Jesus said to them:

Neither will I tell you by what authority I do these things.

§ Then he began to talk to them in parables: A man planted a vineyard and ran a fence about it and dug a pit for the wine press and built a tower, and let it out to farmers and left the country. And when the time came, he sent a slave to the farmers to receive from the farmers some of the fruits of the vineyard. And they took him and lashed him and sent him away empty-handed. And again he sent them another slave; and they broke the head of that one and outraged him. And he sent another; and that one they killed; and many others, lashing some, killing some. He had one more, a beloved son; he was the last he sent them, saying: They will respect my son. But they, the farmers, said among themselves: This is the heir. Come, let us kill him and the inheritance will be ours. And they took him and killed him, and threw him out of the vineyard. What will the lord of the vineyard do? He will come and destroy the farmers, and give the vineyard to others. Have you not read this scripture: The stone that the builders rejected has come to be at the head of the corner. It was made by the Lord, and is wonderful in our sight. They were looking for a way to seize him; also they were afraid of the people. They knew that the parable he told was directed against them. They let him be and went away.

Then they sent him some of the Pharisees and Herodians to try to catch him up in what he said. And they came, and said to him: Master, we know that you are truthful and care for no man, for you are no respecter of persons but teach the way of God truthfully. Is it lawful to pay the assessment to Caesar or not? Shall we give or not give? He knew their hypocrisy and said to them: Why do you tempt me? Bring me a denarius so I may look at it. They brought him one. He said to them: Whose is the image and whose name is inscribed? They said: Caesar's. And Jesus said: Give Caesar what is Caesar's and God what is God's. And they wondered at him.

Sadducees also came to him, who say that there is no resurrection, and they questioned him, saying: Master, Moses wrote for us: If a man's brother dies and leaves a wife, but has no children, the brother should take the wife and raise up issue for his brother. There were seven brothers. The first took a wife, and died and left no issue. And the second took her, and died without leaving issue, and the third likewise. All seven left no issue. Last of all the woman also died. In the resurrection, whose wife shall she be, of these men? For all seven had her as wife. Jesus said to them: Is this not why you go astray, through knowing neither the scriptures nor the power of God? For when they rise from the dead they do not marry nor are they married but are as the angels in heaven. And as for the dead, that they waken, have you not read in the book of Moses, at the bush, how God spoke to him saying: I am the God of Abraham and the God of Isaac and the God of Jacob? God is not God of the dead but of the living. You are far astray.

Then one of the scribes, who had listened to their discussion and knew that he had answered them well, came to him and asked him: Which is the first commandment of all? Jesus answered: The first is: Hear, Israel, the Lord our God the Lord is one; and you shall love the Lord your God with all your heart and all your spirit and all your mind and all your strength. This is the second: You shall love your neighbor as yourself. There is no other commandment greater than these. The scribe said to him: Well said, master; what you said is true, that he is one and there is no other but he; and to love him with all the heart and all the understanding and all strength, and to love one's neighbor as oneself, is worth more than all the burnt offerings and the sacrifices. And Jesus, perceiving that he had answered intelligently, said: You are not far from the Kingdom of God. And no one dared question him after that.

And Jesus spoke forth and said, as he taught in the temple: How is it that the scribes say that the Christ is the son of David? David himself said, under the Holy Spirit: The Lord said to my lord: Sit on my right so that I may put your enemies beneath your feet. David himself calls him lord. Then how can he be his son?

And the masses heard him with pleasure. And in his teaching he said: Turn away from the scribes who desire to walk about in their robes, who desire the salutations in the public places and the first seats in the synagogues and the foremost couches at the dinners, who eat up the houses of the widows, and pray long as an excuse. The greater the condemnation these will receive.

Then he sat down across from the treasury and watched how the multitude put coins into the treasury. And many rich people put in many coins. And there came a poor widow who put in two half pennies, that is, one penny. Calling his disciples to him, he said to them: Truly I tell you, this widow, who is poor, has put in more than all who have put money into the treasury. For they all put in out of their surplus, but out of her deficit she gave all that she had, her whole livelihood.

§ As he was leaving the temple, one of his disciples said to him: See, master, what stones, what buildings! And Jesus said to him: Are you looking at the great buildings? Nothing here will escape destruction and no stone will be left on another. Then he sat down on the Mount of Olives opposite the temple, and Peter and James and John and Andrew asked him privately: Tell us when this shall be, and what will be the sign when all these things are to be accomplished. And Jesus began to tell them: See to it that no one leads you astray. For many will come in my name, saying: I am he. And they will lead many astray. And when you hear of wars and the rumors of wars, do not be frightened. This must be, but the end is not yet. For nation shall rise up against nation and kingdom against kingdom, there will be earthquakes in the lands, there will be famines. This is the beginning of the agony. And look to yourselves. They will turn you over to the councils and you will be lashed in the synagogues, and you will be set before leaders and kings because of me, to testify to them. And first the gospel must be preached to all the peoples. And when they turn you over and bring you to trial, do not take any forethought for what you will say, but whatever is given to you in that hour, say it, for it will not be you who speak but the Holy Spirit. And brother will betray brother to death, and the father his child, and children will rise up against their parents and work their death; and you will be hated by all because of my name. But he who endures to the end will be saved. But when you see the abomination of desolation standing where it should not—and let him who reads this take note of it—then let those who are in Judea flee to the mountains, and let him who is on his housetop not come down or go inside to take up anything from his house, and let him who is in the field not turn back to pick up his coat. Woe to the women who are with child and the women who are nursing in those days. Pray that it will not come in the wintertime; for those days will be an affliction such as there has not been from the beginning of creation, which God created, until now, and may not be again. And if the Lord had not cut short the days, no flesh would be saved; but for the sake of the chosen, whom he chose, he did cut short the days. And then, if someone says to you: See, here is the Christ; see, he is there, do not believe him. For false Christs and false prophets will rise up, and they will present signs and portents to mislead the chosen, if that may be done. Be watchful; I have foretold all to you. But in those days after that affliction, the sun will be darkened and the moon will not give her light, and the stars will be falling out of the sky, and the powers in the skies will be shaken. And then they will see the son of man coming in the clouds with great power and glory; and then he will send out his angels and gather his chosen together from the four winds, from the end of the earth to the end of the sky. From the fig tree learn its parable. When its branch is tender and it puts forth leaves, you know that the summer is near; so also you, when you see these things happening, know that he is near, at your doors. Truly I tell you that this generation will not pass by before all these things are done. The sky and the earth will pass away but my words will not pass away. But concerning that day and the hour none knows, not the angels in heaven or the son, only the father. Be watchful and wakeful; you do not know when the time will come; as when a man has gone on a journey and left his house and given his slaves charge over it, to each his task, and told the doorkeeper he must be watchful. Be watchful then, you do not know when the lord of the house is coming, in the evening or at midnight or at cock-crow or in the morning; lest he come suddenly and find you sleeping. What I say to you I say to all: be watchful.

§ After two days, it would be the Passover and the feast of Unleavened Bread. And the high priests and the scribes were looking for a way to capture him by treachery and kill him; for they said: Not during the festival, for so there will be rioting among the people.

And when he was in Bethany in the house of Simon the leper, and at dinner, a woman came with an alabaster vessel full of ointment of nard, pure and precious; and she broke open the jar and poured the ointment over his head. But there were some who grumbled among themselves: Why was there this waste of ointment? The ointment could have been sold for upward of three hundred denarii and the money given to the poor. And they scolded her. But Jesus said: Let her be. Why are you hard on her? She has done a good

thing for me. For always you have the poor with you,
and you can do them good whenever you will, but you
do not always have me. She did what she could, she
took the opportunity to anoint my body in advance for
my burial. Truly I tell you, wherever the gospel is
preached through all the world, what she did will also
be spoken of, in memory of her.

And Judas Iscariot, he who was one of the twelve,
went off to the high priests, so as to betray him to them.
And they were pleased when they heard him and
promised to give him money. And he looked for an
easy opportunity to betray him.

Now on the first day of Unleavened Bread, when
they used to sacrifice the paschal lamb, his disciples said
to him: Where do you wish us to go and make
preparations for you to eat the feast of the Passover?
He sent forth two of his disciples, and told them: Go
into the city, and a man carrying a pot of water will
meet you. Follow him, and wherever he enters, say to
the master of the house: The master says: Where is my
guest chamber where I can eat the Passover dinner with
my disciples? And he will show you a large upper room,
furnished and ready. There prepare for us. And the
disciples went forth, and went into the city, and found
all as he had told them, and made ready the Passover.
When it was evening, he arrived with the twelve. And
as they were at table and eating, Jesus said: Truly I tell
you that one of you will betray me, the one who is
eating with me. They began to be bitterly hurt, and to
say, one by one: Surely, not I? He said to them: One of
the twelve, the one who dips into the dish with me;
because the son of man goes his way as it has been
written concerning him, but woe to that man through
whom the son of man is betrayed. It were well for that
man if he had never been born. And as they ate, he
took a loaf of bread and blessed it and broke it and gave
it to them and said: Take it; this is my body. And he
took a cup and gave thanks and gave it to them, and
they all drank from it. And he said to them: This is my

blood, of the covenant, which is shed for the sake of many. Truly I tell you that I will not again drink of the produce of the vine, until I drink it, new wine, in the Kingdom of God.

And they sang the hymn and went out to the Mount of Olives. And Jesus said to them You will all be made to fail me; for it is written: I will strike the shepherd, and the sheep will be scattered; but after my resurrection I will lead the way for you into Galilee. But Peter said to him: Even if all fail you, yet I will not. Jesus said to him: Truly I tell you that in this very night, before the cock crows twice, you will disown me three times. But he said very forcefully: Even if I must die with you, I will never disown you. And so said they all.

They came to a place whose name is Gethsemane, and he said to his disciples: Sit down here while I pray. And he took with him Peter and James and John; and then he began to be shaken and distressed, and he said to them: My soul is in anguish to the point of death. Stay here and keep watch. And going forward a little he threw himself on the ground, and prayed that, if it were possible, the hour might pass him by. And he said: Abba, father, for you all things are possible. Remove this cup from me. But not what I wish, but what you wish. He went back and found them sleeping, and said to Peter: Simon, are you sleeping? Were you not strong enough to keep watch for a single hour? Be wakeful, and pray, that you may not be brought to the test. The spirit is eager, but the flesh is weak. And going back again he prayed, in the same words. And coming back again he found them sleeping, for their eyes were heavy, and they did not know how to answer him. And he came a third time and said to them: So you are still asleep and resting. It is enough. The hour has come; behold, the son of man is betrayed into the hands of sinners. Rise up, let us go; see, my betrayer is near.

Immediately, while he was still speaking, Judas came, one of the twelve, and with him a crowd, with swords and clubs, from the high priests and the scribes

and the elders. He who betrayed him had told them the
sign to watch for, saying to them: The one I kiss will be
the man. Seize him, and take him away, carefully. And
right upon his arrival he came up to him and said:
Master; and kissed him. And they laid hands on him
and bound him. But one of his supporters drew his
sword and struck the slave of the high priest and took
off his ear. Then Jesus spoke forth and said to them:
You come out with swords and clubs to arrest me as if I
were a highwayman? Day by day I was near you in the
temple, teaching, and you did not seize me. But let the
scriptures be fulfilled.

And all left him and fled away.

And there was a certain young man who had been
following him, wearing a linen garment over his bare
skin. And they seized him, and he fled naked, leaving
the linen garment behind.

They took Jesus away to the high priest, and all the
high priests and the elders and the scribes assembled.
And Peter had followed him from a distance, into the
courtyard of the high priest, and he was sitting there
with the servingmen and warming himself at the fire.
And the high priests and the entire council were
looking for some evidence against Jesus so that they
could have him killed, and they could find none; for
many brought false witness against him, and their
testimony did not agree. And some stood up and
testified falsely against him, saying: We have heard him
say: I will tear down this temple which was made with
hands, and in three days I will build another, not made
with hands. But not even so did their testimony agree.
Then the high priest stood up among them and
questioned Jesus, saying: Have you no answer? What is
this testimony that they bring against you? But he was
silent and did not answer. Again the high priest
questioned him and said: Are you the Christ, the son of
the Blessed One? Jesus said: I am he, and you will see
the son of man sitting on the right of the power and

coming with the clouds of the sky. The high priest tore his clothing and said: Why do we still need witnesses? Did you hear the blasphemy? What is your view? They all judged that he deserved death. Then some began to spit upon him, and to cover his face and then beat him with their fists and say to him: Prophesy. And the servingmen took him over and beat him.

And while Peter was below in the courtyard there came one of the serving girls of the high priest, and seeing Peter warming himself, she looked at him and said: You also were with the Nazarene, with Jesus. But he denied it, saying: I neither know nor understand what you mean. And he went out into the forecourt. But the girl saw him and began saying once more to those who were standing by: This is one of them. Once more he denied it. And after a little while those who were standing by said to Peter: Truly you are one of them, since you are a Galilaean. Then he began to swear and to say on oath: I do not know the man of whom you speak. And thereupon the cock crowed for the second time. And Peter remembered what Jesus had told him: Before the cock crows twice you will disown me three times. And he threw himself down and wept.

§ Early the next day the high priests with the elders and the scribes and the entire council held a meeting: and they bound Jesus and took him away and gave him over to Pilate. And Pilate asked him: Are you the King of the Jews? He answered him and said: It is you who say it. And the high priests brought many charges against him. And Pilate again asked him: Have you no answer? See how much they charge you with. But Jesus gave no further answer, so that Pilate was amazed.

For the festival, he used to release to them one prisoner, whichever one they asked for. The man called Barabbas was imprisoned among the insurgents who had done murder during the uprising. And the crowd came up and began to demand that he do by them according to his custom. Pilate answered them, saying: Do you wish me to release your King of the Jews? For he perceived that they had handed him over for spite. But the high priests stirred up the crowd, so that he might rather give them Barabbas. Pilate once again spoke to them and said: What then shall I do with the man you call the King of the Jews? And they cried out once more: Crucify him. Pilate said to them: Why? What harm has he done? But they screamed all the more, saying: Crucify him. So Pilate wishing to satisfy the crowd released Barabbas to them, and had Jesus scourged and gave him over to be crucified.

The soldiers led him inside the court, that is, the residence, and they called up their whole battalion. They clothed him in purple and wove a wreath of thorns and put it on him. And they began to acclaim him with: Hail, King of the Jews. And they beat him about the head with a reed, and spat upon him, and going down on their knees they did obeisance to him. And after they had mocked him, they took off the purple and put his own clothes on him. And they led him out, to crucify him. And a certain Simon of Cyrene, the father of Alexander and Rufus, was passing by on his way in from the country, and they impressed him for carrying the cross. And they took him to the place Golgotha, which translated is the Place of the Skull. And they offered him wine mixed with myrrh, which he would not take. And they crucified him, and divided up his clothes, casting lots for them, for who would take which. It was the third hour and they crucified him. And the charge against him was inscribed: The King of the Jews. And with him they crucified two robbers, one on his right and one on his left. And those who passed by blasphemed against him, wagging their heads and saying: Ha, you would tear down the temple and rebuild it in three days, save yourself by coming down from the cross. So likewise the high priests, mocking him together, along with the scribes, said: He saved others, he cannot save himself. Let the annointed, the King of Israel, come down now from the cross, so that we may see and believe. And those who were crucified with him also spoke abusively to him.

And when it was the sixth hour, there was darkness over all the earth until the ninth hour. In the ninth hour Jesus cried out in a great voice: Elōi elōi lama sabachthanei? Which translated is: My God, my God, why have you forsaken me? Then some of those who were standing there said: See, he calls to Elijah. And someone ran up with a sponge soaked in vinegar and put on the end of a reed and offered it to him to drink, saying: Come, let us see if Elijah will come to bring him down. But Jesus uttered a great cry and breathed his last. And the veil of the temple was split in two from top to bottom. And when he saw that he thus breathed his last, the centurion who was posted across from him said: In truth this man was the Son of God. And there were women watching from a distance, among them Mary the Magdalene, and Mary the mother of James the lesser and Joses, and Salome, who when he was in Galilee had followed him and served him, and many others who had come up with him to Jerusalem.

By nightfall, when it was the Day of Preparation, which is the day before the sabbath, there arrived Joseph of Arimathaea, a reputable member of the council who himself was also looking for the Kingdom of God; and he took courage and went into the presence of Pilate and asked for the body of Jesus. But Pilate thought it very strange if he were already dead, and summoning the centurion he asked if he had died yet; and when he learned from the centurion that he had, he presented the corpse to Joseph. And Joseph bought linen, and took him down and wrapped him in the linen, and laid him in a tomb which had been cut in

the rock, and rolled a stone against the door of the
tomb. And Mary the Magdalene and Mary the mother
of Joses were watching where he was laid.

§ And when the sabbath was over, Mary the Magdalene and Mary the mother of James and Salome bought
spices so that they might go and anoint him. And very
early on the first day of the week they went to the tomb,
where the sun had risen. And they were saying to each
other: Who will roll away the stone for us, out of the
door of the tomb? Then looking again they saw that the
stone, which was very large, had been rolled away.
And going into the tomb they saw a young man sitting
in the right-hand part, wearing a white robe. And they
were startled into amazement. But he said to them: Do
not be thus amazed. You are looking for Jesus the
Nazarene, who was crucified. He has risen, he is not
here. See the place where they laid him. But go and tell
his disciples, and Peter: He goes before you into
Galilee. There you will see him, as he told you. And
they went out and fled from the tomb, for trembling
and panic had hold of them. And they said nothing to
anyone, for they were afraid.

[Then after he had risen early on the first day of the
week, he appeared first to Mary the Magdalene, from
whom he had cast out seven demons. She went and told
the news to those who had been with him, who were
mourning and weeping; and they, when they heard that
he was alive and had been seen by her, did not believe
her. After that he appeared to two of them as they were
walking. It was in another form and they were on their
way into the country. And they too went back and told
the news to the others; but neither did they believe
them. Later he appeared to the eleven themselves as
they were at dinner, and he had blame for their lack of
faith and the insensitivity of their hearts, because they
had not believed those who had seen him risen from the
dead. And he said to them: Go out into the whole

world and preach the gospel to all creation. He who believes and is baptized shall be saved, but he who does not believe shall be condemned. And here are the signs that will go with the believers: In my name they will cast out demons, speak with tongues, hold snakes, and if they drink something lethal it cannot harm them, and they will lay their hands on the sick and these will be well.

After talking with them the Lord was taken up into heaven and sat down on the right of God. And they went forth and preached everywhere, the Lord working with them and confirming their message through the signs that accompanied them.]

[They reported briefly to Peter and his companions all that they had been told. And after that Jesus himself sent forth through them, from east to west, the holy and imperishable proclamation of everlasting salvation.]

MATTHEW

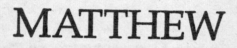

Matthew is believed to date from A.D. 75 at the latest, but incorporating written accounts from an earlier date.

§ THE BOOK OF THE ORIGIN OF JESUS
Christ the son of David the son of Abraham.

Abraham was the father of Isaac, and Isaac of Jacob,
Jacob of Judah and his brothers, and Judah of Perez
and Zarah by Tamar, and Perez of Hezron, and Hezron
of Ram, and Ram of Aminadab, and Aminadab of
Nahshon, and Nahshon of Salmon, and Salmon of Boaz
by Rahab, and Boaz of Obed by Ruth, and Obed of
Jesse, and Jesse of David the King. David was the
father of Solomon by the wife of Uriah, Solomon of
Rehoboam, Rehoboam of Abijah, and Abijah of Asa,
and Asa of Jehosaphat, and Jehosaphat of Joram, and
Joram of Uzziah, and Uzziah of Jotham, and Jotham of
Ahaz, and Ahaz of Hezekiah, Hezekiah of Manasseh,
Manasseh of Amos, and Amos of Josiah, and Josiah of
Jechoniah and his brothers, at the time of the Babyloni-
an migration. After the Babylonian migration Jechoni-
iah was the father of Salathiel, Salathiel of Zerubbabel,

Zerubbabel of Abiud, and Abiud of Eliakim, Eliakim of Azor, and Azor of Zadok and Zadok of Achim, Achim of Eliud, Eliud of Eleazar, Eleazar of Matthan, and Matthan of Jacob, and Jacob of Joseph the husband of Mary, from whom was born Jesus who is called the Christ.

Thus all the generations from Abraham to David are fourteen, and from David until the Babylonian migration fourteen generations, and from the Babylonian migration until Christ fourteen generations.

The birth of Jesus Christ came in this way: Mary his mother was engaged to Joseph, but before they came together she was found to be with child, by the Holy Spirit. And Joseph her husband, being a righteous man and not desiring to make her notorious, wished to put her away secretly. But as he was considering this, behold, the angel of the Lord appeared to him in a dream, saying: Joseph son of David, do not fear to accept Mary your wife, for what is conceived in her is of the Holy Spirit. And she will bear a son, and you shall call his name Jesus; for he shall save his people from their sins. All this was done in order that the word of the Lord might be fulfilled which was spoken through his prophet, saying: Behold, the maiden shall conceive in her womb, and she shall bear a son, and they shall call his name Emmanuel; which translated means, God is with us. And Joseph wakening from his sleep did as the angel of the Lord had told him, and he accepted his wife, and did not know her as a wife until she had borne a son. And he called his name, Jesus.

§ When Jesus was born in Bethlehem in Judaea in the days of Herod the King, behold, Magians from the east came to Jerusalem, saying: Where is he who is born King of the Jews? For we saw his star in the east and have come to worship him. And hearing this King Herod was disturbed, and all Jerusalem with him, and calling together all the high priests and the scribes of the people he asked them where the Christ was born. And they said to him: In Bethlehem of Judaea; for thus it is written by the prophet: You also, Bethlehem, in the land of Judah, are by no means the least among the leaders of Judah; for out of you will come a leader who will be a shepherd of my people, Israel.

Then Herod called in the Magians secretly and found from them the exact time when the star had appeared, and sent them to Bethlehem, saying: Go and learn exactly about the child, and when you find him, bring back the news to me, so that I too may go and worship him. And they after hearing the King went on their way, and behold, the star, which they had seen in the east, led them until it came and stood above the place where the child was. And when they saw the star they were filled with a very great joy. Then going into the house they saw the child with Mary his mother, and they threw themselves down and worshipped him, and opening their strongboxes they proffered him gifts, gold and frankincense and myrrh. Then having been warned in a dream not to turn back to Herod, they went away by another road to their own country.

When they had gone, behold, an angel of the Lord appeared to Joseph in a dream, saying: Awake, take the child and his mother, and escape into Egypt, and remain there until I tell you. For Herod means to seek out the child to destroy him. Then he woke and took the child and his mother by night and went away into Egypt, and was there until the death of Herod; so that there might be fulfilled the word spoken by the Lord through his prophet, saying: Out of Egypt I have called my son.

Then Herod, seeing that he had been outwitted by the Magians, was very angry, and sending out his men, he killed all the boy children in Bethlehem and all its outlying regions, those two years old or less, according to the time he had reckoned from the Magians. Then was fulfilled the word spoken by Jeremiah the prophet, saying: A voice was heard in Rama, weeping and much lamentation, Rachel weeping for her children, and she would not be comforted because they are gone.

Now when Herod died, behold, an angel of the Lord appeared in a dream to Joseph in Egypt, saying: Awake, take the child and his mother and go to the land of Israel; for those who sought the life of the child are dead. And he wakening took the child and his mother and went to the land of Israel. But hearing that Archelaus was King in Judaea in the place of his father Herod, he was afraid to go back there, and being warned in a dream, he withdrew to the region of Galilee, and reaching there settled in a city called Nazareth; so as to fulfill the word spoken by the prophets: He shall be called a Nazarene.

§ In those days came John the Baptist preaching in the desert of Judaea, saying: Repent; for the Kingdom of Heaven is near. He was the one who was mentioned by Isaiah the prophet, saying: The voice of one crying in the desert: prepare the way of the Lord, straighten the roads before him. This John wore clothing made of camel's hair, and a belt of hide around his waist, and his food was locusts and wild honey. At that time Jerusalem came to him, and all Judaea and all the country about Jordan, and they were baptized by him in the river Jordan, confessing their sins. And seeing many of the Pharisees and Sadducees coming to baptism, he said to them: You viper's brood, who warned you to flee from the anger to come? Then produce fruit which is worthy of your repentance; and do not think to say among yourselves: We have Abraham for our father. For I say to you that out of these stones God can raise up children to Abraham. And by now the ax is set against the root of the trees; so that every tree that does not bear good fruit is cut out and thrown into the fire. I baptize you in water for repentance, but he who is coming after me is stronger than I, and I am not fit to carry his shoes; he will baptize you in the Holy Spirit and fire; his winnowing fan is in his hand, and he will clear his threshing floor and gather his grain into his storehouse and burn the chaff in quenchless fire.

Then came Jesus from Galilee to the Jordan and to John to be baptized by him. But he tried to prevent this, saying: I need to be baptized by you. And you come to me? But Jesus answered and said to him: Bear with me now; for so it is right for us to fulfill our whole duty. Then he consented. And when Jesus was baptized, at once he came out of the water, and behold, the skies opened, and he saw the Spirit of God coming down like a dove, descending upon him, and behold, a voice from the skies was heard saying: This is my son whom I love, in whom I am well pleased.

§ Then Jesus was led out into the desert by the Spirit, to be tested by the devil. And he fasted forty days and forty nights, and after that he was hungry. And coming up to him the tempter said: If you are the son of God, speak and make these stones become loaves of bread. But he answered, saying: It is written: not by bread alone shall man live, but in every word that issues through the mouth of God. Then the devil took him to the holy city and set him on the gable of the temple and said to him: If you are the son of God, throw yourself down; for it is written: He will charge his angels concerning you, and on their hands they will support you, so that never may you strike your foot against the stone. Jesus said to him: Again, it is written: You shall not tempt the Lord your God. Once more the devil led him to a very high mountain, and showed him all the kingdoms of the world and their glory, and said to him: All this I will give you if you will throw yourself down and worship me. But Jesus said to him: Go, Satan; for it is written: You shall worship the Lord your God, and shall serve him only. Then the devil let him be; and behold, angels came and served him.

When he heard that John had been betrayed, he

withdrew into Galilee, and leaving Nazareth he came
and settled in Capernaum by the sea, in the districts of
Zebulun and Naphthali; so as to fulfill the word spoken
by Isaiah the prophet, saying: Land of Zebulun and
land of Naphthali, way to the sea, beyond Jordan,
Galilee of the Gentiles, the people who were sitting in
darkness saw a great light, they were sitting in the land
of the shadow of death, and the light dawned on them.

From that time Jesus began to preach and to say:
Repent; for the Kingdom of Heaven is near.

And as he walked by the Sea of Galilee he saw two
brothers, Simon who was called Peter and Andrew his
brother, casting their net into the sea, for they were
fishermen. And he said to them: Come now and follow
me, and I will make you fishers of men. And at once
they left their nets and followed him. And as he went
on from there he saw two more brothers, James the son
of Zebedee and John his brother, in the boat with
Zebedee their father, mending their nets. And he
called them. And at once leaving the boat and their
father they followed him.

And he went all over Galilee teaching in their
synagogues and preaching the gospel of the kingdom
and treating every sickness and every infirmity among
the people. And the fame of him went into all Syria;
and they brought him all who were in bad condition
with complicated diseases and seized with pains, those
afflicted with demons, and epilepsy, and paralytics, and
he healed them. And many multitudes followed him
from Galilee and the Decapolis and Jerusalem and
Judaea and beyond the Jordan.

§ And seeing the multitudes he went up onto the
mountain, and when he was seated, his disciples came
to him, and he opened his mouth and taught them,
saying:

Blessed are the poor in spirit, because theirs is the
Kingdom of Heaven.

Blessed are they who sorrow, because they shall be comforted.

Blessed are the gentle, because they shall inherit the earth.

Blessed are they who are hungry and thirsty for righteousness, because they shall be fed.

Blessed are they who have pity, because they shall be pitied.

Blessed are the pure in heart, because they shall see God.

Blessed are the peacemakers, because they shall be called the sons of God.

Blessed are they who are persecuted for their righteousness, because theirs is the Kingdom of Heaven.

Blessed are you when they shall revile you and persecute you and speak every evil thing of you, lying, because of me. Rejoice and be glad, because your reward in heaven is great; for thus did they persecute the prophets before you.

You are the salt of the earth; but if the salt loses its power, with what shall it be salted? It is good for nothing but to be thrown away and trampled by men. You are the light of the world. A city cannot be hidden when it is set on top of a hill. Nor do men light a lamp and set it under a basket, but they set it on a stand, and it gives its light to all in the house. So let your light shine before men, so that they may see your good works and glorify your father in heaven.

Do not think that I have come to destroy the law and the prophets. I have not come to destroy but to complete. Indeed, I say to you, until the sky and the earth are gone, not one iota or one end of a letter must go from the law, until all is done. He who breaks one of the least of these commandments and teaches men accordingly shall be called the least in the Kingdom of Heaven; he who performs and teaches these commandments shall be called great in the Kingdom of Heaven. For I tell you, if your righteousness is not more abundant than that of the scribes and the Pharisees, you may not enter the Kingdom of Heaven.

You have heard that it was said to the ancients: You shall not murder. He who murders shall be liable to judgment. I say to you that any man who is angry with his brother shall be liable to judgment; and he who says to his brother, fool, shall be liable before the council; and he who says to his brother, sinner, shall be liable to Gehenna. If then you bring your gift to the altar, and there remember that your brother has some grievance against you, leave your gift before the altar, and go first and be reconciled with your brother, and then go and offer your gift. Be quick to be conciliatory with your adversary at law when you are in the street with him, for fear your adversary may turn you over to the judge, and the judge to the officer, and you be thrown into prison. Truly I tell you, you cannot come out of there until you pay the last penny.

You have heard that it has been said: You shall not commit adultery. I tell you that any man who looks at a woman so as to desire her has already committed adultery with her in his heart. If your right eye makes you go amiss, take it out and cast it from you; it is better that one part of you should be lost instead of your whole body being cast into Gehenna. And if your right hand makes you go amiss, cut it off and cast it from you; it is better that one part of you should be lost instead of your whole body going to Gehenna. It has been said: If a man puts away his wife, let him give her a contract of divorce. I tell you that any man who puts away his wife, except for the reason of harlotry, is making her the victim of adultery; and any man who marries a wife who has been divorced is committing adultery. Again, you have heard that it has been said to the ancients: You shall not swear falsely, but you shall make good your oaths to the Lord. I tell you not to swear at all: not by heaven, because it is the throne of God; not by the earth, because it is the footstool for his feet; not by Jerusalem, because it is the city of the great king; not by your own head, because you cannot make one hair of it white or black. Let your speech be yes yes, no no; more than that comes from the evil one.

You have heard that it has been said: An eye for an eye and a tooth for a tooth. I tell you not to resist the wicked man; but if one strikes you on the right cheek, turn the other one to him also; and if a man wishes to go to the law with you and take your tunic, give him your cloak also, and if one makes you his porter for a mile, go with him for two. Give to him who asks, and do not turn away one who wishes to borrow from you. You have heard that it has been said: You shall love your neighbor and hate your enemy. I tell you, love your enemies and pray for those who persecute you, so that you may be sons of your father who is in heaven, because he makes his sun rise on the evil and the good, and rains on the just and the unjust. For if you love those who love you, what reward do you have? Do not even the tax collectors do the same? And if you greet only your brothers, what do you do that is more than others do? Do not even the pagans do the same? Be perfect as your father in heaven is perfect.

§ Take care not to practice your righteousness publicly before men so as to be seen by them; if you do, you shall have no recompense from your father in heaven. Then when you do charity, do not have a trumpet blown before you, as the hypocrites do in the synagogues and the streets, so that men may think well of them. Truly I tell you, they have their due reward. But when you do charity, let your left hand not know what your right hand is doing, so that your charity may be in secret; and your father, who sees what is secret, will reward you. And when you pray, you must not be like the hypocrites, who love to stand up in the synagogues and the corners of the squares to pray, so that they may be seen by men. Truly I tell you, they have their due reward. But when you pray, go into your inner room and close the door and pray to your father, who is in secret; and your father, who sees what is secret, will reward you. When you pray, do not babble as the pagans do; for they think that by saying much they will be heard. Do not then be like them; for your father knows what you need before you ask him. Pray thus, then: Our father in heaven, may your name be hallowed, may your kingdom come, may your will be done, as in heaven, so upon earth. Give us today our sufficient bread, and forgive us our debts, as we also have forgiven our debtors. And do not bring us into temptation, but deliver us from evil. For if you forgive men their offenses, your heavenly father will forgive you; but if you do not forgive men, neither will your father forgive you your offenses. And when you fast, do not scowl like the hypocrites; for they make ugly faces so that men can see that they are fasting. Truly I tell you, they have their due reward. But when you fast, anoint your head and wash your face, so that you may not show as fasting to men, but to your father, in secret; and your father, who sees what is secret, will reward you.

Do not store up your treasures on earth, where the moth and rust destroy them, and where burglars dig through and steal them; but store up your treasures in heaven, where neither moth nor rust destroys them and where burglars do not dig through or steal; for where your treasure is, there also will be your heart. The lamp of the body is the eye. Thus if your eye is clear, your whole body is full of light; but if your eye is soiled, your whole body is dark. If the light in you is darkness, how dark it is. No man can serve two masters. For either he will hate the one and love the other, or he will cling to one and despise the other; you cannot serve God and mammon. Therefore I tell you, do not take thought for your life, what you will eat, or for your body, what you will wear. Is not your life more than its food and your body more than its clothing? Consider the birds of the sky, that they do not sow or harvest or collect for their granaries, and your heavenly father feeds them. Are you not preferred above them? Which of you by taking thought can add one cubit to his growth? And why do you take thought about clothing? Study the lilies in the field, how they grow. They do not toil or spin; yet I tell you, not even Solomon in all his glory was clothed like one of these. But if God so clothes the grass of the field, which grows today and tomorrow is thrown in the oven, will he not much more clothe you, you men of little faith? Do not then worry and say: What shall we eat? Or: What shall we drink? Or: What shall we wear? For all this the Gentiles study. Your father in heaven knows that you need all these things. But seek out first his kingdom and his justice, and all these things shall be given to you. Do not then take thought of tomorrow; tomorrow will take care of itself, sufficient to the day is its own evil.

§ Do not judge, so you may not be judged. You shall be judged by that judgment by which you judge, and your measure will be made by the measure by which you measure. Why do you look at the straw which is in the eye of your brother, and not see the log which is in your eye? Or how will you say to your brother: Let me take the straw out of your eye, and behold, the log is in your eye. You hypocrite, first take the log out of your eye, and then you will see to take the straw out of the eye of your brother. Do not give what is sacred to the dogs, and do not cast your pearls before swine, lest they trample them under their feet and turn and rend you. Ask, and it shall be given you; seek, and you shall find; knock, and the door will be opened for you. Everyone who asks receives, and he who seeks finds, and for him who knocks the door will be opened. Or what man is there among you, whose son shall ask him for bread, that will give him a stone? Or ask him for fish, that will give him a snake? If then you, who are corrupt, know how to give good gifts to your children, by how much more your father who is in heaven will give good things to those who ask him. Whatever you wish men to do to you, so do to them. For this is the law and the prophets.

Go in through the narrow gate; because wide and spacious is the road that leads to destruction, and there are many who go in through it; because narrow is the gate and cramped the road that leads to life, and few are they who find it. Beware of the false prophets, who come to you in sheep's clothing, but inside they are ravening wolves. From their fruits you will know them. Do men gather grapes from thorns or figs from thistles? Thus every good tree produces good fruits, but the rotten tree produces bad fruits. A good tree cannot bear bad fruits, and a rotten tree cannot bear good fruits. Every tree that does not produce good fruit is cut out and thrown in the fire. So from their fruits you will know them. Not everyone who says to me Lord Lord will come into the Kingdom of Heaven, but he who does the will of my father in heaven. Many will say to me on that day: Lord, Lord, did we not prophesy in your name, and in your name did we not cast out demons, and in your name did we not assume great powers? And then I shall admit to them: I never knew you. Go from me, for you do what is against the law.

Every man who hears what I say and does what I say shall be like the prudent man who built his house upon the rock. And the rain fell and the rivers came and the winds blew and dashed against that house, and it did not fall, for it was founded upon the rock. And every man who hears what I say and does not do what I say will be like the reckless man who built his house on the sand. And the rain fell and the rivers came and the winds blew and battered that house, and it fell, and that was a great fall.

And it happened that when Jesus had ended these words, the multitudes were astonished at his teaching, for he taught them as one who has authority, and not like their own scribes.

§ When he came down from the mountain many multitudes followed him. And behold, a leper came and bowed before him, saying: Lord, if you wish, you can make me clean. And he stretched out his hand and touched him, saying: I wish it; be clean. And at once his leprosy was cleansed. And Jesus said to him: Be sure to tell no one, but go and show yourself to the priest and bring him the gift that Moses has ordained, as a proof to them.

When he came into Capernaum there came to him a centurion with a request, saying: Lord, my son is lying paralyzed in my house, in terrible pain. He said to him: I will go and treat him. But the centurion answered and said: Lord, I am not worthy that you should come under my roof; but only say it in a word, and my son will be healed. For I myself am a man under orders, and I have soldiers under me, and I say to this man: Go, and he goes, and to another: Come, and he comes, and to my slave: Do this, and he does it. Jesus hearing him was amazed and said to his followers: Truly I tell you, I have not found such faith in anyone in Israel. I tell you that many from the east and the west will come and feast with Abraham and Isaac and Jacob in the Kingdom of Heaven; but the sons of the kingdom shall be thrown into the outer darkness; and there will be weeping and gnashing of teeth. And Jesus said to the centurion: Go, as you have trusted, so let it befall you. And his son was healed in that hour.

Then Jesus, going into the house of Peter, saw his mother-in-law, who was lying in a fever, and he took her by the hand, and the fever left her; and she got up and served him. And when evening came, they brought him many who were afflicted with demons, and he cast out the spirits by a word, and healed all those who were suffering; so as to fulfill what had been said by the prophet Isaiah, saying: He took up our sicknesses and carried off our diseases.

Then Jesus, seeing a great multitude about him, gave the word to go to the other side. And one scribe came to him and said: Master, I will follow you wherever you go. And Jesus said to him: Foxes have holes, and the birds of the sky have nests, but the son of man has no place to lay his head. And another, one of his disciples, said to him: Lord, give me leave first to go and bury my father. But Jesus said to him: Follow me, and leave the dead to bury their own dead.

When he went aboard the ship, his disciples followed him. And behold, there was a great upheaval on the sea, so that the ship was hidden by the waves; but he himself was asleep. And they came and waked him, saying: Lord, save us, we are perishing. And he said to them: Why are you frightened, you men of little faith? Then he rose up and admonished the winds and the sea, and there was a great calm. But the people wondered, saying: What sort of man is this, that the winds and the sea obey him? And when he crossed over into the country of the Gadarenes there met him two men possessed by demons, coming out of the tombs, very wild, so that none could force a way past on that road. And behold, they cried out, saying: What have we to do with you, son of God? Have you come thus before your time to torment us? A long way from them was a herd of many swine, feeding. And the demons entreated him, saying: If you throw us out, send us into the herd of swine. And he said to them: Go. And they came out and went into the herd of swine; and behold, the whole herd rushed over the cliff into the sea and died in the waters. Then the swineherds fled and when they came to their city told all the story of those who had been possessed by demons. And behold, all the city came out to meet Jesus, and when they saw him they begged him to go away from their territory.

§ Then he went aboard a ship and crossed over and came to his own city. And behold, they brought him a paralytic who was laid on a bed. And Jesus, seeing their faith, said to the paralytic: Take heart, my child, your sins are forgiven. And behold, some of the scribes said among themselves: This man blasphemes. Then Jesus, knowing their thoughts, said: Why do you think evil in your hearts? Which then is easier: to say, Your sins are forgiven, or to say, Rise up and walk? But so that you may know that the son of man has authority on earth to forgive sins . . . Then he said to the paralytic: Rise up, take your bed and go to your house. And he rose up and went to his house. And the multitude seeing this were frightened and glorified God, who gave such authority to men.

And Jesus, going on from there, saw a man sitting in the tollhouse, named Matthew, and said to him: Follow me. And he stood up and followed him. And it happened as he dined in the house, behold, many tax collectors and sinners came and dined with Jesus and his disciples. And when they saw this the Pharisees said to his disciples: Why does your teacher eat with tax collectors and sinners? He heard them and said: The strong do not need a physician, but those who are in poor health. Go and learn the meaning of: I want mercy, not sacrifice; for I did not come to summon the righteous, but the sinners. Then the disciples of John came to him and said: Why do we and the Pharisees fast, but your disciples do not fast? And Jesus said to them: Surely the members of the wedding party cannot mourn while the bridegroom is with them? The days will come when the bridegroom is taken away from them, and then they will fast. No one sews a patch of unfulled cloth on an old coat; for the filling pulls from

the coat and makes the tear worse. Nor do they put new
wine in old skins; if they do, the skins break, and the
wine spills, and the skins are destroyed; but they put
new wine in new skins, and both are kept whole.

As he said this, behold, an official came and bowed
down before him and said: My daughter died just now.
But come and put your hand on her, and she will live.
Jesus rose up and followed him, and his disciples
followed. And behold, a woman who had been bleeding for twelve years came from behind and touched the
border of his mantle; for she said to herself: If I only
touch his mantle, I shall be healed. But Jesus turned
and saw her and said: Take heart, my daughter; your
faith has healed you. And the woman was well from
that hour. Then Jesus went into the house of the official
and saw the flute players and the noisy crowd, and said:
Go away, for the girl has not died, but she is asleep.
And they laughed at him. But when the crowd had
been put out, he went in and took her hand, and the girl
woke. And the story of this went out to the whole of
that country.

Then as Jesus went on from there, two blind men
followed him, crying out and saying: Pity us, son of
David. As he went into the house, the blind men came
up with him, and Jesus said to them: Do you believe
that I can do this? They said to him: Yes, Lord. Then he
touched their eyes and said: As you have faith, so let it
be with you. And their eyes were opened. Then Jesus
spoke severely to them, saying: See that nobody hears
of this. But they went out and spread the news of him to
the whole of that country. As they went out, behold,
men brought him a deaf-mute who was possessed by a
demon. And when the demon was driven out, the
deaf-mute talked. Then the multitude wondered, saying: Never was anything seen like this in Israel. But the
Pharisees said: He drives out demons through the
prince of demons.

Now Jesus went about through all the cities and
the villages, teaching in their synagogues and preach-

ing the gospel of the kingdom and healing every sickness and every infirmity. And when he saw the multitudes he was moved with pity for them, because they had been distracted and turned loose like sheep without a shepherd. Then he said to his disciples: The harvest is abundant, but the laborers few. Beg the master of the harvest to send out laborers to his harvest.

§ Then calling to him his twelve disciples, he gave them authority over unclean spirits, to cast them out, and to treat every sickness and every infirmity. And these are the names of the twelve apostles: First, Simon, who was called Peter, and Andrew his brother, and James the son of Zebedee, and John his brother, Philip and Bartholomew, Thomas and Matthew the tax collector, James the son of Alphaeus and Thaddeus, Simon the Cananaean and Judas the Iscariot, even he who betrayed him. These twelve Jesus sent forth and gave them instructions, saying:

Do not go on the road to the Gentiles, and do not go into any city of the Samaritans. Make your way rather to the lost sheep of the house of Israel. As you go, preach and say that the Kingdom of Heaven is near. Heal the infirm, raise up the dead, make lepers clean, cast out demons. You have taken a free gift; give a free gift. Do not keep gold or silver or bronze in your money belts, or a bag for the journey or two garments or shoes or a staff. The laborer is worthy of food and clothing. Whatever city or village you enter, find out who within it is worthy; stay with him until you go on. As you enter his house, greet it; and if the house is worthy, let your peace be upon it, and if it is not worthy, let your peace return upon yourselves. And when one does not receive you or listen to your words, as you go out of that house or that city, shake the dust of it from your feet. Truly I tell you, it will be more tolerable for the land of Sodom and Gomorrah on the day of judgment than for that city. See, I send you out like sheep into the midst of wolves; be then crafty like snakes and innocent like doves. Beware of people; for they will hand you over to the council boards, and they will flog you in their synagogues, and you will be brought before the leaders and the kings, because of me, to bear witness before them and the Gentiles. But when they hand you over, do not think about how you will speak; that will be given to you at the time when you speak; for it will not be you who speak but the spirit of your father speaking through you. Brother will hand brother over to death, father will hand over child, and children will stand up against their parents and cause their death. You will be hated by all because of my name; and he who endures it to the end will be saved. When they persecute you in one city, flee to the next one; for truly I tell you, you will not be through with the cities of Israel before the son of man comes. The disciple is not above the teacher, or the slave above his master; it is enough for the disciple that he be as his teacher and for the slave that he be as his master. If then they call the head of the house Beelzebub, how much more will they so call his domestics. Then do not be afraid of them; for there is nothing concealed that shall not be revealed, and nothing secret that shall not be known. What I say to you in the dark, say in the light; what is said in your ear, proclaim on the housetops. And have no fear of those who kill the body but cannot kill the soul; fear rather him who can destroy both soul and body in Gehenna. Are not two sparrows sold for a penny? And one of them will not fall to the ground without the knowledge of your father. Also, the very hairs of your head are all numbered. Then do not fear; you are worth many sparrows. If any man shall acknowledge me before men, I shall acknowledge him before my father in heaven; if any shall deny me before men, I shall deny him before my father in heaven. Do not think that I have come to bring peace upon the earth. I have not come to bring peace, but a sword. I have come to set a man against his father, and a daughter against her mother, and a bride against her mother-in-law, and the household of a man will be his enemies. He who loves father or mother more than me is not worthy of me; and he who loves son or daughter more than me is not worthy of me; and he who does not take his cross and come along behind me is not worthy of me. He who finds his life shall lose it, and he who loses his life because of me shall find it. He who receives you receives me, and he who receives me receives him who sent me forth. He who receives a prophet in the name of a prophet shall have the reward of a prophet, and he who receives a just man in the name of a just man shall have the reward of a just man. And he who gives one of these small ones a cup of cold water to drink, if only in the name of a disciple, truly I tell you, he shall not lose his reward.

§ Then it came about that when Jesus had finished instructing his twelve disciples, he went away from there to teach and preach in their cities. But John in his prison heard of the works of the Christ, and sent his disciples to him, and through them asked him: Are you the one who is to come, or shall we look for another? Jesus answered and said to them: Go and tell John what you are seeing and hearing. The blind see again and the lame walk, lepers are made clean and deaf-mutes hear, and the dead rise up and beggars are told good news. And blessed is he who does not go astray where I am concerned. As these went away Jesus began to speak about John to the multitudes: What did you come out into the desert to see? A reed shaken by the wind? But what did you come out to see? A man wrapped in soft clothing? Behold, those who wear soft clothing are in the houses of the kings. But why did you come out? To see a prophet? Yes, I tell you, and more than a prophet. This is he about whom it was written: Behold, I send forth my messenger before your face, who will make your way ready before you. Truly I tell you, among men born of women there has not risen a greater one than John the Baptist; but one who is only a lesser one in the Kingdom of Heaven is greater than he. From the days of John the Baptist until now the Kingdom of Heaven has been forced and the violent have seized it. For all the prophets, and the law, prophesied until John; and if you wish to accept it, he himself is Elijah, who was to come. He who has ears, let him listen. To what shall I liken this generation? It is like children sitting in the public places who call out to others and say: We played the flute, but you did not dance; we lamented and you did not beat yourselves. For John came neither eating nor drinking and they say: He has a demon. The son of man came eating and drinking and they say: See, the man is an eater and wine drinker, a friend of tax collectors and sinners. And wisdom is justified by what it has done.

Then he began to blame the cities in which his greatest powers had been shown, because they had not repented: Woe to you, Chorazin. Woe to you, Bethsaida. For if there had been shown in Tyre and Sidon the powers that have been shown among you, long since they would have repented in sackcloth and ashes. But I tell you, it will be more tolerable for Tyre and Sidon on the day of judgment than it will be for you. And you, Capernaum, will you be exalted to heaven? You will go down to Hades. For if in Sodom there had been shown the powers that have been shown among you, Sodom would have remained until today. But I tell you that it will be more tolerable for the land of Sodom on the day of judgment than it will be for you.

At that time Jesus spoke and said: I thank you, father, lord of heaven and earth, because you have hidden these things from the clever and the understanding, and revealed them to the simple; yes, father, that thus it has been your pleasure in your sight. All was given to me by my father, and no one knows the son except the father, and no one knows the father except the son, and anyone to whom the son wishes to reveal it. Come to me, all who toil and are burdened, and I will give you rest. Take my yoke upon you and learn from me, because I am gentle and humble at heart, and you will find rest for your souls; for my yoke is good and my burden is light.

§ At that time Jesus walked on the sabbath through the sown fields; and his disciples were hungry, and began to pick the ears of grain and eat them. But the Pharisees saw it and said to him: See, your disciples are doing what it is forbidden to do on the sabbath. But he said to them: Have you not read what David did when he was hungry, and those with him? How he went into the house of God, and they ate the show bread, which he was not permitted to eat, nor those with him, but only the priests? Or have you not read in the law that on sabbath days the priests in the temple profane the sabbath, and are not guilty? I tell you that here is a thing greater than the temple. But if you knew what this means: I wish mercy, not a sacrifice; then you would not have condemned the guiltless. For the son of man is lord of the sabbath. And passing on from there he went into the synagogue, and behold, there was a man with a withered arm. And they questioned him, saying: Is it lawful to heal on the sabbath? They meant to bring a charge against him. But he said to them: Will there be one of you who owns one sheep, and if it falls down a hole on the sabbath, will not take hold of it and pull it out? How much better a man is than a sheep. Thus it is permitted to do good on the sabbath. Then he said to the man: Stretch out your arm. And he stretched it, and it became sound, like the other arm. But the Pharisees went outside and began plotting against him to destroy him.

Jesus seeing this went away from them, and many followed him, and he healed them all, and charged them not to divulge what he was doing; so as to fulfill the word spoken by the prophet Isaiah, saying: Behold, my son, whom I have chosen, whom I love, and my soul is well pleased with him. I will put my spirit into him, and he will announce the judgment to the nations. He will not fight or cry out, nor will any hear his voice in the public places. He will not break the reed that is bent or quench the flax that is smoking, until he issues his judgment in triumph. And in his name the nations shall have hope.

Then there was brought to him a man possessed by a demon, blind and a deaf-mute, and he healed him, so that the deaf-mute talked and saw. Then all the multitudes were astonished and said: Is this not the son of David? But the Pharisees heard them and said: This man does not drive out demons except through Beelzebub, the prince of demons. He knew their thoughts and said to them: Every kingdom that is divided against itself is made desolate, and every city or house that is divided against itself will not stand. And if Satan drives out Satan, he is divided against himself. How then shall his kingdom stand? If through Beelzebub I drive out demons, through whom do your sons drive them out? Therefore they shall be your judges. But if I drive out demons by the spirit of God, then the Kingdom of God has come to you. Or how can one enter the house of the strong man and seize his goods, unless he first binds the strong man and then plunders his house? He who is not with me is against me, and he who does not join my meetings dispels them. Therefore, I tell you this, every sin and blasphemy shall be forgiven to men, but the blasphemy of the Spirit shall not be forgiven. And if one speaks a word against the son of man, it shall be forgiven him; but if one speaks against the Holy Spirit, it shall not be forgiven him, neither in this age nor the next. Either make the tree good and its fruit good, or make the tree bad and its fruit bad; for from the fruit the tree is known. You viper's brood, how can you say what is good when you are bad? For from what overflows the heart the mouth speaks. The good man issues good from his good storehouse, and the bad man issues bad from his bad storehouse. I tell you, every idle word men speak they shall account for on the day of judgment; for from your words you shall be justified, and from your words judgment shall be given against you.

Then some of the scribes and Pharisees answered him and said: Master, we wish to see a sign from you. He answered and said to them: A corrupt and adulterous generation asks for a sign, and no sign shall be given to it unless it be the sign of Jonah the prophet. For as Jonah was in the belly of the whale three days and three nights, so the son of man shall be in the heart of the earth three days and three nights. The men of Nineveh shall stand up on the day of judgment with this generation and condemn it; because they repented upon the proclamation of Jonah, and behold, there is more than Jonah here. The Queen of the South shall rise up on the day of judgment with this generation and condemn it; because she came from the ends of the earth to listen to the wisdom of Solomon, and behold, there is more than Solomon here. But when the unclean spirit goes out of a man, it wanders through waterless regions looking for a place to rest, and finds none. Then it says: I will return to my house that I came out from; and it comes and finds it free and swept and furnished. Then it goes and picks up seven more spirits worse than itself, and they go and settle there; and the end for that man is worse than the beginning. Thus it will be also with this evil generation.

While he was still talking with the multitudes, behold, his mother and his brothers stood outside, desiring to speak with him. And someone said to him: See, your mother and your brothers are standing outside and desire to speak with you. But he answered and said to the man who reported this: Who is my mother, and who are my brothers? And pointing his hand toward his disciples, he said: These are my

mother and my brothers. For whoever does the will
of my father in heaven is my brother and sister and
mother.

§ On that day Jesus went out of the house and sat
beside the sea; and a great multitude gathered before
him, so that he went aboard a ship and sat there, and all
the multitude stood on the shore. And he talked to
them, speaking mostly in parables: Behold, a sower
went out to sow. And as he sowed, some of the grain
fell beside the way, and birds came and ate it. Some fell
on stony ground where there was not much soil, and it
shot up quickly because there was no depth of soil, but
when the sun came up it was parched, and because it
had no roots it dried away. Some fell among thorns,
and the thorns grew up and stifled it. But some fell
upon the good soil and bore fruit, some hundredfold,
some sixtyfold, some thirtyfold. He who has ears, let
him hear. Then his disciples came to him and said: Why
do you talk to them in parables? He answered them and
said: Because it is given to you to understand the
secrets of the Kingdom of Heaven, but to them it is not
given. When a man has, he shall be given, and it will be
more than he needs; but when he has not, even what he
has shall be taken away from him. Therefore I talk to
them in parables, because they have sight but do not
see, and hearing but do not hear or understand. And
for them is fulfilled the prophecy of Isaiah, saying: With
your hearing you shall hear and not understand, and
you shall use your sight and look but not see. For the
heart of this people is stiffened, and they hear with
difficulty, and they have closed their eyes; so that they
may never see with their eyes, or hear with their ears
and with their hearts understand and turn back, so that
I can heal them.

Blessed are your eyes because they see, and your ears
because they hear. Truly I tell you that many prophets
and good men have longed to see what you see, and not

seen it, and to hear what you hear, and not heard it. Hear, then, the parable of the sower. To every man who hears the word of the Kingdom and does not understand it, the evil one comes and seizes what has been sown in his heart. This is the seed sown by the way. The seed sown on the stony ground is the man who hears the word and immediately accepts it with joy; but he has no root in himself, and he is a man of the moment, and when there comes affliction and persecution, because of the word, he does not stand fast. The seed sown among thorns is the man who hears the word, and concern for the world and the beguilement of riches stifle the word, and he bears no fruit. And the seed sown on the good soil is the man who hears the word and understands it, who bears fruit and makes it, one a hundredfold, one sixtyfold, and one thirtyfold.

He set before them another parable, saying: The Kingdom of Heaven is like a man who sowed good seed in his field. And while the people were asleep, his enemy came and sowed darnel in with the grain, and went away. When the plants grew and produced a crop, the darnel was seen. Then the slaves of the master came to him and said: Master, did you not sow good grain in your field? Where does the darnel come from? He said to them: A man who is my enemy did it. His slaves said: Do you wish us to go out and gather it? But he said: No, for fear that when you gather the darnel you may pull up the grain with it. Let them both grow until harvest time, and in the time of harvest I shall say to the harvesters: First gather the darnel, and bind it in sheaves for burning, but store the grain in my granary.

He set before them another parable, saying: The Kingdom of Heaven is like a grain of mustard, which a man took and sowed in his field; which is the smallest of all seeds, but when it grows, it is the largest of the greens and grows into a tree, so that the birds of the air come and nest in its branches.

He told them another parable: The Kingdom of
Heaven is like leaven, which a woman took and buried
in three measures of dough, so that it all rose.

All this Jesus told the multitudes in parables, and he
did not talk to them except in parables; so as to fulfill
the word spoken by the prophet, saying: I will open my
mouth in parables, and pour out what has been hidden
since the creation. Then he sent away the multitudes
and went to the house. And his disciples came to him and
said: Make plain to us the parable of the darnel in the
field. He answered them and said: The sower of the good
seed is the son of man; the field is the world; the good
seed is the sons of the Kingdom; the darnel is the
sons of the evil one, and the enemy who sowed it is
the devil; the harvest time is the end of the world, and
the harvesters are angels. Then as the darnel is gathered and burned in the fire, so it is at the end of the
world. The son of man will send out his angels, and
they will gather from his Kingdom all that misleads,
and the people who do what is not lawful, and cast
them in the furnace of fire; and there will be weeping
and gnashing of teeth. Then the righteous men will
shine forth like the sun in the Kingdom of their
father. He who has ears, let him hear. The Kingdom
of Heaven is like a treasure hidden in the field, which
a man found and hid, and for joy of it he goes and
sells all he has and buys that field. Again, the Kingdom
of Heaven is like a trader looking for fine pearls; he
found one of great value, and went and sold all he
had and bought it. Again, the Kingdom of Heaven is
like a dragnet cast into the sea and netting every kind
of fish; and when it is full they draw it out and sit on
the beach and gather the good ones in baskets, but the
bad they throw away. So will it be at the end of the
world. The angels will go out and separate the bad
from the midst of the righteous, and cast them in
the furnace of fire; and there will be weeping and
gnashing of teeth. Do you understand all this? They
said to him: Yes. And he said to them: Therefore every

scribe who is learned in the Kingdom of Heaven is like a man who is master of a house, who issues from his storehouse what is new and what is old.

Then it happened that when Jesus was through with these parables, he went away from there, and went to his own country and taught them in their synagogue, so that they were astonished, and said: Where has this man found this wisdom and these powers? Is not this the son of the carpenter? Is not his mother called Mary, and his brothers James and Joseph and Simon and Judas? And are not all his sisters with us? From where does this man derive all these powers? And they made it difficult for him. Jesus said to them: No prophet is rejected except in his own country and his own house. And he did not show his powers much there because of their lack of faith.

§ At this time Herod the tetrarch heard the rumors about Jesus, and said to his children: This is John the Baptist. He has risen from the dead, and therefore powers are at work in him. For Herod had seized John and bound him and put him in prison, because of Herodias, the wife of Philip his brother. For John said to him: It is not lawful for you to have her. And Herod wished to kill him, but he was afraid of the people, because they held him as a prophet. But when it was Herod's birthday, the daughter of Herodias danced before them and pleased Herod, and he agreed with an oath to give her whatever she asked. And she, guided by her mother, said: Give me, here on a platter, the head of John the Baptist. The king was grieved, but because of his oath, and the guests at dinner, he ordered that it should be granted, and sent word and had John beheaded in the prison. Then the head was brought on a platter and given to the girl, and she took it to her mother. Then John's disciples came and took away his body and buried it, and went and told the news to Jesus.

When Jesus heard, he withdrew from there on a ship to a deserted place, privately; and the multitudes heard and followed him on foot from the cities. When he came ashore, he saw a great crowd, and was sorry for them, and healed those among them who were afflicted. Then when it was evening his disciples came to him, saying: This is a lonely place and the time is late; then send the people away so that they can go back to their villages and buy food. But Jesus said to them: There is no need for them to go. Give them something to eat yourselves. They said to him: We have nothing here but five loaves and two fish. He said: Bring them here to me. Then he told the people to take their places on the grass, and took the five loaves and the two fish, and looked up into the sky and gave a blessing, and broke the loaves and gave them to his disciples, and the disciples gave them to the people. And they all ate and were fed, and they picked up what was left over from the broken pieces, twelve baskets full. Those who ate were perhaps five thousand men, not counting women and children.

Then he made the disciples board the ship and precede him to the other side while he dismissed the multitude. And when he had dismissed the multitude, he went up on the mountain, by himself, to pray. When it was evening he was alone there. The ship was now many furlongs out from the land, battered by the waves, for the wind was against them. And in the fourth watch of the night he came toward them, walking on the sea. The disciples saw him walking on the sea and were shaken, saying it was a phantom, and from this fear they cried out. But at once Jesus talked to them, saying: Take heart, it is I; do not fear. Peter answered him and said: Lord, if it is you, bid me go to you on the water. He said: Come. Peter stepped down from the ship and walked on the water and went toward Jesus. But when he saw the storm he was frightened, and began to sink, and cried out, saying: Lord, save me. At once Jesus reached out his hand and took hold of him, and said: You have little faith. Why did you hesitate? And when they went aboard the ship, the wind fell. They who were on the ship worshipped him and said: Truly you are the son of God.

Then they crossed over and went to the country of Gennesaret, and the people of that region recognized him and sent word to all the country about, and brought to him all those who were afflicted, and begged of him that they might touch just the border of his mantle. And those who touched it were healed.

§ Then Pharisees and scribes came to Jesus from Jerusalem, saying: Why do your disciples go against the tradition of our elders? For they do not wash their hands when they eat bread. And he answered them and said: Why do you also go against the commandment of God because of your own tradition? For God said: Give due right to your father and mother; and: Let him who speaks rudely to his father or mother be put to death. But you say: If one says to his father or mother: Whatever profit you might have had from me is a gift of God; then such a one will not have to give due right to his father or mother. And you have made void the word of God, because of your tradition. Hypocrites, Isaiah prophesied well concerning you, saying: This people honors me with the lips, but their heart is far away from me; they worship me vainly, teaching doctrines which are the precepts of men.

Then summoning the multitude he said to them: Hear and understand. It is not what goes into the mouth that defiles a man but what comes out of the mouth; that defiles a man. Then his disciples came to him and said: Do you know that the Pharisees who heard this word objected to it? He answered and said: Every plant which was not planted by my father in heaven shall be uprooted. Let them go. They are blind guides of blind men; when blind man guides blind man, both will fall into the pit. Peter answered him and said:

Explain the parable to us. He said: Are even you still unable to understand? Do you not see that everything that goes into the mouth passes to the belly and is voided into the privy, but what comes out of the mouth comes from the heart, and that defiles a man. For from the heart come vile thoughts, murders, adulteries, fornications, thefts, false testimonies, blasphemies. These are what defile a man. To eat with unwashed hands does not defile a man.

Then Jesus left there and went away to the regions of Tyre and Sidon. And behold, a Canaanite woman from those parts came out and cried to him, saying: Pity me, son of David. My daughter is sadly vexed with a demon. But he said not a word in answer. Then his disciples came up to him and pressed him, saying: Send her away, for she follows us crying. He answered and said: I was not sent forth except after the lost sheep of the house of Israel. But she came and bowed before him, saying: Lord, help me. He answered and said: It is not well to take the bread of the children and throw it to the dogs. But she said: Yes, Lord, for even the dogs eat from the crumbs that fall from the table of their masters. Then Jesus answered and said to her: Woman, your faith is great. Let it be as you wish. And her daughter was healed from that hour.

Then Jesus went from there and came beside the Sea of Galilee, and going up on the mountain he sat there. And there came to him great multitudes, having with them their lame, crippled, blind, deaf and dumb, and many others; and they flung them at his feet; and he healed them, so that the multitude were astonished when they saw deaf-mutes speaking, cripples made sound, and lame men walking about, and blind men seeing; and they glorified the God of Israel. But Jesus summoned his disciples to him and said: I have pity for the multitude, because it is now three days they have stayed with me, and they have nothing to eat; and I do not wish to send them away hungry, for fear they will give out on the way. The disciples said: How shall we come by enough bread in the desert to feed such a multitude? And Jesus said to them: How many loaves do you have? They said: Seven, and a few little fish. Then he gave the word to the people to take their places on the ground, and took the loaves and the fish, and gave thanks, amd broke them up and gave them to his disciples, and his disciples gave them to the people. And all ate and were fed, and they picked up what was left over from the broken pieces, seven baskets full. Those who ate were four thousand men, not counting women and children. Then he sent away the people and went aboard the ship, and came to the regions of Magadan.

§ Then Pharisees and Sadducees came to him and made trial of him and asked him to show them a sign from the sky. He answered them and said: When it is sunset, you say: Fair weather, for the sky is red. And when it is dawn: Stormy today, for the sky is red and threatening. Do you know how to judge the face of the sky, and can you not judge the signs of the times? A corrupt and adulterous generation asks for a sign, and no sign shall be given to it, unless it be the sign of Jonah. Then he left them and went away.

When the disciples crossed to the other side they forgot to take bread. And Jesus said to them: Be watchful and beware of the leaven of the Pharisees and Sadducees. Then they talked among themselves, saying: We did not bring bread. Jesus perceived it and said: Why do you talk among yourselves, you men of little faith, about having no bread. Do you not yet see, do you not remember the fiye loaves of the five thousand and all the baskets you gathered? Or the seven loaves of the four thousand and all the baskets you gathered. How can you not see that I was not talking to you about bread? But beware of the leaven of the Pharisees and

Sadducees. Then they understood that he had not told them to beware of the leaven of bread, but of the teaching of the Pharisees and Sadducees.

When Jesus came to the regions of Caesarea Philippi, he questioned his disciples, saying: Who do men say the son of man is? They said: Some say John the Baptist, some Elijah, and others say Jeremiah or one of the prophets. He said to them: And you, who do you say I am? And Simon Peter said: You are the Christ, the son of the living God. Jesus answered him and said: Blessed are you, Simon Bariona; for it was not flesh and blood that revealed this to you but my father who is in heaven. And I tell you, you are Peter, the Rock, and upon this rock I will build my church, and the gates of Hades shall have no power against it. I shall give you the keys of the Kingdom of Heaven, and what you close upon earth shall be closed in heaven, and what you open on earth shall be open in heaven.

Then he warned his disciples to tell no one that he was the Christ.

From that time, Jesus began to show his disciples that he must go to Jerusalem, and suffer much from the elders and the high priests and the scribes, and be killed, and rise up on the third day. But Peter laid his hand upon him and tried to warn him, and said: Lord, be of good cheer; this shall not happen to you. He turned to Peter and said: Go behind me, Satan; you would put me off my way, because you do not think the thoughts of God but the thoughts of men. Then Jesus said to his disciples: If anyone wishes to go after me, let him deny himself and take up his cross and follow me. For he who wishes to save his life will lose it; and he who loses his life for my sake shall find it. For what will it advantage a man if he gains the whole world but must pay with his life? Or what will a man give that is worth as much as his life? The son of man is to come in the glory of his father among his angels, and then he will give to each according to what each has done. Truly I tell you that there are some of those who stand here who will not taste of death until they see the son of man coming in his Kingdom.

§ Then after six days Jesus took with him Peter and James and John the brothers of James, and led them up on a high mountain, by themselves. And he was transfigured before them, and his face blazed like the sun, and his clothing became white as light. And behold, Moses and Elijah were seen talking with him. But Peter spoke forth and said to Jesus: Lord, it is good for us to be here. If you wish, I will make three shelters here, one for you and one for Moses and one for Elijah. While he was still speaking, behold, a shining cloud covered them, and behold, a voice from the cloud saying: This is my son whom I love, in whom I am well pleased. Listen to him. When the disciples heard, they threw themselves upon their faces and were greatly afraid. And Jesus came to them and laid his hands upon them and said: Rise up and do not fear. And lifting their eyes they saw no one except Jesus himself alone.

Then as they were coming down from the mountain Jesus enjoined them and said: Do not speak of the vision until the son of man is raised from the dead. And his disciples asked him and said: Why then do the scribes say that Elijah must come first. He answered and said: Elijah will come and will set all right again. But I tell you that Elijah has already come, and they did not know him, and did with him what they wished; thus also is the son of man to suffer at their hands. Then the disciples understood that he spoke to them about John the Baptist.

Then as they came to the multitude there came a man who knelt to him and said: Lord, have pity on my son, for he is epileptic and in evil case; for often he falls into the fire, and often into the water. And I brought him to your disciples, and they were not able to heal him. Jesus answered and said: O generation without faith and perverse, how long shall I be with you? How long

shall I endure you? Bring him here to me. And Jesus
scolded him, and the demon went out of him, and the
boy was healed from that hour. Then his disciples came
to Jesus privately and said: Why were we not able to
cast it out? He said to them: Because of your little faith.
Truly I tell you, if you have faith as large as a grain of
mustard, you will say to this mountain: Move from here
to there; and it will move, and nothing will be
impossible to you.

Now as they gathered in Galilee, Jesus said to them:
The son of man is to be given over into the hands of
men and they will kill him, and on the third day he will
rise. And they were greatly saddened.

Then when they came to Capernaum, those who
took up the two-drachma tax came up to Peter and
said: Does not your teacher pay the two drachmas? He
said: Yes. And he was going into the house, Jesus
intercepted him and said: What do you think, Simon?
From whom do the kings of the earth take their taxes
and their assessment? From their sons or from strangers? When he said: From strangers, Jesus said to him:
Thus their sons go free. But so that we may cause them
no trouble, go to the sea and let down your hook, and
take the first fish that comes up, and open its mouth and
you will find a stater. Take it and give it to them, for
you and me.

§ In that time, his disciples came to Jesus and said:
Who is greater in the Kingdom of Heaven? Then he
called a child to him and set him in the midst of them,
and said: Truly I tell you, if you do not turn about and
become as children are, you shall not enter the
Kingdom of Heaven. He then who makes himself small
as this child is, he shall be the greater in the Kingdom of
Heaven. And if one accepts one child like this in my
name, he accepts me. But if one leads astray one of
these little ones who have faith in me, it is better for
him to have a millstone hung about his neck and be

drowned in the sea. Woe to the world from the troubles which shall be caused. For it is necessary for the troubles to come, but woe to him through whom the trouble comes. If your hand or foot makes you go amiss, cut it off and throw it from you; for it is better to go into life one-handed or lame than with both hands and both feet to be thrown into everlasting fire. And if your eye makes you go amiss, take it out and throw it from you; for it is better for you to go into life with one eye than with both eyes to be thrown into Gehenna. Take care that you do not despise one of these little ones; for I tell you that their angels in heaven forever look upon the face of my father in heaven. What do you think? If a man has a hundred sheep, and one of them strays, will he not let the ninety-nine go on the mountain, and go and look for the one that has strayed? And if it befalls him to find it, truly I tell you, he takes more joy over it than over the ninety-nine that did not stray. Thus there is no intention on the part of your father, who is in heaven, that one of these little ones should be lost.

If your brother does you wrong, go and charge him with it between you and him alone. If he listens to you, you have won your brother over. But if he does not listen to you, take along with you one or two more, so that everything said may be on the lips of two or three witnesses. And if he will not listen to them, tell it to the congregation. And if he will not listen even to the congregation, let him be to you as the Gentile and the tax collector. Truly I tell you, all that you close on earth shall be closed in heaven, and all that you open on earth shall be open in heaven. Again I tell you, if two of you agree on earth concerning everything they ask for, it shall be granted them by my father in heaven. For where there are two or three gathered together in my name, there I am in their midst.

Then Peter came to him and said: Lord, how many times shall my brother do me wrong, and I forgive him? As many as seven times? Jesus said to him: I tell you, not as many as seven times, but as many as seventy times seven. Thus the Kingdom of Heaven has been likened to a man who is a king, who wished to settle accounts with his slaves, and as he began to cast up accounts, there was brought to him one who was in his debt for ten thousand talents. When he could not pay it, the master said he must be sold, and his wife and children and all he had, and payment made. Then the slave threw himself down and worshipped him, saying: Delay your anger against me, and I will pay you back all. And the master took pity on his slave and let him go and forgave him his debt. That slave went out and found a fellow slave who owed him a hundred denarii, and seized him and choked him and said: Pay me back what you owe me. His fellow slave threw himself down before him and begged him, saying: Delay your anger against me and I will pay you back. But he would not, but went and threw him into prison until he should pay his debt. When his fellow slaves saw this they were much grieved and went and explained to their master all that had happened. Then the master called the man before him and said to him: Wicked slave, I forgave you all that other debt, since you begged me to. Should you not then have had pity on your fellow slave, as I myself pitied you? And the master in anger handed him over to the torturers until he could pay back all that he owed him. Thus also will my father in heaven do to you, unless each of you forgives his brother, from your heart.

§ Then it came about that when Jesus had done with these sayings, he removed from Galilee and went into the border districts of Judaea, across Jordan. And many multitudes followed him, and he treated them.

Then Pharisees came to him, making trial of him and saying: Is it lawful for a man to divorce his wife, for any cause? He answered and said: Have you not read that from the beginning the creator made them male and female, and said: Because of this, a man will leave his father and mother and cling to his wife, and they will be two in one flesh. So that they are no longer two, but one flesh. Then what God has joined together, let man not separate. They said to him: Why then did Moses decree that one might give a note of divorce, and divorce her. He said to them: Moses, looking toward the hardness of your hearts, permitted you to divorce your wives; but it was not so from the beginning. And I tell you that he who divorces his wife, except for harlotry, and marries another, is committing adultery. His disciples said to him: If this is the case with man and wife, it is better not to marry. He said to them: Not all can accept this saying, but those to whom it is given. For there are sexless men who have been so from their mother's womb, and there are sexless men who have been made sexless by other men, and there are sexless men who have made themselves sexless for the sake of the Kingdom of Heaven. Let him who can accept, accept.

Then children were brought to him, so that he could lay his hands on them and pray for them. But his disciples scolded them. But Jesus said: Let the children be and do not prevent them from coming to me. For of such is the Kingdom of Heaven. And he laid his hands on them, and went away from there.

Then, behold, there was one who came to him and said: Master, what shall I do that is good, so that I may have life forever? He said to him: Why do you ask me about good? One only is good. But if you wish to enter life, keep the commandments. He said to him: Which commandments? Jesus said: That you shall not murder, or commit adultery, or steal, or bear false witness; honor your father and your mother, and love your neighbor as you love yourself. The young man said to him: I have kept all these commandments. What more must I do? Jesus said to him: If you wish to be perfect, go sell what belongs to you and give it to the poor, and you shall have a treasury in heaven. And come and follow me. When the young man heard what he said, he went sadly away; for he was one who had many possessions. But Jesus said to his disciples: Truly I tell you that it will be hard for a rich man to enter the Kingdom of Heaven. And again I tell you that it is easier for a camel to enter the eye of a needle than for a rich man to enter the Kingdom of Heaven. When his disciples heard this, they were greatly astonished, and said: Who then can be saved? Jesus looked at them and said: For men it is impossible, but for God all things are possible. Then Peter took him up and said: See, we have given up everything and followed you. What then will there be for us? Jesus said to them: Truly I tell you, in the next life, when the son of man is seated on the throne of his glory, you who have followed me shall be seated, you also, upon twelve thrones, and judge the twelve tribes of Israel. And everyone who has given up houses or brothers or sisters or father or mother or children or lands for the sake of my name, shall have them back many times over and inherit life everlasting. And many who are first shall be last, and many who are last shall be first.

§ For the Kingdom of Heaven is like a man, the master of a house, who went out in the early morning to hire laborers for his vineyard. He agreed with the laborers for a denarius a day and sent them off to his vineyard. Then going out about the third hour he saw others standing idle in the marketplace, and said to them: Go on, you also, into my vineyard, and I will pay you whatever is fair. And they went. And going out again about the sixth and the ninth hour he did likewise. And about the eleventh hour he went out and found more men standing there, and said to them: Why are you standing thus idle all day? They said to them: Because nobody hired us. He said to them: Go on, you also, into my vineyard. Then when it was twilight the master of the vineyard said to his overseer: Call the laborers and pay them their wages, beginning with the last to come and going on to the first. And those who had come at the eleventh hour came and were paid a denarius each. And those who had been hired first came and thought they would receive more; and they also were paid a denarius each. But when they were paid they murmured against the master of the house, saying: Those who came last did one hour's work, and you have made them the equals of us, who bore the heaviness of the day and the heat. But he answered one of them and said: Friend, I do you no wrong. Did you not agree with me on one denarius? Take your wages and go. But I desire to give this last man the same as I gave you. Can I not do as I wish with what is my own? Or does your eye hurt because I am kind?

Thus they who are last shall be first and they who are first shall be last.

Then as Jesus set out to go up to Jerusalem he took the twelve with him, alone, and on the way he said to them: Behold, we are going to Jerusalem, and the son of man will be given over into the hands of the high priests and the scribes and they will condemn him to death, and give him over to the Gentiles to mock and flog and crucify, and on the third day he will rise.

At that time there came to him the mother of the sons of Zebedee with her sons, and bowed before him and had something to ask of him. He said to her: What do you wish? She said: Tell me that these, my two sons, shall sit on your right and on your left in your Kingdom. Jesus answered and said: You do not know what you are asking. Can you drink the cup that I am to drink? They said: We can. He said to them: You shall drink my cup; but for you to sit on my right and on my left, that is not mine to give, but it is for those who have been appointed by my father. Hearing this, the other ten were indignant over the two brothers. But Jesus called them to him and said: You know that the leaders of the Gentiles are lords over them, and their great men exercise power over them. It is not thus with you; but he who wishes to be great among you shall be your servant, and he who wishes to be first among you shall be your slave; as the son of man came not to be served but to serve, and to give his own life for the redemption of many.

Now as they were going out from Jericho a great crowd followed him. And behold, two blind men sitting by the road, hearing that Jesus was going by, cried aloud and said: Lord, have pity on us, son of David. But the people told them angrily to be quiet, but they cried the louder, saying: Lord, have pity on us, son of David. Jesus stopped and spoke to them and said: What do you wish me to do for you? They told him: Lord, let our eyes be opened. Jesus pitied them, and laid his hands on their eyes, and at once they saw, and followed him.

§ Then as they came near Jerusalem and arrived at Bethphage, at the Mount of Olives, Jesus sent two of his disciples ahead, saying to them: Go on into the village that lies before you, and presently you will find a donkey, tethered, and a foal with her. Untie them and bring them to me. And if anyone says anything to you, say that their master needs them, and he will send them at once. This was done so as to fulfill the word spoken by the prophet, saying: Say to the daughter of Zion: Behold, your king comes to you, modest and riding on a donkey and with a foal, the son of a beast of burden. His disciples went and did as Jesus told them, and brought the donkey and the foal, and piled clothing on them, and he sat on this. And most of the crowd strewed clothing on their own in the road, and others cut branches from the trees and strewed them in the road. And the crowds who went before him and who came after him cried aloud, saying: Hosanna to the son of David. Blessed is he who comes in the name of the Lord. Hosanna in the highest. And when he entered Jerusalem, all the city was disturbed, and said: Who is this? And the multitude answered: This is the prophet Jesus of Nazareth in Galilee.

And Jesus went into the temple and drove out all who bought and sold in the temple, and overturned the tables of the money changers and the stalls of the sellers of doves, and said to them: It is written: My house shall be called a house of prayer, and you are making it a den of robbers. And the blind and the lame came to him in the temple, and he healed them. When the high priests and the scribes saw the wonders he performed, and that the boys cried out in the temple and said: Hosanna to the son of David, they were angry and said to him: Do you hear what they are saying? But Jesus said to them: Yes. Have you never read that from the mouths of children and babies you have composed praise?

Then he left them and went out of the city, into Bethany, and spent the night there. Early in the morning he came back to the city, and he was hungry. And seeing a single fig tree beside the road, he went to it, and found nothing on it except only leaves, and said to it: Let there be no more fruit from you forevermore. And at once the fig tree dried up. His disciples seeing it were astonished and said: How did the fig tree suddenly dry up? Jesus answered them and said: Truly I tell you, if you have faith and do not deliberate, you can not only do what was done to the fig tree but you can even say to this mountain: Rise up and throw yourself into the sea, and it will happen: and all that you ask for by prayer, if you have faith, you shall receive.

Now when he had gone into the temple and was teaching there, the high priests and the elders of the people came to him saying: By what authority do you do this, and who gave you this authority? Jesus answered and said to them: I too will ask you to tell me one thing, and if you tell me, I will tell you by what authority I do this. Whence came the baptism of John? From heaven or from men? They discussed this among themselves, saying: If we tell him: From heaven, he will say to us: Then why did you not believe him? But if we tell him: From men, then we have the people to fear, for they all hold John to be a prophet. And they answered Jesus and said: We do not know. He answered them in turn: Neither will I tell you by what authority I do this. What do you think? A man had two sons. He went to the first and said: My son, go out today and work in the vineyard. He answered and said: So I will, master; and did not go. He went to the second and spoke likewise; and he answered and said: I do not wish to; but later he repented and did go. Which of the two did his father's will? They said: The second. Jesus said to them: Truly I tell you that the tax collectors and the harlots shall go before you into the Kingdom of God. For John came to you in the way of righteousness, and you did not believe him; but the tax collectors and the harlots believed him; and when you saw it you did not repent, so as to believe him.

Hear one more parable. There was a man who was lord of a manor, and he planted a vineyard, and ran a fence about it and dug a pit for the wine press in it, and built a tower, and let it out to farmers, and left the country. When the time of the harvest was near, he sent his slaves to the farmers to take the harvest. And the farmers took his slaves, and one they lashed, and one they killed, and one they stoned. Again he sent slaves, more than the first ones, and they dealt with them in the same way. After this he sent his son, saying: They will respect my son. But when the farmers saw the son, they said among themselves: This is the heir. Come, let us kill him and take his inheritance. And they took him and cast him out of the vineyard and killed him. Now, when the lord of the vineyard comes, what will he do to those farmers? They said: He will destroy them evilly, as they are evil, and let the vineyard to other farmers, who will render him the harvests in their due time. Jesus said to them: Have you never read in the scriptures: The stone that the builders rejected has come to be at the head of the corner. It was made by the Lord, and is wonderful in our sight. Therefore I tell you that the Kingdom of God shall be taken away from you and given to a nation that produces its harvest. [And he who falls on that stone shall be broken; and he upon whom it falls shall be crushed by it.] And when the high priests and the Pharisees heard his parables they knew that he spoke of them; and they were looking for a way to seize him, but they feared the populace, since these held him to be a prophet.

§ Then Jesus spoke forth again and talked to them in parables, saying: The Kingdom of Heaven is like a king who held a wedding for his son. And he sent out his slaves to summon the invited guests to the wedding, and they would not come. Again he sent forth more slaves, saying to them: Tell the invited guests: See, I have made the dinner ready, my oxen and calves are sacrificed, and all is ready; come to the wedding. But they paid no heed and went their ways, one to his own lands, one to his house of business, but the others seized the slaves and outraged them and killed them. Then the king was angry and sent out his armies and destroyed those murderers and burned their city. Then he said to his slaves: The wedding feast is ready, but the invited guests were not worthy. Go out then to the street corners and invite any you find there, to the wedding. And those slaves went out into the streets and brought in all they found, bad and good, and the wedding hall was filled with guests at the tables. The king came in to see them at dinner, and saw one man who was not wearing a wedding garment; and he said to him: My friend, how did you come in here without a wedding garment? The man was speechless. Then the king said to his servants: Tie his feet and his hands and cast him into the outer darkness. There will be wailing and gnashing of teeth. For many are invited but few are accepted.

Then the Pharisees went and held a consultation, in order to catch him up in what he said. They sent their disciples along with the Herodians, and they said: Master, we know that you are truthful, and you teach the way of God truthfully, and you care for no man, for you are no respecter of persons. Tell us then what you think. Is it lawful to pay the assessment to Caesar, or not? Jesus guessed at their treachery and said: Hypocrites, why do you tempt me? Show me the coin for the assessment. They showed him a denarius. He said: Whose is the image, and whose name is inscribed? They said: Caesar's. Then he said to them: Then give Caesar what is Caesar's and God what is God's. When they heard this, they were left wondering, and let him be, and went away.

On that day there came to him Sadducees, who say that there is no resurrection. And they questioned him, saying: Master, Moses said: If a man dies without children, his brother shall marry his wife and raise up issue for his brother. But among us there were seven brothers. The first married and died without issue, and left his wife to his brother; and so also did the second and third until all seven had married her. Last of all the woman died. So in the resurrection, whose wife will she be, of the seven? For they all had her as wife. Jesus answered and said to them: You are far astray and do not know the scriptures, nor yet the power of God. For in the resurrection they do not marry, nor are they married, but are as the angels in heaven. But as to the resurrection of the dead, have you not read the word spoken to you by God, saying: I am the God of Abraham and the God of Isaac and the God of Jacob. God is not God of the dead but of the living. Hearing this the multitude were struck with wonder at his teaching.

But when the Pharisees heard that he had silenced

the Sadducees, they assembled together, and one of
them who was versed in the law questioned him,
making trial of him: Master, in the law, which is the
great commandment? He said: That you shall love the
Lord your God in all your heart and all your spirit and
all your mind. That is the great commandment, and the
first. There is a second, which is like it: You shall love
your neighbor as yourself. On these two commandments all the law and the prophets depend. And when
the Pharisees were gathered together, Jesus questioned
them, saying: What do you think concerning the
Christ? Whose son is he? They said to him: The son of
David. He said: How then did David call him in the
spirit, Lord, when he said: The Lord said to my Lord:
Sit on my right, so that I may put your enemies beneath
your feet. But if David calls him Lord, how can he be
his son? And none of them could answer him a word,
nor did anyone dare from that day to question him any
more.

§ Then Jesus spoke to the people and to his disciples,
saying: The scribes and the Pharisees sit in the chair of
Moses. Do and observe all that they tell you, but do not
do as they do; for they speak, and do nothing. They tie
up heavy bundles and put them on the shoulders of
men, but they will not use one finger to carry them. All
they do is done for show, before people; they spread
their phylacteries and wear large tassels, they love the
foremost couch at the dinners and the first seats in the
synagogues, and the salutations in the marketplace, and
being called rabbi by the people. Do not let yourselves
be called rabbi; for you have one teacher, but you are
all brothers. And do not call anyone your father on
earth; for you have one father, in heaven. And do not
let yourselves be called instructors, since you have one
instructor, the Christ. He who is greater than you shall
be your servant. He who exalts himself shall be brought
low, and he who lowers himself shall be exalted.

Woe to you, scribes and Pharisees, hypocrites, because you shut the Kingdom of Heaven in the face of mankind; for neither do you go in yourselves, nor do you let those who are trying to enter go in. Woe to you, scribes and Pharisees, hypocrites, because you sweep the sea and the dry land to make one convert, and when it is done, you make him a son of Gehenna twice over as much as yourselves. Woe to you, blind guides who say: If one swears by the temple, it is nothing, but if one swears by the gold of the temple, he is bound. Fools and blind men, which is greater, the gold or the temple that hallows the gold? Again you say: If one swears by the altar, it is nothing, but if one swears by the offering upon the altar, he is bound. Blind, for which is greater, the offering or the altar that hallows the offering? So one who swears by the altar swears by it and all that is on it; and one who swears by the temple swears by it and by him who dwells in it; and one who swears by heaven swears by the throne of God and by him who sits upon it. Woe to you, scribes and Pharisees, hypocrites, because you pay a tenth on the mint and the anise and the cumin, and have passed over what is weightier in the law, the judgment and the mercy and the faith. These you should have cultivated, nor yet passed over the other things. Blind guides, who filter out the gnat but swallow the camel whole. Woe to you, scribes and Pharisees, hypocrites, because you scour the outside of the cup and the dish, but inside they are filled with rapacity and incontinence. Blind Pharisees, scour first the inside of the cup, so that the outside may be also clean. Woe to you, scribes and Pharisees, hypocrites, because you are like tombs that are whitewashed, which show handsome on the outside, but inside they are full of dead bones and all uncleanness. So you too on the outside seem to men to be just, but in the inside you are full of hypocrisy and lawlessness. Woe to you, scribes and Pharisees, hypocrites, because you build the tombs of the prophets and adorn the monuments of the just, and say: If we had

been in the days of our fathers, we should not have
been guilty of the blood of the prophets. Thus you bear
witness against yourselves that you are the sons of those
who murdered the prophets. Fill out, then, the measure
of your fathers. Serpents, viper's brood, how can you
escape the judgment of Gehenna? Therefore, see, I
send you the prophets and the wise men and the
scribes; and some of them you will kill and crucify, and
some of them you will lash in your synagogues and
chase from city to city, so that upon you shall descend
all righteous blood that has been poured out upon
earth, from the blood of Abel the righteous to the
blood of Zachariah the son of Barach, whom you
murdered between the temple and the altar. Truly I tell
you, all this shall descend upon this generation. Jerusalem Jerusalem, who kill the prophets and stone those
who have been sent to you, how many times have I
wished to gather in your children, as a bird gathers her
fledglings under her wings, and you would not let me.
Behold, your house is lost. For I tell you, you shall not
see me again, until you say: Blessed is he who comes in
the name of the Lord.

§ And Jesus left the temple and was going on his way,
and his disciples came to him, to show him the buildings
of the temple. But he answered them and said: Do you
not see all this? Truly I tell you, nothing here shall
escape destruction and no stone will be left on another.
Then he sat down upon the Mount of Olives, and his
disciples came to him privately and said: Tell us, when
shall this be, and what is the sign of your presence and
the end of the world? Jesus answered and said to them:
See to it that no one leads you astray. For many will
come in my name, saying: I am the Christ. And they
will lead many astray. You will hear wars and rumors of
wars. Be watchful, do not be frightened. For this must
be, but the end is not yet. Nation shall rise up against
nation and kingdom against kingdom, and there shall

be famines and earthquakes, place by place; all these things are the beginnings of the agony. Then they will hand you over for persecution, and kill you, and you will be hated by all the nations because of my name. And at this time many shall be driven astray and betray and hate each other, and many false prophets shall rise up, and they shall lead many astray; and through abundance of lawlessness the love of many shall grow cold. He who endures to the end shall be saved. And this gospel of the kingdom shall be preached in all the inhabited world in testimony to all the nations, and then the end will come. Thus when you see the abomination of desolation, that was told by Daniel the prophet, established in the holy place—and let him who reads this take note of it—then let those who are in Judaea flee to the mountains, and let him who is on the housetop not come down to take up what is in his house, and let him who is in the field not turn back to pick up his coat. Woe to the women who are with child and the women who are nursing in those days. Pray that your flight may not come in the wintertime, nor on the sabbath. For at that time there will be great affliction, such as there has not been since the beginning of creation and cannot be again. And if those days had not been cut short, there would be no flesh saved; but because of the chosen, those days will be shortened. Then, if anyone says to you: Here is the Christ, or here; do not believe him. For false Christs will rise up and false prophets, and they will present great signs and portents so as to mislead even the chosen, if that may be done. See, I have warned you. If then they say to you: See he is in the desert; do not go out; or, see, he is in the countinghouses; do not believe. For as the lightning goes out from the east and shines as far as the west, thus shall be the coming of the son of man. Where the carcass is, there will the eagles be gathered. And at once after the affliction of those days the sun will be darkened and the moon will not give her light, and the stars will fall from the sky, and the powers of the skies will be shaken. And then will appear the sign of the son of man in the sky, and then all the tribes of the earth will beat themselves, and see the son of man coming upon the clouds with power and great glory, and he will send out his angels with a great trumpet, and they will gather the chosen together from the four winds and from end to end of the sky. From the fig tree learn its parable; when its branch is tender and it puts forth leaves, you know that the summer is near; so too when you see all these things, you know that he is near, at your doors. Truly I tell you that this generation will not pass before all these things are done. The sky and the earth will pass away, but my words cannot pass away. But concerning that day and hour none knows, not the angels of heaven nor the son, none but the father alone. For as the days of Noah, thus will be the coming of the son of man. For as in those days before the flood there were people eating and drinking, marrying and making marriages, until the day when Noah went aboard his ark, and they did not know, until the flood came and took them all away; thus also will be the coming of the son of man. Then there will be two in the field, and one taken and one left; two women grinding at the mill, and one taken and one left. Be watchful then, because you do not know on what day your Lord will come. But you know this, that if the master of the house had known the time when the burglar would come, he would have stayed awake and would not have let his house be broken into. Therefore make yourselves ready, because in the hour when you do not expect him the son of man will come. Who then is the faithful and prudent slave whom the master set over his household, to give them their food when it is due? Blessed is that slave whom his master, when he comes, will find doing so. Truly I tell you that he will put him in charge of all his possessions. But if that other, bad slave says in his heart: My master is long coming; and begins to beat his fellow slaves, and eat and drink with the drunkards; the master of that slave will come on the day when he does not expect him and in the hour when he is unaware, and cut him to ribbons, and make his lot one with the hypocrites; and there will be wailing and gnashing of teeth.

§ Then the Kingdom of Heaven will be like ten girls who took their lamps and went out to meet the bridegroom. And five of them were thoughtless, and five were thoughtful. For the thoughtless ones, when they took their lamps, did not take oil with them, and the thoughtful ones took oil in their flasks along with their lamps. When the bridegroom was late they all grew sleepy and slept. But in the middle of the night there was a great outcry: Behold, the bridegroom; go out to meet him. Then all those girls woke up and trimmed their lamps, but the thoughtless ones said to those who were thoughtful: Give us some of your oil, since our lamps are going out. But the thoughtful ones answered, saying: There would never be enough for us and for you. Better, go to those who sell it and buy it for yourselves. But while they were gone to buy it, the bridegroom arrived, and those who were ready went in with him to the wedding, and the door was shut. Then later came the other girls, saying: Lord, lord, open to us. But he answered and said: Truly I tell you, I do not know you. Be watchful then, since you do not know the day, or the hour.

For it is like a man who made a journey, and called in his own slaves and handed over to them all his properties. And to one he gave five talents, to one two, to one one, each according to his ability, and went away. At once the one who had received five talents went into business with them, and made five more; so also the one who had received two made another two. But the man who had received one went away and dug a hole in the ground and hid the money of his master in it. Then after a long time the master of those slaves came back and cast up accounts with them. And the one who had received five talents came forward and delivered five talents more, saying: Master, you gave me five talents; see, I have made five talents more. His master said to him: Well done, good and trusty slave; you were trusty in small amounts, I will set you in charge of much. Come in and share your master's festivities. Then he who had received two talents came forward and said: Master, you gave me two talents; see, I have made two talents more. His master said to him: Well done, good and trusty slave; you were trusty in small amounts, I will set you in charge of much. Come in and share your master's festivities. Then he who had received one talent came forward and said: Master, I knew that you were a hard man, that you harvest where you did not sow, that you gather where you did not scatter the seed; and I was afraid and went away and buried your talent in the ground; see, you have what is yours. His master answered and said to him: Wretched timid slave! Did you know that I harvest where I did not sow, that I gather where I did not scatter the seed? You should have put the money out with the bankers, and I could have gone and taken back my own, with interest. Take away his talent and give it to him who has the ten talents; for to everyone who has shall be given, even in excess; but from him who has not, even what he has shall be taken away. And cast this useless slave into the outer darkness; there will be wailing and gnashing of teeth.

When the son of man comes in his glory, and all the angels with him, then he will sit upon the throne of his glory, and all the nations shall be gathered before him, and he will sort them one from another, as the shepherd separates the sheep from the goats, and he will station the sheep on his right hand, and the goats on his left. Then the king will say to those who are on his right: Come, you who are the blessed of my father, inherit the kingdom which has been made ready for you from the beginning of the world. For I was hungry and you fed me, I was thirsty and you gave me to drink, I was a stranger and you took me in, I was naked and you clothed me, I was sick and you visited me, I was in prison and you came to me. Then the just will answer him, saying: Lord, when did we see you hungry and feed you, or thirsty and give you to drink? When did we see you a stranger and take you in, or naked and clothe you? When did we see you sick or in prison and come to you? And the king will answer and say to them: Truly I tell you, inasmuch as you have done it for any one of the least of these my brothers, you have done it for me. Then he will say to those on his left: Go from me, cursed, to the everlasting fire which has been made ready by the devil and his angels. For I was hungry and you did not feed me, I was thirsty and you did not give me to drink, I was a stranger and you did not take me in, I was naked and you did not clothe me, I was sick and in prison and you did not visit me. And they will answer him, saying: Lord, when did we see you hungry or thirsty or a stranger or naked or sick or in prison and not take care of you? Then he will answer them and say: Truly I tell you, inasmuch as you have failed to do this for one of these who are least, you have failed to do it for me. And these shall go to everlasting punishment, but the just to everlasting life.

§ Then it happened, when Jesus had done with all these sayings, that he said to his disciples: You know that after two days the Passover comes, and the son of man will be handed over to be crucified. Then the high priests and the elders of the people gathered in the courtyard of the high priest who was called Caiaphas, and they made plans to capture Jesus by treachery and kill him. But they said: Not during the festival, for fear there may be rioting among the people.

Now when Jesus was in Bethany, in the house of Simon the leper, there came to him a woman with an alabaster vessel full of precious ointment and anointed his head with it as he reclined at dinner. When his disciples saw this they were displeased and said: Why this waste? It could have been sold for a great price and the money given to the poor. Jesus was aware of them and said: Why are you hard on the woman? She has done a good thing to me. For always you have the poor with you, but you do not always have me. When she anointed my body with this ointment, it was for my burial. Truly I tell you, wherever this gospel is preached through all the world, she will be spoken of, and what she did, in memory of her.

And at that time one of the twelve, he who was called Judas Iscariot, went to the high priests and said: What are you willing to give me if I betray him to you? And they paid him thirty pieces of silver. And from that time he looked for an opportunity to betray him.

On the first day of the feast of unleavened bread, his disciples came to Jesus and said: Where do you wish us to make preparations for you to eat the feast of the Passover? He said: Go to the city, to the house of a certain man, and say to him: The teacher says: My time is near. I shall keep the Passover at your house, with my disciples. And his disciples did as Jesus instructed them, and made ready the Passover. When it was evening, he took his place at dinner with the twelve disciples. And as they were eating he said: Truly I tell you that one of you will betray me. They were bitterly hurt and began each one to say: Surely it is not I, Lord? He answered and said: The one who dips his hand in the dish with me, he is the one who will betray me. The son of man goes his way as it has been written for him to do, but woe to that man through whom the son of man is betrayed. It would have been well for that man if he had never been born. Judas, who had betrayed him, answered and said: Master, it is not I? Jesus said to him: It is you who said it. As they ate, Jesus took a loaf of bread, and blessed it, and broke it, and gave it to his disciples, and said: Take it; eat it; this is my body. And he took a cup and gave thanks and gave it to them, saying: Drink from it, all; for this is my blood, of the convenant, which is shed for the sake of many, for the remission of sins. But I tell you, from now on I shall not drink of this produce of the vine, until that day when I drink it with you, new wine, in the kingdom of my father.

And they sang the hymn and went out to the Mount of Olives. Then Jesus said to them: All of you will be made to fail me in the course of this night. For it is written: I will strike the shepherd, and the sheep of his flock will be scattered. But after my resurrection I will lead the way for you into Galilee. Peter spoke forth and said: Though all the others fail you, I will never fail you. Jesus said to him: Truly I tell you that on this night before the cock crows you will disown me three times. Peter said to him: Even if I must die with you, I will never disown you. And so spoke all the disciples.

Then Jesus went with them to a place called Gethsemane; and he said to his disciples: Sit down here, while I go over there and pray. He took with him Peter and the two sons of Zebedee; and then he was in pain and distress. And he said to them: My soul is in anguish to the point of death. Stay here and keep watch with me. Then he went a little farther, and threw himself down on his face, and said in prayer: Father, if it is possible, let this cup pass me by; except only, let it be not as I wish, but as you wish. Then he went back to his disciples and found them asleep, and said to Peter: Are you not then strong enough to keep watch with me for a single hour? Be wakeful, and pray that you may not be brought to the test. The spirit is eager, but the flesh is weak. Again a second time he went off and prayed, saying: Father, if it is not possible for this cup to pass me by, but I must drink it, let your will be done. Then he came back and again found them sleeping, for their eyes were heavy; and leaving them he went back and prayed a third time, saying the same words as before. Then he came back to the disciples and said to them: So you are still asleep, and resting. Behold, the hour is near, and the son of man is betrayed into the hands of sinners. Rise up, let us go; see, my betrayer is near.

And while he was still speaking, behold, Judas came, one of the twelve, and with him a great crowd, with swords and clubs, from the high priests and the elders of the people. And he who betrayed him told them the signal, saying: The one I kiss will be the man. Seize him. And at once he came up to Jesus and said: Hail, master; and kissed him. Jesus said to him: My friend, why are you here? Then they came up and laid hands on Jesus and bound him. And behold, one of those who were with Jesus put out his hand and drew his sword, and struck the slave of the high priest and took off his ear. Then Jesus said: Put away your sword where it belongs; for all who take up the sword shall die by the sword. Or do you not believe that I have the power to call upon my father, and he will at once send more than twelve legions of angels? But then, how to fulfill what has been written, that these things must be. At that time Jesus said to the multitude: You come out to arrest me with swords and clubs as if I were a highwayman? Day by day I sat in the temple, teaching, and you did not seize me.

But all this took place so that what was written by the prophets should be fulfilled.

At that time all his disciples left him and fled away.

But they who had seized Jesus brought him to the house of Caiaphas the high priest, where the scribes and elders were assembled. But Peter followed him at a distance as far as the courtyard of the high priest, and went inside and sat with the servingmen, to watch the event. And the high priests and the entire council were looking for some false evidence against Jesus, so that they might have him killed, and they could find none, though many false witnesses came forward. But later two came forward and spoke, saying: This man said this: I am able to tear down the temple of God and rebuild it within three days. Then the high priest stood up and said to him: Have you no answer? What is the testimony these bring against you? But Jesus remained silent. And the high priest said to him: I charge you by

the living God that you tell us whether you are the
Christ, the son of God. Jesus said to him: It is you who
said it. But now I say to you, presently you shall see the
son of man sitting on the right of the power and walking
upon the clouds of the sky. Then the priest rent his
clothing, saying: He has blasphemed. Why do we still
need witnesses? Behold, you have heard the blasphemy. What is your decision? They answered and said:
He has deserved death. Then they spat in his face and
struck him with their fists and beat him, saying: Tell us,
Christ, by prophecy, who hit you?

But Peter was sitting outside in the courtyard, and a
serving girl came up to him and said: You also were
with Jesus the Galilaean. But he denied it before them
all, saying: I do not know what you mean. And as he
went out to the gate another girl saw him and said to
those who were there: This man was with Jesus the
Nazarene. And again he denied it, with an oath, saying:
I do not know the man. After a little those who were
standing by came up to Peter and said: Truly you are
one of them, for your way of speaking makes it clear.
Then he began to swear with many oaths, saying: I do
not know the man. And thereupon the cock crew. And
Peter remembered the words of Jesus when he said:
Before the cock crows you will disown me three times.
And he went out and wept bitterly.

§ When morning came, all the high priests and elders
of the people held a meeting against Jesus, to have him
killed. And they bound him and took him away and
gave him over to Pilate the governor.

Then when Judas, who had betrayed him, saw that
he had been condemned, he repented and proffered the
thirty pieces of silver back to the high priests and the
elders, saying: I did wrong to betray innocent blood.
They said: What is that to us? You look to it. And he
threw down the silver pieces in the temple and went
away, and when he was alone he hanged himself. The

high priests took up the silver pieces and said: We cannot put them in the treasury, since it is blood money. Then they took counsel together and with the money they bought the potter's field to bury strangers in. Therefore that field has been called the Field of Blood, to this day. Then was fulfilled the word spoken by Jeremiah the prophet, saying: I took the thirty pieces of silver, the price of him on whom a price was set, whom they priced from among the sons of Israel, and I gave the money for the field of the potter, as my Lord commanded me.

Now Jesus stood before the governor, and the governor questioned him, saying: Are you the King of the Jews? Jesus answered: It is you who say it. And while he was being accused by the high priests and the elders he made no answer. Then Pilate said to him: Do you not hear all their testimony against you? And he made no answer to a single word, so that the governor was greatly amazed.

For the festival, the governor was accustomed to release one prisoner for the multitude, whichever one they wished. And they had at that time a notorious man, who was called Barabbas. Now as they were assembled Pilate said to them: Which one do you wish me to release for you, Barabbas, or Jesus, who is called Christ? For he knew that it was through malice that they had turned him over. Now as he was sitting on the platform, his wife sent him a message, saying: Let there be nothing between you and this just man; for I have suffered much today because of a dream about him. But the high priests and the elders persuaded the crowd to ask for Barabbas and destroy Jesus. Then the governor spoke forth and said to them: Which of the two shall I give you? They answered: Barabbas. Pilate said to them: What then shall I do with Jesus, who is called Christ? They all said: Let him be crucified. But Pilate said: Why? What harm has he done? But they screamed all the more, saying: Let him be crucified. And Pilate, seeing that he was doing no good and that the disorder was growing, took water and washed his hands before the crowd, saying: I am innocent of the blood of this man. You see to it. And all the people answered and said: His blood is upon us and upon our children. Then Pilate gave them Barabbas, but he had Jesus flogged, and gave him over to be crucified.

Then the soldiers of the governor took Jesus to the residence, and drew up all their battalion around him. And they stripped him and put a red mantle about him, and wove a wreath of thorns and put it on his head, and put a reed in his right hand, and knelt before him and mocked him, saying: Hail, King of the Jews. And they spat upon him and took the reed and beat him on the head. And after they had mocked him, they took off the mantle and put his own clothes on him, and led him away to be crucified. And as they went out they found a man of Cyrene, named Simon. They impressed him for carrying the cross.

Then they came to a place called Golgotha, which means the place of the skull, and gave him wine mixed with gall to drink. When he tasted it he would not drink it. Then they crucified him, and divided up his clothes, casting lots, and sat there and watched him. Over his head they put the label giving charge against him, where it was written: This is Jesus, the King of the Jews. Then there were crucified with him two robbers, one on his right and one on his left. And those who passed by blasphemed against him, wagging their heads, and saying: You who tear down the temple and rebuild it in three days, save yourself, and come down from the cross, if you are the son of God. So too the high priests, mocking him along with the scribes and the elders, said: He saved others, he cannot save himself. He is King of Israel, let him come down from the cross and we will believe in him. He trusted in God, let him save him now, if he will; for he said: I am the son of God. And the robbers who were crucified with him spoke abusively to him in the same way.

But from the sixth hour there was darkness over all

the earth until the ninth hour. But about the ninth hour Jesus cried out in a great voice, saying: *Elei elei lema sabachthanei?* Which is: My God, my God, why have you forsaken me? But some of those who were standing there heard and said: This man calls to Elijah. And at once one of them ran and took a sponge, soaked it in vinegar and put it on the end of a reed, and gave it to him to drink. But the rest said: Let us see if Elijah comes to save him.

Then Jesus cried out again in a great voice, and gave up his life. And behold, the veil of the temple was split in two from top to bottom, and the earth was shaken, and the rocks were split, and the tombs opened and many bodies of the holy sleepers rose up; and after his resurrection they came out of their tombs and went into the holy city, and were seen by many. But the company commander and those with him who kept guard over Jesus, when they saw the earthquake and the things that happened, were greatly afraid, saying: In truth this was the son of God. And there were many women watching from a distance there, who had followed Jesus from Galilee, waiting on him. Among them were Mary the Magdalene, and Mary the mother of James and Joseph, and the mother of the sons of Zebedee.

When it was evening, there came a rich man of Arimathaea, Joseph by name, who also had been a disciple of Jesus. This man went to Pilate and asked for the body of Jesus. Then Pilate ordered that it be given up to him. And Joseph took the body and wrapped it in clean linen, and laid it in his new tomb, which he had cut in the rock, and rolled a great stone before the door of the tomb, and went away. But Mary the Magdalene and the other Mary were there, sitting before the tomb. On the next day, which is the day after the Day of Preparation, the high priests and the Pharisees gathered in the presence of Pilate, and said: Lord, we have remembered how that impostor said while he was still alive: After three days I shall rise up. Give orders, then, that the tomb be secured until after the third day,

for fear his disciples may come and steal him away and
say to the people: He rose from the dead. And that will
be the ultimate deception, worse than the former one.
Pilate said to them: You have a guard. Go and secure it
as best you can. And they went and secured the tomb,
sealing it with the help of the guard.

§ Late on the sabbath, as the light grew toward the
first day after the sabbath, Mary the Magdalene and the
other Mary came to visit the tomb. And behold, there
was a great earthquake, for the angel of the Lord came
down from heaven and approached the stone and rolled
it away and was sitting on it. His look was like lightning,
and his clothing white as snow. And those who were on
guard were shaken with fear of him and became like
dead men. But the angel spoke forth and said to the
women: Do not you fear; for I know that you look for
Jesus, who was crucified. He is not here. For he rose
up, as he said. Come here, and look at the place where
he lay. Then go quickly and tell his disciples that he has
risen from the dead, and behold, he goes before you
into Galilee. There you will see him. See; I have told
you. And quickly leaving the tomb, in fear and great
joy, they ran to tell the news to his disciples. And
behold, Jesus met them, saying: I give you greeting.
They came up to him and took his feet and worshipped
him. Then Jesus said to them: Do not fear. Go and tell
my brothers to go into Galilee, and there they will see
me. And as they went on their way, behold, some of the
guards went into the city and reported to the high
priests all that had happened. And they met with the
elders and took counsel together, and gave the soldiers
a quantity of money, saying: Say that the disciples came
in the night and stole him away while we were sleeping.
And if this is heard in the house of the governor, we
shall reason with him, and make it so that you have
nothing to fear. And they took the money and did as

they were instructed. And this is the story that has been spread about among the Jews, to this day.

Then the eleven disciples went on into Galilee, to the mountain where Jesus had given them instructions to go; and when they saw him, they worshipped him; but some doubted. And Jesus came up to them and talked with them, saying: All authority has been given to me, in heaven and on earth. Go out, therefore, and instruct all the nations, baptizing them in the name of the Father and the Son and the Holy Spirit, teaching them to observe all that I have taught you. And behold, I am with you, all the days until the end of the world.

LUKE

Luke is believed by the majority of authorities to be "Luke, the beloved physician" of *Colossians* 4.14. This gospel is generally dated somewhere about A.D. 85, after the fall of Jerusalem in A.D. 70.

§ SINCE MANY HAVE UNDERTAKEN TO COM-
pose an account of those things which have been fulfilled among us, as those who saw for themselves from
the beginning and became servants of the word have
handed it down to us, it seemed good for me also, since
I have followed everything closely from the first, to
write it out in order for you, most exalted Theophilus,
so that you may learn the truth concerning those stories
of which you have been informed.

In the days of Herod, king of Judaea, there was a
certain priest, by name Zachariah, of the division of
Abiah; and his wife came from the daughters of Aaron,
and her name was Elizabeth. They were both righteous
people in the sight of God, going blamelessly in all the
commandments and judgments of the Lord. And they
had no child, because Elizabeth was barren; and they
were both well advanced in their days. Now it happened that during his priestly duty, when it was the turn

of his division to be in the presence of God, according
to the custom of the priesthood, he was the one allotted
to go into the temple of the Lord and burn the incense.
And all the multitude of people was praying outside at
the hour of the incense; and he had a vision of an angel
of the Lord standing at the right of the altar for the
incense. And Zachariah was shaken when he saw him,
and fear fell upon him. But the angel said to him: Do
not fear, Zachariah; since your entreaty has been
heard, and your wife Elizabeth shall bear you a son,
and you shall call his name John; and he will be your
joy and your pride, and many will rejoice at his birth.
For he will be great in the sight of the Lord, and he will
never drink wine or strong drink, and he will be filled
with the Holy Spirit while still in the womb of his
mother, and he will turn many of the sons of Israel
toward the Lord their God; and he will go before him in
his presence in the spirit and power of Elijah, to turn
the hearts of fathers toward their children, and the
disobedient to the wisdom of the righteous; to prepare
a people which will be ready for the Lord. And
Zachariah said to the angel: How shall I know this?
For I am an old man, and my wife is advanced in her
days. And the angel answered him and said: I am Gabriel. I stand in the presence of God; and I was sent
to talk to you to bring you this good news. And behold, you will be silent and unable to speak until the
day when these things come to pass, because you did
not believe my words, which will be fulfilled in their
time.

Now the people were waiting for Zachariah, and they
wondered at the time he took in the temple. But when
he came out he could not speak to them, and they
realized that he had seen a vision in the temple; and he
kept nodding to them, and remained speechless. And it
happened that when the days of his service were
completed he went back to his own house. And after
these days Elizabeth his wife conceived; and she kept
herself in concealment for five months, saying: Thus

has the Lord done by me in the days when he consented
to take away the reproach that was mine among men.

In the sixth month the angel Gabriel was sent to a
city of Galilee, whose name is Nazareth, to a virgin
engaged to a man named Joseph, of the house of
David; and the name of this virgin was Mary. And
going into her presence, he said: Hail, favored one; the
Lord is with you. She was disturbed at what he said and
asked herself what this greeting might mean. And the
angel said to her: Do not fear, Mary, for you have
found favor with God; and behold, you shall conceive
in your womb and bring forth a son, and you shall call
his name Jesus. He will be great, and called son of the
Highest, and the Lord God will give him the throne of
David his forefather, and he will be king over the house
of Jacob through the ages, and of his Kingdom there
will be no end. But Mary said to the angel: How shall
this be, since I know no man? And the angel answered
and said to her: The Holy Spirit will come to you, and
the power of the highest will overshadow you. Therefore the offspring will be called holy, the son of God.
And behold, Elizabeth your kinswoman, she also has
conceived a son, in her old age, and this is the sixth
month for her who had been called barren; because
nothing at all will be impossible for God. Mary said:
Here is the slave of the Lord. May it happen to me as
you have said. And the angel left her.

And Mary rose up in those days and journeyed in
haste into the hill country, to a city of Judah, and
entered the house of Zachariah and greeted Elizabeth.
And it happened that when Elizabeth heard the
greeting of Mary, the child leaped in her womb, and
Elizabeth was filled with the Holy Spirit, and she spoke
out with a great cry and said: Blessed are you among
women, and blessed the fruit of your womb. And how
did it befall me that the mother of my Lord should
come to me? For behold, when the sound of your
greeting came to my ears, the child leapt for joy in my
womb. And blessed is she who believed that there will

be fulfillment of what was told her from the Lord. Then
Mary said: My soul exalts the Lord, and my spirit
rejoices in God my savior, because he cast down his
eyes to the low estate of his slave girl. Behold, after
now all the generations will bless me; because the
mighty one has done great things for me, and his name
is holy; and his mercy is for generations and generations, for those who fear him. He has taken power into
his arm, and scattered the proud in the imagination of
their hearts. He has pulled down the dynasts from their
thrones, and raised up the humble; he has filled the
hungry with good things, and sent the rich away empty.
He has reached out his hand to Israel his servant,
through the memory of mercy; as he said to our fathers,
to Abraham and his seed forever.

And Mary remained with her for about three
months, and then returned to her own house.

For Elizabeth her time was completed, and she bore
a son. And her neighbors and relatives heard that the
Lord had made great his mercy in her case, and they
rejoiced with her. And it came about that on the eighth
day they came to circumcise the baby; and they were
calling him by the name of his father, Zachariah. Then
his mother spoke forth and said: No, but he shall be
called John. And they said to her: There is no one in
your kindred who is called by that name. And they
made signs to his father, to learn what he wished him to
be called. And he asked for a tablet and wrote, saying:
John is his name. And all were amazed. But his mouth
was set free at once, and his tongue, and he spoke
praising God. And fear came upon all those who lived
about them, and in all the hill country of Judaea all
these sayings were repeated, and those who heard them
laid them in their hearts, saying: What will this child
be? The hand of the Lord is with him. And Zachariah
his father was filled with the Holy Spirit, and he
prophesied, saying: Praised be the Lord God of Israel,
because he visited his people and wrought their deliverance, and raised up our horn of salvation in the house

of David, his servant; as he spoke through the mouth of his holy prophets from of old; safety from our enemies and the hand of all those who hate us, to work mercy with our fathers and to remember his holy convenant; the oath he swore to Abraham our father, to grant that we be rescued without fear from the hand of our enemies, to serve him in piety and righteousness before his presence all our days. And you, child, will be called prophet of the highest, and go before the presence of the Lord to make ready his ways, to grant to his people knowledge of their salvation through the remission of their sins; through the compassionate mercy of our Lord whereby the sunrise shall shine upon us from on high, to illuminate those who sit in darkness and the shadow of death, to guide our feet into the way of peace.

And the child grew and became strong in spirit; and he was in the desert until the day of his appearance before Israel.

§ It happened in those days that a decree went forth from Augustus Caesar that all the world should be enrolled in a census. This was the first census, when Quirinius was governor of Syria. And all went to be enrolled, each to his own city. And Joseph also went up from Galilee, from the city of Nazareth, to Judaea, to the city of David which is called Bethlehem, because he was of the house and family of David; to be enrolled with Mary his promised wife, who was pregnant. And it happened that while they were there her time was completed, and she bore a son, her first-born, and she wrapped him in swaddling clothes and laid him in a manger, because there was no room for them in the inn. And there were shepherds in that region, camping out at night and keeping guard over their flock. And an angel of the Lord stood before them, and the glory of the Lord shone about them, and they were afraid with a great fear. The angel said to them: Do not be afraid;

behold, I tell you good news, great joy which shall be
for all the people; because this day there has been born
for you in the city of David a savior who is Christ the
Lord. And here is a sign for you; you will find a baby
wrapped in swaddling clothes and lying in a manger.
And suddenly with the angel there was a multitude of
the heavenly host, praising God and saying: Glory to
God in the highest and peace on earth among men of
good will. And it happened that after the angels had
gone off from them into the sky, the shepherds began
saying to each other: Let us go to Bethlehem and see
this thing which has happened, which the Lord made
known to us; and they went, hastening, and found
Mary and Joseph, and the baby lying in the manger;
and when they had seen, they spread the news about
what had been told them concerning this baby. And all
who heard wondered at what had been told them by the
shepherds; and Mary kept in mind all these sayings as
she pondered them in her heart. And the shepherds
returned, glorifying and praising God over all they had
heard and seen, as it had been told them.

And when eight days were past, for his circumcision,
his name was called Jesus, as it was named by the angel
before he was conceived in the womb.

And when the days for their purification according to
the Law of Moses had been completed, they took him
up to Jerusalem to set him before the Lord, as it has
been written in the Law of the Lord: Every male child
who opens the womb shall be called sacred to the Lord;
and to give sacrifice as it is stated in the Law of the
Lord, a pair of turtle doves or two young pigeons. And
behold, there was a man in Jerusalem whose name was
Simeon, and this man was righteous and virtuous and
looked forward to the consolation of Israel, and the
Holy Spirit was upon him; and it had been prophesied
to him by the Holy Spirit that he should not look upon
his death until he had looked on the Lord's Anointed.
And in the spirit he went into the temple; and as his
parents brought in the child Jesus so that they could do

for him what was customary according to the law, Simeon himself took him in his arms and blessed God and said: Now, Lord, you release your slave, in peace, according to your word; because my eyes have looked on your salvation, what you made ready in the presence of all the peoples; a light for the revelation to the Gentiles, and the glory of your people, Israel. And his father and his mother were in wonder at what was being said about him. And Simeon blessed them and said to Mary his mother: Behold, he is appointed for the fall and the rise of many in Israel; and as a sign which is disputed; and through your soul also will pass the sword; so that the reasonings of many hearts may be revealed. And there was Anna, a prophetess, the daughter of Phanuel, of the tribe of Asher. And she was well advanced in years, having lived with her husband seven years from the time of her maidenhood, and now she was eighty-four years a widow. And she did not leave the temple, serving night and day with fastings and prayers. And at this same time she came near and gave thanks to God and spoke of the child to those who looked forward to the deliverance of Jerusalem.

And when they had done everything according to the Law of the Lord, they went back to Galilee, to their own city, Nazareth.

And the child grew in stature and strength as he was filled with wisdom, and the grace of God was upon him.

Now his parents used to journey every year to Jerusalem for the feast of the Passover. And when he was twelve years old, when they went up according to their custom for the festival and had completed their days there, on their return the boy Jesus stayed behind in Jerusalem, and his parents did not know it. And supposing that he was in their company they went a day's journey and then looked for him among their relatives and friends, and when they did not find him they turned back to Jerusalem in search of him. And it happened that after three days they found him in the

temple sitting in the midst of the masters, listening to
them and asking them questions. And all who heard
him were amazed at his intelligence and his answers.
And they were astonished at seeing him, and his
mother said to him: Child, why did you do this to us?
See, your father and I have been looking for you, in
distress. He said to them: But why were you looking for
me? Did you not know that I must be in my father's
house? And they did not understand what he had said
to them. And he returned with them and came to
Nazareth, and was in their charge. And his mother kept
all his sayings in her heart. And Jesus advanced in
wisdom and stature, and in the favor of God and men.

§ In the fifteenth year of the reign of Tiberius Caesar,
when Pontius Pilate was governor of Judaea, and
Herod was tetrarch of Galilee, and Philip his brother
was tetrarch of the region of Ituraea and Trachonitis,
and Lysanias was tetrarch of Abilene, when Annas,
with Caiaphas, was high priest, the word of God came
to John the son of Zachariah in the desert. And he went
into all the region about Jordan preaching the baptism
of repentance for the remission of sins, as it is written in
the book of the words of Isaiah the prophet: The voice
of one crying in the desert, prepare the way of the
Lord, make straight the roads before him. Every
watercourse will be filled, and every mountain and hill
will be brought low; and the crooked will turn straight
and the rough roads will turn smooth; and all flesh will
look on the salvation of God. And he said to the
multitudes that came out to be baptized by him: You
viper's brood, who warned you to flee from the anger to
come? Then produce fruits that are worthy of your
repentance; and do not begin to say among yourselves:
We have Abraham for our father. For I say to you that
out of these stones God can raise up children to
Abraham. And by now the ax is set against the root of

the trees; so that every tree that does not bear fruit is cut out and thrown into the fire. And the people questioned him saying: What then shall we do? He answered and said to them: Let him who has two tunics share with him who has none, and let him who has food do likewise. And tax collectors also came to him to be baptized and said to him: Master, what shall we do? He said to them: Collect nothing except what is assigned to you. And soldiers in service also questioned him, saying: And we too, what shall we do? And he said to them: No extortion, no false accusation, and live on your wages. And as the people had great hopes and all were wondering in their hearts about John, whether he might even be the Messiah, John spoke forth saying to all: I baptize you with water; but one is coming who is stronger than I, and I am not fit to untie the fastening of his shoes. He will baptize you in the Holy Spirit and in fire. His winnowing fan is in his hand, to clear his threshing floor and gather his grain into his storehouse, and he will burn the chaff in quenchless fire.

There was much else also that he advised the people to do as he announced the good news. But Herod the tetrarch, who had been reproved by him in the matter of Herodias his brother's wife, and for all his other misdeeds, added this one to the rest: he had John confined in prison.

And it happened that in the baptizing of all the people Jesus also was baptized; and as he prayed the sky opened and the Holy Spirit in bodily form like a dove descended upon him, and there came a voice from the sky saying: You are my son, whom I love, in whom I am well pleased.

And Jesus when he began was about thirty years old, and was the son, as it was believed, of Joseph, the son of Heli, the son of Mathat, the son of Levi, the son of Melchi, the son of Jannai, the son of Joseph, the son of Matathias, the son of Amos, the son of Nahum, the son of Esli, the son of Naggai, the son of Maath, the son of

Matathias, the son of Semein, the son of Josech, the
son of Joda, the son of Joanan, the son of Rhesa, the
son of Zerubbabel, the son of Salathiel, the son of Neri,
the son of Melchi, the son of Addi, the son of Cosam
the son of Elmadam, the son of Er, the son of Jesus,
the son of Eliezer, the son of Jorim, the son of Mathat, the son of Levi, the son of Symeon, the son of
Judah, the son of Joseph, the son of Jonam, the son of
Eliacim, the son of Melea, the son of Menna, the son
of Matatha, the son of Nathan, the son of David, the
son of Jesse, the son of Jobed, the son of Boaz, the
son of Sala, the son of Nahshon, the son of Aminadab,
the son of Admin, the son of Arni, the son of Hezron, the son of Perez, the son of Judah, the son of
Jacob, the son of Isaac, the son of Abraham, the son
of Terah, the son of Nachor, the son of Serug, the
son of Reu, the son of Peleg, the son of Eber, the son
of Sala, the son of Cainan, the son of Arphaxad, the
son of Shem, the son of Noah, the son of Lamech,
the son of Methuselah, the son of Enoch, the son
of Jared, the son of Mahahaleel, the son of Cainan,
the son of Enos, the son of Seth, the son of Adam,
the son of God.

§ And Jesus, filled with the Holy Spirit, turned away
from Jordan and was guided by the spirit in the desert
for forty days, being tested by the devil. And he ate
nothing in those days, and when they were finished he
was hungry. And the devil said to him: If you are the
son of God, tell this stone to become bread. Jesus said
to him in answer: It is written: Not by bread alone shall
man live. Then he led him on high and showed him all
the kingdoms of the world in a flash of time; and the
devil said to him: I will give you this power entire and
the glory of these things, because this has been turned
over to me, and I give it to whom I will. If then you will
worship me, it shall all be yours. Jesus answered and
said to him: It is written: You shall worship the Lord

your God, and shall serve him only. Then he took him
to Jerusalem and set him on the gable of the temple,
and said to him: If you are the son of God, throw
yourself down from here; for it is written: He will
charge his angels concerning you, to guard you; and
that: Upon their hands they will support you, so that
never may you strike your foot against the stone. And
Jesus answered and said to him: It is said: You shall not
tempt the Lord your God. So when he had done with
every temptation, the devil left him until a better
time.

And Jesus, in the power of the Spirit, returned to
Galilee; and rumor about him went through the entire
region; and he himself taught in their synagogues,
honored by all. And he came to Nazareth, where he
had been raised, and entered the synagogue as was his
custom on the day of the sabbath, and stood up to read.
And he was handed the book of the prophet Isaiah, and
opening the book he found the place where it was
written: The spirit of the Lord is upon me, because of
which he has anointed me, to bring good news to the
poor; he sent me forth to announce release to captives,
and eyesight to the blind; to set those who are broken at
liberty; to proclaim the accepted year of the Lord. And
folding the book he gave it back to the servant and sat
down; and the eyes of all who were in the synagogue
were fixed upon him. And he began to say to them:
Today this scripture is fulfilled in your hearing. And all
spoke well of him and marveled at the grace in the
words that came from his mouth, and said: Is not this
the son of Joseph? And he said to them: Surely you will
tell me the parable: Physician, cure yourself; do here
also in your own country all we have heard of that was
done in Capernaum. And he said: Truly I tell you, no
prophet is accepted in his own country. But this is true
that I tell you: There were many widows in Israel in the
days of Elijah, when the sky was closed for three years
and six months, so that there was famine in all the land;
but to none of them was Elijah sent, but only to a

widowed woman of Sarepta in Sidon. And there were many lepers in Israel in the time of Elisha the prophet, but none of them was made clean except Naaman the Syrian. And all those in the synagogue were filled with anger when they heard this, and they rose up and cast him out of the city, and they took him to the brink of the cliff on which was built their city, to fling him over. But he passed through their midst and went on his way.

And he went down to Capernaum, a city of Galilee. And he was teaching them on the sabbath, and they were astonished at his teaching, because he spoke with authority. And in the synagogue there was a man who had the spirit of an unclean demon and he cried out in a great voice: Ha. What is there between us and you, Jesus of Nazareth? Did you come to destroy us? I know you, who you are, God's holy one. Jesus reproved him, saying: Be silent and go out from him. And the demon flung him down in their midst and came out of him, without doing him any harm. And wonder came upon all and they talked among themselves, saying: What is this speech, that in authority and power he gives orders to unclean spirits, and they come out? And the rumor of him went forth to every place in the region.

But he rose up and left the synagogue and went into the house of Simon. The mother-in-law of Simon was suffering from a great fever, and they besought him for her sake. He stood over her and reproved the fever, and it left her; and at once she stood up and served them. And when the sun set, all those who had people sick with various sicknesses brought them to him, and he laid his hands on each one of them, and healed them. And also demons came out of many, crying out and saying: You are the son of God. But he forbade them and told them not to speak, because they knew that he was the Christ. When day came he went out to a deserted place, and the multitudes went looking for him, and came up with him, and held him back so that he could not go from them. But he said to them: I must bring the good news of the Kingdom of God to the other cities also, since for this I was sent forth. And he went preaching through the synagogues of Judaea.

§ It happened that, while the crowd was pressing upon him and listening to the word of God, he himself was standing by the Lake of Gennesaret, and he saw two boats standing beside the lake, but the fishermen had disembarked and were washing their nets. He went aboard one of the boats, which was Simon's, and asked him to take him out a little way from the land, and he sat in the boat and taught the multitudes. And when he was through speaking, he said to Simon: Go on out into the deep water and let down your nets and fish. Simon answered and said: Master, all through the night we wore ourselves out and got nothing; but on your word I will let down our nets. And when they did so, they netted a great haul of fish, and their nets were breaking. And they beckoned to their partners in the other boat to come and help them. And they came, and both boats were filled so they began to sink. Seeing this, Simon Peter flung himself at the knees of Jesus and said: Go from me, for I am a sinful man, Lord. For amazement had seized him and all who were with him over the haul of fish they had taken, and also James and John, the sons of Zebedee, who were partners with Simon. And Jesus said to Simon: Do not be afraid. From now on your catch will be men. And they beached their boats and left everything and followed him.

It happened that he was in one of the cities, and behold, there was a man covered with leprosy; and when he saw Jesus, he flung himself down on his face and implored him, saying: Lord, if you wish you can make me clean. And he stretched out his hand and touched him, saying: I wish it; be clean. And immediately the leprosy left him. And he told him not to tell anyone; but go and show yourself to the priest, and bring him the gift for your purification that Moses ordained, in witness to these things. But the word went around all the more about him, and multitudes came together to hear him and to be healed of their sicknesses. But he for a while was withdrawn into the desert, praying.

And it happened on one of those days, he himself was teaching, and also there were Pharisees seated there and teachers of the law, who had come out from every village of Galilee and Judaea, and from Jerusalem; and the power of the Lord was with him, to heal. And behold, men carrying on a bed a man who was paralyzed, and they tried to carry him inside and set him before Jesus. And failing to find any way to get him in through the crowd, they went up on top of the house and let him down, bed and all, between the tiles and into the middle, before Jesus. And he, seeing their faith, said: Fellow, your sins are forgiven you. Then the scribes and the Pharisees began to discuss this, saying: Who is this man who speaks blasphemies? Who can forgive sins, except God alone? Jesus realized what they were saying to each other, and spoke forth and said to them: Why do you question in your hearts? Which is easier, to say: Your sins are forgiven you, or to say: Arise and walk about? But so that you may know that the son of man has authority on earth to forgive sins—he said to the paralyzed man: I say to you, rise, take up your bed and go to your house. And at once he stood up before them all, and lifted up what he had been laid on, and went away to his house, glorifying God. And they were all transported, and they glorified God and were filled with fear and said: We have seen incredible things today.

And after that he went forth and saw a tax collector named Levi sitting in the tollhouse, and said to him: Follow me. And he left everything and got up and followed him. And Levi held a great reception for him in his house; and there was a throng of tax collectors and others who dined with them. Then the Pharisees and their scribes muttered to his disciples: Why do you eat and drink with tax collectors and sinners? Jesus answered and said to them: The healthy do not need a physician but those who are in poor health. I did not come to summon the just to repentance, but the sinners. But they said to him: The disciples of John fast often and say prayers, and so likewise do the disciples of the Pharisees, but yours eat and drink. But Jesus said to them: Surely you cannot make the members of the wedding party fast while the bridegroom is with them? But the days will come, and when the bridegroom is taken away from them, then in those days they will fast. And he told them a parable: No one tears a piece from a new coat to put on an old coat; if he does, he will be tearing the new one, and the patch from the new will not fit the old. And no one puts new wine into old skins; if he does, the new wine will break the skins and the wine will all be spilled and the skins will be destroyed; but new wine is to be put into new skins. And no one drinking old wine wants new; for he says: The old is good.

§ It happened on the sabbath he went walking through the sown fields, and his disciples picked and ate the ears of grain, rubbing them in their hands. And some of the Pharisees said: Why do you do what is forbidden on the sabbath? Jesus answered and said to them: Have you not read what David did when he was hungry and those with him? How he went into the house of God and took the show bread and ate it and gave it to those who were with him; which is not lawful for any to eat except only the priests? And he said to them: The son of man is lord of the sabbath.

And it happened that on another sabbath he went into the synagogue and taught; and there was a man there, and his right arm was withered. And the scribes and the Pharisees were watching him to see whether he healed on the sabbath, so that they might find a charge to bring against him. But he read their thoughts and said to the man with the withered arm: Rise up and stand in our midst. And he rose and stood there. And Jesus said to them: I ask you, is it lawful to do good or evil on the sabbath, to save a life or destroy it? And he looked around at them all and said to the man: Stretch out your arm. And he did, and his arm became sound. They were filled with fury, and talked with each other about what they could do to Jesus.

And it happened in those days that he went out to the mountain to pray, and he spent all the night in prayer to God. And when it was day, he summoned his disciples, and chose twelve of them, whom he also named apostles: Simon, whom he also named Peter, and Andrew his brother, and James and John and Philip and Bartholomew, and Matthew and Thomas, and James the son of Alphaeus and Simon, who was called the zealot, and Judas the son of James, and Judas Iscariot, who turned traitor: and went down with them and stood in a place in the plain: and there was a great crowd of his disciples, and a great multitude of the people from all of Judaea and Jerusalem and the seaboard of Tyre and Sidon, who had come to hear him and be healed of their sicknesses: and those troubled with unclean spirits were cured of them: and all the multitude sought to touch him, because power went forth from him and he healed all. And he himself, raising his eyes to his disciples, said:

Blessed are you who are poor, because yours is the Kingdom of God.

Blessed are you who are hungry now, because you shall be fed.

Blessed are you who weep now, because you shall laugh.

Blessed are you when men hate you, and when they segregate you and blame you and cast out your name as wicked, because of the son of man. Rejoice on that day and frolic, for behold your reward is great in heaven. For in the same way their fathers treated the prophets.

But woe to you who are rich, because you have had all your consolation.

Woe to you who are filled now, because you shall be hungry.

Woe to you who laugh now, because you shall mourn and weep.

Woe when all men speak well of you, for in the same way their fathers treated the false prophets.

But I say to you who hear me, love your enemies, do well by those who hate you, praise those who curse you, pray for those who revile you. When one strikes you on the cheek, offer him the other; if one seizes your coat, do not keep him from taking your shirt also. Give to any who asks you and from him who takes what is yours ask for nothing back. And as you wish men to do by you, so do by them. And if you love those who love you, what thanks do you have? For even the sinners love those who love them. And if you do good to those who do good to you, what thanks do you have? For even the sinners do the same. And if you lend to those from whom you hope for a return, what thanks do you have? Even sinners lend to sinners so they may get an equal return. But love your enemies and do good and lend without hope of return; and your reward will be great, and you will be sons of the Highest, because he is good to the ungrateful and the wicked. Be compassionate as your father is compassionate; and do not judge, and you shall not be judged; and do not condemn, and you shall not be condemned. Forgive, and you will be forgiven. Give, and it will be given you. They will pour into your lap good measure, pressed down, shaken down, running over. For by the measure by which you measured it will be measured back to you.

And he told them a parable: Surely a blind man cannot guide a blind man? Will they not both fall into the pit? Nor is the disciple above the teacher, but every disciple will end by being like his teacher. Why do you look at the straw that is in the eye of your brother, and not perceive the log that is in your own eye? How can you say to your brother: Brother, let me take out the straw that is in your eye? When you cannot see the log that is in your eye? You hypocrite, first take the log out of your eye, and then you can see to take the straw out of the eye of your brother. There is no good tree that bears rotten fruit, nor again a rotten tree that bears good fruit. For every tree is known from its own fruit; men do not gather figs from thorns, or harvest grapes from brambles. The good man brings forth good from the good treasure house of his heart, and the bad brings forth bad from the bad. For out of the fullness of his heart his mouth speaks. Why do you call me Lord and not do what I say? Whenever any man comes to me and listens to my words and does as I say, I will show you what that man is like. He is like a man building a house who dug deep down and placed his foundation upon the rock; and the flood came and the river burst out against that house, and could not shake it because it was well built. But the man who listens to me but does not do as I say is like a man who built his house on the ground, without any foundation, and the river burst forth against it, and at once it collapsed, and the ruin of that house was great.

§ After he had completed all his discourse for the people to hear, he went to Capernaum. And the slave of a certain centurion, who was prized by him, was sick and about to die. When he heard about Jesus, he sent the elders of the Jews to him, asking him to come and rescue his slave. When they came to Jesus they entreated him earnestly, saying: This man for whom you will do this is worthy of it, for he loves our people and he himself built our synagogue. And Jesus went along with them. And when he was no long way from the house, the centurion sent friends from the house saying to him: Lord, do not trouble yourself, for I am not fit to have you come under my roof. Therefore I did not take it upon myself to come to you. But say it in a word, and let my servant be healed. For I myself am a man set under orders, and I have soldiers under me, and I say to this man: Go, and he goes, and to another: Come, and he comes, and to my slave: Do this, and he does it. Jesus hearing this wondered at him, and turned about and said to the crowd that was following him: I tell you, I have not found such faith in Israel. And those who had been sent to him returned to the house and found the slave in good health.

And it happened after this that he went to a city called Nain, and his disciples and a great multitude went along with him. As he approached the gate of the city, behold, there was a dead man being carried out, the only son of his mother, and she was a widow; and a good crowd from the city was with her. And when he saw her the Lord took pity on her and said to her: Weep no more. And he went up and laid hands on the coffin, and those who were carrying it stopped; and he said: Young man, I tell you, rise up. And the corpse sat up and began to talk, and he gave him to his mother. And fear seized all of them, and they glorified God, saying: A great prophet is risen among us, and: God has looked on his people. And the word about him went forth over all Judaea and all the land about.

John's disciples brought him news about all these things. And John summoned two of his disciples and sent them to the Lord, saying: Are you the one who is to come or shall we look for another? And when the men reached him, they said: John the Baptist sent us to you, saying: Are you the one who is to come or shall we look for another? In that time he healed many from diseases and afflictions and evil spirits, and he gave to many who were blind the joy of sight. He answered them and said: Go and tell John what you have seen and heard. The blind see again, the lame walk, lepers are made clean and deaf-mutes hear, the dead rise up, beggars are told good news; and blessed is he who does not go wrong where I am concerned. When the

messengers of John went away, he began to speak to
the multitudes about John: What did you come out into
the desert to see? A reed shaken by the wind? But what
did you come out to see? A man dressed in soft
clothing? Behold, those who are in splendid clothing
and luxury are in the houses of the kings. But what did
you come out to see? A prophet? Yes, I tell you, and
more than a prophet. This is he about whom it was
written: Behold, I send forth my messenger before your
face, who will make ready your way before you. I tell
you, among men born of women there is none greater
than John; but one who is a lesser one in the Kingdom
of God is greater than he. (And all the people who
listened, and the tax collectors, called God righteous,
since they had been baptized with the baptism of John;
but the Pharisees and the legalists rejected the will of
God for themselves, since they had not been baptized
by him.) To what shall I liken the people of this
generation, and what are they like? They are like
children sitting in the public places who call to each
other, who say: We played the flute for you and you did
not dance; we lamented and you did not weep. For
John came neither eating bread nor drinking wine, and
you say: He has a demon. The son of man came eating
and drinking, and you say: See, this man is an eater and
a wine drinker, a friend of tax collectors and sinners.
And wisdom is justified from all its children.

One of the Pharisees asked him to dine with him; and
he went into the house of the Pharisee and reclined for
dinner. And behold, there was a woman of the town
who was a sinner; and when she learned that he was
dining in the house of the Pharisee, she brought a jar of
ointment and stood behind by his feet, weeping, and
with her tears she began to wash his feet, and dried
them with her hair and kissed his feet and anointed him
with the ointment. The Pharisee who had invited him
saw this and said to himself: If this were a prophet, he
would have known who she was and what sort of
woman is handling him, that she is a sinner. Jesus spoke

forth and said to him: Simon, I have something to say to you. He said: Speak, master. There were two who were in debt to a certain lender. One owed him five hundred denarii, the other fifty. When they could not repay him, he forgave both. Then which of them will love him more? Simon answered and said: I suppose the one whom he forgave the greater amount. He said: You judge rightly. Then turning to the woman he said to Simon: Do you see this woman? I came into your house, you did not give me water for my feet. But she washed my feet with her tears and dried them with her hair. You gave me no kiss. But she from the time when I came in did not leave off kissing my feet. You did not anoint my head with oil; but she anointed my feet with ointment. In thanks for which, I tell you, her sins are forgiven, which are many, because she loved much. But one who is forgiven little loves little. And he said to her: Your sins are forgiven. And those who were dining with him began to say among themselves: Who is this who even forgives sins? But he said to the woman: Your faith has saved you. Go in peace.

§ And it happened after this that he was traveling, city by city and village by village, preaching and bringing the good news of the Kingdom of God; both himself and the twelve with him, and there were certain women who had been healed of evil spirits and sicknesses, Mary who was called the Magdalene, from whom seven demons had been driven, and Joanna the wife of Chuza, Herod's steward, and Susannah and many others. These ministered to them from their own possessions. And when a great multitude gathered and the people of the city came out also, he spoke to them through a parable: The sower went out to sow his seed. And as he sowed it, some fell beside the way, and it was trodden down and the birds of the sky ate it. And some fell on the rock, and after growing it withered because it had no moisture. And some fell in the midst of thorns, and the thorns grew together and stifled it. And some fell upon good soil and grew and bore fruit, a hundredfold. When he had told them this, he said: He who has ears to hear, let him hear. His disciples asked him what that parable was. And he said: To you it is given to understand the secrets of the Kingdom of God, but to the rest in parables, so that though they have sight they may not see and though they have hearing they may not understand. But this is the parable. The seed is the word of God. Those who fall beside the way are those who hear, and then the devil comes and plucks the word from their heart, so that they may not believe and be saved. Those on the rock are those who when they hear the word accept it with joy, and these have no root, who believe for the time and in the time of trial give way. What falls among the thorns, that means those who listened, and then as they go along they are stifled by concerns and money and the pleasures of life, and bring nothing to fulfillment. And what falls on the good soil, that means those who when they hear the word keep it fast in their good and worthy hearts, and bear fruit for their steadfastness.

No one lights a lamp and covers it with stuff or puts it under a bed, but one puts it on a stand, so that those who come in may see the light. For there is nothing hidden which will not be manifest, and nothing obscure which will not be known and come to light. Look to it how you listen. For when a man has, it will be given him, and if one has not, even what he thinks he has will be taken away from him.

His mother and his brothers came to see him, and they could not reach him because of the crowd. Word was brought to him: Your mother and your brothers are standing outside, and wish to see you. He answered and said to them: My mother and my brothers are these people, who listen to the word of God and perform it.

It happened on one of these days that he went aboard a ship, he and his disciples, and said to them: Let us cross to the other side of the lake. And they put out, and as they sailed he fell asleep. And a great wind storm descended upon the lake, and they were filling, and in peril. They went to him and woke him, saying: Master, master, we are lost. But he woke, and reproved the wind and the waves on the water, and they stopped, and it fell calm. And he said to them: Where is your faith? And they were afraid, and wondered, saying to each other: Who is this who gives orders even to the winds and the water, and they obey him?

And they put in at the country of the Gerasenes, which is across from Galilee. And as he stepped ashore a man from the city met him, a man beset by demons; for some time he had worn no clothing, and would not stay in a house, but only among the tombs. When he saw Jesus he cried out aloud and threw himself down before him and said, in a great voice: What have I to do with you, Jesus son of the most high? I pray you, do not torture me. For he had been commanding the unclean spirit to go out of the man. For at many times it had seized upon him, and he had been bound in chains and shackles and kept under guard, and he would break his bonds and go driven by the demon into the desert. But Jesus asked him: What is your name? And he said: Legion; because many demons had entered him. And they begged him not to order them to vanish into the bottomless pit. But there was a considerable herd of swine feeding there on the hillside. And they begged him to give them leave to enter into these; and he gave them leave. And when the demons came forth from the man they entered into the swine, and the whole herd rushed over the cliff into the lake and were drowned. And when those who were herding them saw what had happened, they fled and brought the news to the city and the countryside. And they came out to see what had happened, and came to Jesus, and they saw the man, from whom the demons had gone forth, sitting at the feet of Jesus, clothed and in his right mind: and they were afraid. Those who had seen it told them how the possessed man had been saved. And the whole popula-

tion of the region of the Gerasenes asked him to go
away from them, because they were constrained by a
great fear; and he went to the ship and returned. The
man from whom the demons had gone forth begged to
be with him; but he dismissed him, saying: Go back to
your house and describe what God has done for you.
And he went through the whole city announcing what
Jesus had done for him.

As Jesus returned the multitude welcomed him, for
they were all expecting him. And behold, a man came
to him whose name was Jairus; and this man was a
leader in the synagogue, and he threw himself at the
feet of Jesus and begged him to enter his house,
because he had an only daughter about twelve years
old, and she was dying. As he went the people were
crowding close about him. And there was a woman who
had been bleeding for twelve years, who could not be
healed by anyone. She came behind him and touched
the hem of his mantle, and immediately her flow of
blood stopped. And Jesus said: Who is the one who
touched me? When they all denied that they had, Peter
said: Master, the crowds are squeezing you and pressing in upon you. But Jesus said: Someone touched me,
for I felt the power going forth from me. And when the
woman saw that she had not gone unnoticed, she came,
trembling, and threw herself down before him, and in
the presence of all the people she told why she had
touched him and how she had been healed at once.
And he said: My daughter, your faith has saved you.
Go in peace. While he was still talking, a man came
from the house of the leader of the synagogue, saying:
Your daughter is dead: do not trouble the master any
longer. But when Jesus heard, he answered him: Have
no fear, only believe, and she will be saved. And he
entered the house, and would not let anyone come in
with him except Peter and John and James and the
father of the child, and her mother. And all were
weeping and mourning for her. But he said: Do not
weep, for she has not died, but she is asleep. And they

laughed at him, knowing that she had died. But he took her hand and spoke and said: Child, awake. And her breath came back, and at once she stood up, and he directed that something be given her to eat. And her parents were astonished; but he told them to tell no one what had happened.

§ And calling together the twelve, he gave them power and authority against all demons, and to treat sicknesses, and he sent them out to preach the Kingdom of God and to heal, and he said to them: Take nothing with you for the journey, no staff, no bag, no bread, no money, nor have two tunics. And if you go into a house, stay there and make your excursions from there. And when any will not receive you, as you go out of that city shake the dust from your feet, in testimony against them. And they went forth and went through the villages preaching the gospel and healing people everywhere.

And Herod the tetrarch heard of all that was happening, and he was perplexed because it was said by some that John was risen from the dead, and by some that Elijah had appeared, and by others that one of the ancient prophets had risen up. And Herod said: John I beheaded. But who is this about whom I hear such things? And he sought to see him.

And the apostles returned and told him what they had done. And taking them with him he withdrew privately to a city called Bethsaida. And the multitudes learned of it and followed him. And he welcomed them and talked to them about the Kingdom of God, and those who needed treatment he healed. And the day began to decline; and the twelve came to him and said: Dismiss the people, so that they can go to the villages and farms which are round about and put up there and find something to eat, since here we are in a deserted place. But he said to them: Give them something to eat yourselves. But they said: We have nothing but five loaves and two fish; unless we go and buy food for all these people. For there were some five thousand men. But he said to his disciples: Place them by companies, by about fifties. And they did so and placed them all. And taking the five loaves and the two fish he looked up into the sky, and blessed them and broke them and gave them to his disciples to set before the multitude. And they ate and all were fed, and what was left of the broken pieces was picked up, twelve baskets.

It happened that while he was praying, alone, his disciples joined him, and he questioned them, saying: Who do the masses say I am? And they said in answer: John the Baptist; but others say Elijah, and others that one of the ancient prophets has risen up. He said to them: And you, who do you think I am? Peter answered and said: The Christ of God. But he warned them and directed them to tell this to no one, saying: The son of man must suffer much, and be rejected by the elders and the high priests and the scribes, and be killed, and rise up on the third day. And he said to all: If anyone wishes to go after me, let him deny himself and take up his cross day by day and follow me. For he who wishes to save his life will lose it; and he who loses his life for my sake, will save it. For what will it advantage a man if he gains the whole world, but loses himself or is punished? For he who is ashamed of me and my words, of him will the son of man be ashamed when he comes in the glory of himself and his father and the holy angels. But I tell you truly, there are some of those who stand here who will not taste of death until they see the Kingdom of God.

And it happened about eight days after these sayings that taking with him Peter and John and James he went up the mountain to pray. And it happened while he was praying that the look of his face became different, and his clothing was flashing white. And behold, two men were talking with him. They were Moses and Elijah, and they were seen in their glory as they spoke of his outward journey which he was to complete in Jerusalem. Now Peter and those with him had been heavy with sleep; but wakening they saw his glory, and the two men who were standing with him. And it happened as they were going from him that Peter said to Jesus: Master, it is good for us to be here, and let us make three shelters, one for you and one for Moses and one for Elijah. He did not know what he was saying. But as he was saying this there came a cloud, and it covered them; and they were frightened as they went into the cloud. And a voice came from the cloud, saying: This is my son, the chosen; listen to him. And in the coming of the voice Jesus was found to be alone. And they kept silence and reported to no one, in those days, anything of what they had seen.

And it happened on the next day, as they came down from the mountain, a great multitude met them. And behold, out of the crowd a man cried out, saying: Master, I beg you to look upon my son; because he is my only child, and see, a spirit takes hold of him, and suddenly he screams, and it racks him with foaming and bruises him and barely leaves him. And I begged your disciples to cast him out, and they were not able to. Jesus answered and said: O generation without faith and perverse, how long shall I be with you and endure you? Bring your son here. While he was still coming forward the demon tore him and convulsed him. But Jesus reproved the unclean spirit and healed the boy and gave him back to his father. And all were astounded at the greatness of God.

And as all were wondering over all the things he was doing, he said to his disciples: Store these words in your ears; for the son of man is about to be betrayed into the hands of men. But they did not understand this saying, and it was hidden from them so that they might not be aware of it, and they were afraid to ask him about this saying. But there arose a dispute among them as to which was the greater; and Jesus, knowing the disputation of their hearts, took a child and set him beside himself and said to them: He who accepts this child in my name accepts me, and he who accepts me accepts him who sent me. For he who is smaller among you all, that one is great.

And John spoke forth and said: Master, we saw a man driving out demons in your name, and we tried to stop him, because he was not one of our following. Jesus said to him: Do not stop him; for he who is not against you is for you.

And it happened in the filling out of the days before his assumption, that he himself set his face toward the journey to Jerusalem and also that he sent messengers out before his presence. And they on their journey entered a village of the Samaritans, to make things ready for him. And they would not receive him, because his face was set on the journey to Jerusalem. And learning of this the disciples James and John said: Lord, do you wish us to summon fire to come down from heaven and consume them? But Jesus turned on them and reproved them. And they went to another village.

And as they journeyed along the way, a man said to him: I will follow you wherever you go. And Jesus said to him: Foxes have holes, and the birds of the sky have nests, but the son of man has no place to lay his head. And he said to another: Follow me. But the man said: Give me leave first to go and bury my father. But he said to him: Leave the dead to bury their own dead, but you go and announce the Kingdom of God. And another man said: I will follow you, Lord; but first allow me to take leave of the people in my house. But Jesus said to him: No one who has put his hand to the plow and then looked back is fit for the Kingdom of God.

§ After this the Lord appointed seventy other men and sent them out two by two before his presence to every city and place where he was going to go. And he said to them: The harvest is abundant, but the laborers few.

Beg the master of the harvest to send out laborers to his harvest. Go forth. See, I send you out like sheep into the midst of wolves. Take no purse, no bag, no shoes, and greet no one on the road. Whenever you enter any house, say: Peace to this house. And if a son of peace is there, your peace will stay with him; and if not, it will return to you. Remain in the same house, eating and drinking what they give you, for the laborer is worthy of his wages. Do not move about from house to house. And when you go into any city, and they receive you, eat what is put before you, and treat the sick who are there, and say to them: The Kingdom of God has come near you. But when you go into any city and they do not receive you, as you go into the open places of that city say: Even the dust of your city which has stuck to our feet we wipe off, against you. Only know this, that the Kingdom of God is near. I tell you that on the Day it will be more tolerable for Sodom than for that city. Woe to you, Chorazin. Woe to you, Bethsaida. For if there had been shown in Tyre and Sidon the powers that have been shown among you, long since they would have repented in sackcloth and ashes. But for Tyre and Sidon it will be more tolerable at the judgment than it will be for you. And you, Capernaum, will you be exalted to the sky? You will go down to Hades.

He who listens to you listens to me, and he who rejects you rejects me. And he who rejects me rejects him who sent me.

And the seventy returned in joy, saying: Lord, even the demons submit to us in your name. He said to them: I saw Satan falling from the sky like a flash of lightning. See, I have given you authority to tread on snakes and scorpions, and against every power of the enemy, and nothing can injure you. Except do not rejoice in this, that the spirits submit to you, but rejoice because your names are written in heaven.

In that same hour, he rejoiced in the Holy Spirit and said: I thank you, father lord of heaven and earth, because you have hidden these things away from the clever and the understanding, and revealed them to the simple. Yes, father, that thus it has been your pleasure in your sight. All was given to me by my father, and no one knows who is the son except the father, and who is the father except the son and anyone to whom the son wishes to reveal it. And he turned to the disciples and said to them alone: Blessed are the eyes that have seen what you have seen. For I tell you that many prophets and kings have wished to see what you have seen, and have not seen it, and to hear what you have heard and have not heard it.

And behold, a man versed in the law stood up, making trial of him and saying: Master, what shall I do to inherit everlasting life? He said to him: What is written in the law? How do you read it? The man answered and said: You shall love the Lord your God from all your heart and in all your spirit and in all your strength and in all your mind; and you shall love your neighbor as yourself. He said to him: You have answered right. Do this and you will live. But the man, wishing to justify himself, said to Jesus: And who is my neighbor? Jesus answered and said: There was a man who went down from Jerusalem to Jericho and fell in with robbers who stripped him and beat him and went away leaving him half dead. And by chance a priest went down that road, and when he saw him passed by on the other side; and so likewise a Levite coming to the place and seeing him passed by on the other side. But a certain Samaritan came there on his journey, and when he saw him he pitied him, and went to him and bound up his wounds, pouring oil and wine on them, and set him on his own beast and took him to an inn, and took care of him. And on the next day he put out two denarii and gave them to the innkeeper and said: Take care of him, and any extra expense you have I will repay you on my return journey. Which of these three do you think was the neighbor of the man who fell among robbers? He said: The man who treated him with mercy. Jesus said to him: Go on, you also, and do likewise.

And it happened on their journey that he came to a certain village; and there was a woman, Martha by name, who took him into her house. And she had a sister named Mary who sat at the feet of the Lord and listened to what he was saying. But Martha was distracted with much serving, and she stood near him and said: Lord, does it not matter to you that my sister has left me to serve all by myself? Tell her to help me. But the Lord answered and said to her: Martha, Martha, you worry and are troubled over much, but there is need of few things, or only one. For Mary has chosen the good portion, which shall not be taken away from her.

§ And it happened that while he was praying in a certain place, when he stopped, one of his disciples said to him: Lord, teach us to pray, as John also taught his disciples. He said to them: When you pray, say: Father, may your name be hallowed. May your kingdom come. Give us our sufficient bread day by day; and forgive us our sins, for we also forgive everyone who is our debtor. And do not bring us into temptation.

And he said to them: Which of you will have a friend and go to him in the middle of the night and say to him: My friend, lend me three loaves, because a friend has come in from the road to visit me and I have nothing to set before him? And he answers from inside and says: Stop making difficulties for me. Now the door is locked, and my children are in bed with me. I cannot get up and give it to you. I tell you, if he will not get up and give it to the man because he is his friend, he will wake up and give him what he needs because of his insistence. And I tell you, ask, and it shall be given you; seek, and you shall find; knock, and the door will be opened for you. For everyone who asks receives, and he who seeks finds, and for him who knocks the door is opened. Or who is there among you whose son will ask his father for a fish, and he will give him a snake? Or ask for an egg, and will give him a scorpion? If then you, who are corrupt, know how to give good gifts to your children, by how much more your father in heaven will give the Holy Spirit to those who ask him.

He was casting out a deaf-mute demon, and it happened as the demon went out the deaf-mute talked. And the people marveled, but some of them said: It is through Beelzebub the prince of the demons that he drives out the demons. But others, making trial of him, demanded of him a sign from heaven. But he knew their thoughts and said to them: Every kingdom that is divided against itself is made desolate, and house that is against house collapses. And if even Satan is divided against himself, how shall his kingdom stand? Since you say that through Beelzebub I drive out the demons. But if I drive out the demons through Beelzebub, through whom do your sons drive them out? Therefore they will be judges of you. But if through the finger of God I drive out demons, then the Kingdom of God has come suddenly upon you. When the strong man, well armed, guards his own estate, his possessions are in peace; but when one stronger than he attacks and overcomes him, he takes away the armor in which he had trusted, and he gives away his spoils. He who is not with me is against me; and he who does not gather with me, scatters. When the unclean spirit goes forth from a man, it wanders through waterless regions looking for a place to rest, and when it does not find one it says: I will return to my house that I came out from; and it comes and finds it swept and furnished. Then it goes and picks up other spirits worse than itself, seven of them, and they go in and settle there; and the end for that man is worse than the beginning.

While he was saying this, it happened that a woman in the crowd raised her voice and cried to him: Blessed is the womb that carried you, and the breasts that you sucked. But he said to her: Blessed rather are those who listen to the word of God and obey it.

As the crowds gathered he began to say: This generation is a corrupt generation. It asks for a sign, but no sign shall be given it unless it be the sign of Jonah. For as Jonah was a sign to the people of Nineveh so is the son of man to this generation. The Queen of the South will rise up on the day of judgment with the men of this generation, and condemn them; because she came from the ends of the earth to listen to the wisdom of Solomon, and behold, there is more than Solomon here. The men of Nineveh will arise on the day of judgment with this generation and condemn it; because they repented upon the proclamation of Jonah, and behold, there is more than Jonah here. No one lights a lamp and then puts it in a hiding place or under a basket, but on a lampstand, so that those who come in may see the light. The lamp of the body is your eye. When your eye is clear, the whole of your body is also full of light; but when it is soiled, your body also is in darkness. Consider then whether the light in you may not be darkness. If then your whole body is full of light, having no part that is dark, it will all be light as when the lamp illuminates you with its beam.

While he was talking, a Pharisee asked him to dine with him; and when he entered, he took his place at table. And the Pharisee seeing this was surprised that he had not washed before the meal. But the Lord said to him: Now you Pharisees scour the outside of the cup and the plate, but what is inside you teems with rapacity and corruption. You fools. Did not he who made the outside make the inside also? But give away what is inside as charity, and see, all is clean with you. But woe to you Pharisees, because you pay a tenth on the mint and the rue and every kind of potherb, but you pass over the judgment and the love of God; but you should have done that, without neglecting the other. Woe to you Pharisees, because you love the first seats in the synagogues and the salutations in the public places. Woe to you, because you are like concealed unmarked graves, and people walk upon you without knowing it. One of those expert in the law spoke up and said to him: Master, in saying this you attack us also. But he said: And woe to you, experts in the law, because you load people with burdens that are hard to carry, and you yourselves do not put a finger to the burdens. Woe to you, because you build the tombs of the prophets, but your fathers killed them. But you are witnesses, and you join in approval of their actions, because they killed them and you build their tombs. Therefore even the wisdom of God has said: I will send them prophets and apostles, and some of these they will kill and persecute, so that the blood of all the prophets that has been spilled since the establishment of the world may be exacted from this generation, from the blood of Abel to the blood of Zachariah who was killed between the altar and the temple. Yes, I tell you, it will be exacted from this generation. Woe to you, experts in the law, because you have taken away the key to knowledge. You did not go in yourselves, and you prevented those who tried to go in. And when he went away from them, the scribes and Pharisees began to hate him terribly, and to try to make him speak carelessly about more matters, lying in wait to catch him up on something he might let fall.

§ As the multitude gathered by tens of thousands, so that they trampled each other, he began to speak first to his disciples: Guard yourselves against the leaven, that is, the hypocrisy, of the Pharisees. There is nothing concealed that shall not be revealed, nothing secret that shall not be known. Because of which, what you say in the dark will be heard in the light, and what you have said in someone's ear in inner rooms will be proclaimed on the housetops. But I say to you, my friends, do not fear those who kill the body but are able to do nothing more after that. I will show you which one to fear. Fear the one who has authority after killing you to throw you into Gehenna. Yes, I tell you, fear that one. Are not five sparrows sold for two coppers? And not one of them is forgotten in the sight of God. But even the hairs of your heads are all numbered. Have no fear; you are worth many sparrows. I tell you, everyone who will acknowledge me before men the son of man will acknowledge before the angels of God; but he who denies me in the sight of men shall be denied in the sight of God. And everyone who speaks a word against the son of man shall have it forgiven him; but for the one who blasphemes against the Holy Spirit it shall not be forgiven. And when they bring you before the synagogues and the powers and the authorities, do not be concerned about how you will defend yourselves and what you will say; for the Holy Spirit will teach you in that very hour what you must say.

Someone in the crowd said to him: Master, tell my brother to divide the inheritance with me. But he said to him: My good man, who appointed me your judge or your arbitrator? And he said to them: Look to it and keep yourselves from all greed, because a man's life does not consist in the abundance of his possessions. And he told them a parable, saying: There was a certain rich man whose land was fruitful. And he deliberated within himself, saying: What shall I do, since I have no place where I can store all my crops? And he said: Here is what I will do. I will tear down my granaries and build bigger ones, and I will bring all my grain and my goods together there, and I will say to my soul: Soul, you have many good things stored away, for many years. Rest, eat, drink, enjoy yourself. But God said to him: You fool, they demand that soul of you tonight. Who will have what you provided? So much for him who stores up treasures for himself rather than being rich for God.

And he said to his disciples: Therefore I tell you, do not take thought for your life, what you will eat, or for

your body, what you will wear. For life is more than
food, and the body is more than clothing. Think of the
ravens, that they do not sow or harvest, they have
neither storehouse nor granary, and God feeds them.
How much more are you worth than the birds! Which
of you by taking thought can add one cubit to his
growth? If then you cannot achieve the least, why are
you concerned about the rest? Think of the lilies, how
they grow. They do not toil or spin; yet I tell you, not
even Solomon in all his glory was clothed like one of
these. But if God so arrays the grass in the field which
grows today and tommorow is thrown in the oven, how
much more will he array you, you men of little faith!
Do not you then keep searching for what you can eat
and what you can drink, and do not be troubled, for all
the nations of the world search for these things, and
your father knows that you need them; only search for
his kingdom, and all these things will be added also. Do
not fear, little flock; because your father has been well
pleased to give you the kingdom. Sell what you own
and give it away as charity; make yourselves purses
that do not wear out, an infallible treasure house in
heaven, where no thief attacks, no moth corrupts;
for where your treasure is, there also will be your
heart.

Let your loins be girt up and your lamps burning, and
yourselves like men who are expecting their master
when he comes back from the wedding, so that when he
comes and knocks they can open promptly to him.
Blessed are those slaves whom this master returning
finds wide awake; truly I tell you, he will gird himself
up and set them down to dine and go about and wait on
them. And if he comes in the second watch or the third
and finds them thus, blessed are they. But know this,
that if the master of the house had known at what time
the thief was coming, he would have been watchful and
not let his house be broken into. And you, be ready,
because the son of man comes in the hour when you do
not expect him. Peter said: Lord, are you telling this

parable to us or to all? And the Lord said: Who is the faithful steward, the prudent one, whom his master will set over the servants of his household to give them their measure of food when it is due? Blessed is that slave whom his master arriving finds doing thus; truly I tell you that he will put him in charge of all his possessions. But if that slave says in his heart: My master is late returning; and begins to beat the menservants and the maidservants, and to eat and drink and get drunk; the master of that slave will come on a day when he does not expect him in the hour when he is unaware, and cut him to ribbons, and make his lot one with the unfaithful. That slave who knows the will of his master, and does not make ready or act according to his will, will be beaten with many strokes; but the one who knows nothing and does what deserves whipping will be beaten with few strokes. Everyone to whom much is given will have much required of him; from him to whom much was entrusted they will demand more.

I came to cast fire upon the earth, and what is my will if it has already been lit? I have a baptism to undergo, and how I am oppressed until it is done with. Do you think that I came to give peace on earth? No, I tell you, dissension rather. For from now there will be five in one house at odds with each other, three against two and two against three, and father will be at odds with son and son with father, mother with daughter and daughter with mother, mother-in-law with her daughter-in-law and daughter-in-law with mother-in-law.

And he said to the multitudes: When you see a cloud rising in the west, you say at once: Rain is coming. And so it happens. And when you see the south wind blowing, you say: There will be hot weather. And so it happens. You hypocrites, you know how to read the face of the earth and the sky, but how is it you do not know how to read this time? And why do you not judge what is right of your own will. As you go with your adversary at law to the magistrate, make an effort to be reconciled with him on the way there, for fear he may

drag you before the judge, and the judge turn you over
to the bailiff, and the bailiff throw you in prison. I tell
you, you cannot come out of there until you pay the last
penny.

§ At that time some people came to him and brought
him news about the Galilaeans whose blood Pilate had
mixed with their sacrifices. And he answered and said
to them: Do you suppose that these Galilaeans,
because they suffered this, were sinners as compared
with the rest of the Galilaeans? No, I tell you, but
unless you repent, you will all be destroyed like them.
Or those eighteen when the tower at Siloam fell on
them and killed them. Do you suppose they were guilty
as compared with all the rest of the people who live in
Jerusalem? No, I tell you, but unless you repent you
will all be destroyed in the same way. And he told them
this parable: A man had a fig tree planted in his
vineyard, and he went looking for fruit on it and did not
find any. And he said to the gardener: It is three years
now since I began coming and looking for fruit on this
fig tree without finding it. Cut it down. Why should it
be wasting the soil? But he answered and said to him:
Master, let it go for this year too, until I have cultivated
it and put manure on it. And if it bears fruit after that,
well: . . . but if it does not, you will cut it down.

He was teaching in one of the synagogues on the
sabbath. And behold, there was a woman who had had
a spirit of infirmity for eighteen years, and she was bent
over and unable to straighten up at all. And Jesus saw
her and spoke to her and said: Woman, you are loosed
from your infirmity, and laid his hands on her. And
immediately she straightened up and glorified God. But
the head of the synagogue, angered because Jesus had
given treatment on the sabbath, said to the congregation: There are six days in which one must work. Come
then and be healed on those days and not on the day of

the sabbath. The Lord answered him and said: You hypocrites, does not each of you on the sabbath loose his ox or his donkey from the crib and lead him to water? And she, who is a daughter of Abraham, whom Satan had kept bound for eighteen years, must she not be loosed from this bondage on the day of the sabbath? And when he said this, all who were set against him were put to shame, and all the masses were happy over all the glorious things that came to be through him.

Then he said: What is the Kingdom of God like, and to what shall I liken it? It is like a grain of mustard, which a man took and sowed in his garden, and it grew and became a tree, so that the birds of the air came and nested in its branches. And again he said: To what shall I liken the Kingdom of God? It is like leaven, which a woman took and buried in three measures of dough, so that it all rose.

And he journeyed through the cities and villages, teaching and making his way toward Jerusalem. And a man said to him: Lord, will those who are saved be few? And he said to them: Struggle to go in through the narrow door, because many, I tell you, try to get in and are not able to, from the time when the master of the house wakens and bars the door, and you begin to stand outside and knock on the door, saying: Lord, open to us. And he will answer and say to you: I do not know you or where you come from. Then you will begin to say: We ate and drank in your presence, and you taught in our public places. Then he will speak and say to you: I do not know where you come from. Go away from me, all you workers of iniquity. There will be weeping and gnashing of teeth, when you see Abraham and Isaac and Jacob and all the prophets in the Kingdom of God, and yourselves cast outside. And they will come from the east and the west, and the north and the south, and be feasted in the Kingdom of God. And behold, they are last who will be first, and they are first who will be last.

In the same hour some Pharisees came to him and said: Go and make your way from here, because Herod wants to kill you. And he said to them: Go and say to that fox: Look, I cast out demons and effect my cures today and tomorrow, and the third day I am done. But I must go forward today and tomorrow and the next day, because there is no way for a prophet to be killed outside Jerusalem. Jerusalem, Jerusalem, who kills the prophets and stones those who have been sent to her! How often I have wished to gather your children together as a bird gathers her brood under her wings, and you were unwilling. Behold, your house is deserted. I tell you, you cannot see me until you say: Blessed is he who comes in the name of the Lord.

§ And it happened that when he went to the house of one of the leading Pharisees, and dined, that they were watching him closely. And behold, there was a man before him who suffered from dropsy. And Jesus spoke forth and said to the legal experts and the Pharisees: Is it lawful or not to give treatment on the sabbath? They held their peace. He took hold of him, and healed him, and dismissed him. And he said to them: Which of you will have a son, or an ox, fall down a well, and will not immediately pull him out on the day of the sabbath? And they were not able to answer that.

And he told the guests a parable, applying it to the way they apportioned their places of honor, and said to them: When you are invited by someone to a wedding, do not recline in the first place, for fear someone he honors more than you may have been invited by him, and he who invited you both may come and say to you: Give this man the place. And then you will begin, with shame, to occupy the last place. But when you are invited, go and set yourself in the last place, so that when your host comes he will say to you: My friend, come on up higher. Then you will have dignity in the

sight of all your fellow guests; because everyone who
exalts himself will be humbled, and he who humbles
himself will be exalted.

And he said to the man who had invited him: When
you give a lunch or a dinner, do not invite your friends,
or your brothers, or your relatives, or your rich
neighbors, lest they too invite you in return and some
recompense befall you. But when you are receiving,
invite the poor and the maimed and the lame and the
blind; and you will be blessed, because they are not
able to repay you; for it will be repaid you at the
resurrection of the righteous.

Hearing this, one of his fellow guests said: Blessed is
he who dines in the Kingdom of God. Jesus said to him:
A certain man was holding a great feast, and he invited
many, and at the time for the feast he sent out his slave
to say to those who were invited: Come, since everything is now ready. Then they all at once began to make
excuses. The first one said to him: I have bought a piece
of land and I must go out and look at it; I pray you,
hold me excused. Another said: I have bought five yoke
of oxen, and I am on my way to try them out. I pray
you, hold me excused. And another said: I took a wife
in marriage, and therefore I cannot come. And the
slave came back and reported all this to his master.
Then the master of the house was angry and said to his
slave: Go out quickly into the squares and streets of the
city and bring here the poor and the maimed and the
blind and the lame. And the slave said: Master, what
you ordered has been done, and there is still room.
And the master said to his slave: Go out to the
highways and the hedgerows and force them to come
in, so that my house may be full; for I tell you that not
one of those other men who were invited shall taste of
my feast.

Many multitudes followed him along the way, and he
turned and said to them: If someone comes to me and
does not hate his father and mother and wife and

children and brothers and sisters, and even his own life also, he cannot be my disciple. He who does not take up his cross and come after me cannot be my disciple. For which of you who desires to build a tower does not first sit down and reckon the cost, to see if he has enough for its completion? For fear that, after he has set down the foundation and cannot finish it, all the people watching him may begin to tease him and say: This man began to build, and he could not finish. Or what king, on his way to encounter another king in battle, will not first sit down and think out whether with his ten thousand he is strong enough to meet the man who comes against him with twenty thousand? If he is not, while the other is still far off, he sends an embassy to ask for peace. So, therefore, any of you who does not renounce all his possessions cannot be my disciple. Salt is good: but if the salt loses its power, with what will it be seasoned? It is fit for neither the land nor the dunghill. They throw it out. He who has ears to hear, let him hear.

§ All the tax collectors and the sinners kept coming around him, to listen to him. And the Pharisees and the scribes muttered, saying: This man receives sinners and eats with them. But he told them this parable, saying: Which man among you who has a hundred sheep and has lost one of them will not leave the ninety-nine in the wilds and go after the lost one until he finds it? And when he does find it, he sets it on his shoulders, rejoicing, and goes to his house and invites in his friends and his neighbors, saying to them: Rejoice with me, because I found my sheep which was lost. I tell you that thus there will be joy in heaven over one sinner who repents, rather than over ninety-nine righteous ones who have no need of repentance. Or what woman who has ten drachmas, if she loses one drachma, does not light the lamp and sweep the house and search diligently until she finds it? And finding it she invites in her friends and neighbors, saying: Rejoice with me, because I found the drachma I lost. Such, I tell you, is the joy among the angels of God over one sinner who repents.

And he said: There was a man who had two sons. And the younger of them said to his father: Father, give me my appropriate share of the property. And the father divided his substance between them. And not many days afterward the younger son gathered everything together and left the country for a distant land, and there he squandered his substance in riotous living. And after he had spent everything, there was a severe famine in that country, and he began to be in need. And he went and attached himself to one of the citizens of that country, who sent him out into the fields to feed the pigs. And he longed to be nourished on the nuts that the pigs ate, and no one would give to him. And he went and said to himself: How many hired servants of my father have plenty of bread while I am dying of hunger here. I will rise up and go to my father and say to him: Father, I have sinned against heaven and in your sight, I am no longer worthy to be called your son. Make me like one of your hired servants. And he rose up and went to his father. And when he was still a long way off, his father saw him and was moved and ran and fell on his neck and kissed him. The son said to him: Father, I have sinned against heaven and in your sight, I am no longer worthy to be called your son. But his father said to his slaves: Quick, bring the best clothing and put it on him, and have a ring for his hand and shoes for his feet, and bring the fatted calf, slaughter him, and let us eat and make merry because this man, my son, was a dead man and came to life, he was lost and he has been found. And they began to make merry. His older son was out on the estate, and as he came nearer to the house he heard music and dancing, and he called over one of the servants and asked what was going on. He told him: Your brother is here, and your father slaughtered the fatted calf, because he got him back in good health. He was angry and did not want to go in. But his father came out and entreated him. But he answered and said to his father: Look, all these years I have been your slave and never neglected an order of yours, but you never gave me a kid so that I could make merry with my friends. But when this son of yours comes back, the one who ate up your livelihood in the company of whores, you slaughtered the fatted calf for him. But he said to him: My child, you are always with me, and all that is mine is yours; but we had to make merry and rejoice, because your brother was a dead man and came to life, he was lost and has been found.

§ And he said to his disciples: There was a rich man who had a steward, and this steward was accused to his master of wasting the property. And he called him and said to him: What is this I hear about you? Give the statement of your stewardship, since you can no longer be the steward. And the steward said to himself: What shall I do now that my master has taken away my stewardship from me? I am not strong enough to dig, I am ashamed to beg. Now I have seen what to do, so that I can be removed from my stewardship but people will still take me into their houses. And he called in each one of his master's debtors, and he said to the first one: How much do you owe my master? And he said: A hundred measures of oil. He said to him: Take your note and sit down quickly and write fifty. Then he said to another: And how much do you owe? He said: A hundred measures of grain. He said to him: Take your note and write eighty. And the master praised the steward for his dishonesty because he had acted prudently; because the sons of this age are wiser than the sons of light for this generation that is theirs. And I tell you, make friends for yourselves by means of the mammon of dishonesty, so that when it gives out they may receive you into everlasting tabernacles. He who is trustworthy in the least matter is also trustworthy in the great one, and he who is dishonest in the least matter is also dishonest in the great one. If then you were not trustworthy in the dishonest mammon, who will entrust the true to you? And if you were not trustworthy in what belonged to others, who will give you what is yours? No servant can serve two masters. For he will either hate the one and love the other, or he will cling to the one and despise the other. You cannot serve God and mammon.

The Pharisees, who are fond of money, heard all this and they sneered at him. He said to them: You are the ones who justify yourselves in the eyes of men, but God knows your hearts; because what is exalted among men is an abomination in the eyes of God. Until John, it was the law and the prophets; but from then on, the good news of the Kingdom of God is announced, and everyone tries to force his way into it. But it is easier for heaven and earth to pass away than for one letter end of the law to fail. Everyone who divorces his wife and marries another is committing adultery, and he who marries a woman divorced from her husband is committing adultery.

There was a certain rich man, and he would put on purple and fine linen and feast in his splendor day after day. And a beggar, Lazarus by name, would throw himself down at his door, covered with sores, and longing to eat of the crumbs that fell from the rich man's table. And the very dogs would come out and lick his sores. And it happened that the beggar died, and he was transported by angels to recline close by Abraham; and the rich man died and was buried. And in Hades he lifted up his eyes, being in torment, and from far away he could see Abraham, and Lazarus reclining close by him. And he called out and said:

Father Abraham, have pity and send Lazarus to dip his
fingertip in water and refresh my tongue, because I am
in agony in this flame. But Abraham said: My child,
remember that you got your share of good things in
your life, and Lazarus likewise his misfortunes. But
now he is thus comforted and you are in pain. And in
any case, there is a great chasm fixed between us and
you, so that those who wish to cross over to you are not
able to, nor can they cross from there to us. Then he
said: I beg you then, father, to send him to my father's
house, for I have five brothers, to warn them so that
they may not come into this place of torment. But
Abraham said: They have Moses and the prophets. Let
them listen to them. But he said: No, father Abraham,
but if someone goes to them from the dead, they will
repent. But he said to him: If they do not listen to
Moses and the prophets, they will not be persuaded
though one rise from the dead.

§ And he said to his disciples: It is impossible that
there should come no causes to make man go astray;
but woe to him through whom they come. It is better
for him to have a millstone hung around his neck and
be thrown into the sea than to cause one of these little
ones to go astray. Watch yourselves. If your brother
does wrong, charge him with it, and if he repents,
forgive him. And if he does you wrong seven times in a
day and seven times turns to you and says: I repent, you
shall forgive him. The apostles said to the Lord: Give
us more faith. But the Lord said: If you have faith the
size of a grain of mustard, you could have said to this
sycamine tree: Be uprooted and grow in the sea; and it
would have obeyed you. Or which of you has a slave
who plows or herds the flocks and will say to him when
he comes in from the fields: Come now and eat with
me? Will he not rather say: Prepare me something to
dine on, and tuck yourself up and wait on me while I

eat and drink, and after that you eat and drink? Surely
he does not feel thankful to the slave because he has
done as he was told? So you, when you have done all
that you were told to, should say: We are worthless
slaves. What we have done was what we were obliged
to do.

And it happened on his journey to Jerusalem that he
passed between Samaria and Galilee. And as he went
into a certain village ten men who were lepers met him,
and they stood at a distance, and raised their voices,
saying: Jesus, master, pity us. And when he saw them
he said: Go and show yourselves to the priests. And it
happened that as they went they became clean. And
one of them, seeing that he was healed, turned,
glorifying God in a great voice, and fell on his face at
his feet, thanking him. And this man was a Samaritan.
Jesus answered him and said: Were not all ten made
clean? Where are the nine? Were none found turning
back and glorifying God except only this alien? And he
said to him: Rise and go. Your faith has saved you.

When he was asked by the Pharisees when the
Kingdom of God was to come, he answered them and
said: The Kingdom of God is not coming in an
observable way, nor will they say: Look, it is here; or:
There. For see, the Kingdom of God is inside you. And
he said to his disciples: Days will come when you will
long to see one of the days of the son of man, and you
will not see it. And they will say to you: Look, it is
there; or: See, this way. Do not follow them. For as the
lightning flashes and lights up, from one side to the
other, what is under the sky, such will be the son of
man. But first he must suffer much and be rejected by
this generation. And as it was in the days of Noah, so
will it be in the days of the son of man. They ate, they
drank, they married, they were given in marriage, until
the day when Noah went into the ark and the flood
came and destroyed them all. Or as it was in the days of
Lot. They ate, they drank, they bought, they sold, they

planted, they built houses. But on the day when Lot
went out from Sodom, it rained fire and sulphur from
the sky and destroyed them all. It will be the same way
on the day when the son of man is revealed. On that
day, if one is on his roof and his goods are in the house,
let him not come down to take them up: and so likewise
let him who is in the field not turn back. Think of Lot's
wife. He who tries to preserve his life will lose it, and
he who loses it will bring it to life. I tell you, on that
night there will be two in one bed, and one will be
taken and the other left; there will be two women
grinding at the same place, and one will be taken and
the other left. And they answered and said to him:
Where, Lord? He said to them: Where the body is,
there will the eagles be gathered.

§ And he told them a parable about the need to be
always praying and not weakening, saying: In a certain
city there was a judge who neither feared God nor
heeded man. But there was a widow in that city and she
kept going to him and saying: Vindicate me against my
adversary. And for a time he would not, but later he
said to himself: Even though I neither fear God nor
heed man, because this widow gives me trouble I will
vindicate her, so that she may not end by wearing me
out with her visits. And the Lord said: Hear what this
judge of injustice says. Will God not accomplish the
vindication of his chosen ones who cry out to him day
and night? Will he be patient in their case? I tell you
that he will accomplish their vindication with speed.
But when the son of man comes, will he find faith on
earth?

And he told this parable against those who were
confident that they were righteous and despised all
others: Two men went out to the temple to pray; one
was a Pharisee, the other a tax collector. And the
Pharisee stood and prayed thus within himself: O God,

I thank you that I am not like the rest of mankind—
rapacious, dishonest, adulterous—or even like this tax
collector. I fast twice a week, I pay a tithe on all I have.
But the tax collector, standing at a distance, would not
even raise his eyes to the sky, but beat his breast and
said: O God, have mercy upon sinful me. I tell you, this
man went back to his house justified as compared with
the other; because everyone who exalts himself will be
humbled, and he who humbles himself will be exalted.

They brought him even their babies for him to touch.
And seeing this the disciples scolded them. But Jesus
called them to him and said: Let the children come to
me and do not prevent them: for of such is the
Kingdom of God. Truly I tell you, he who does not
receive the Kingdom of God like a child may not enter
into it.

And an official questioned him, saying: Good master, what must I do to inherit life everlasting? Jesus said
to him: Why do you call me good? No one is good but
God alone. You know the commandments: Do not
commit adultery, do not murder, do not steal, do not
bear false witness, honor your father and your mother.
But he said: I have kept all these from my youth.
Hearing this Jesus said to him: You have one thing
missing. Sell all you have and give it to the poor, and
you shall have a treasury in heaven; and come and
follow me. He was greatly pained when he heard this,
for he was very rich. Watching him, Jesus said: How
hard it is for those with money to enter the Kingdom of
God. For it is easier for a camel to enter the eye of a
needle than for a rich man to enter the Kingdom of
God. But his listeners said: And who can be saved? He
said: What is impossible for men is possible for God.
But Peter said: See, we have given up all that was our
own and followed you. But he said to them: Truly I tell
you, there is no one who has given up house or wife or
brothers or parents or children for the sake of the
Kingdom of God who will not receive many times as

much in this time, and in the age to come life
everlasting.

Then taking the twelve aside he said to them:
Behold, we are going up to Jerusalem, and all that has
been written by the prophets about the son of man will
be fulfilled. He will be given over to the Gentiles, and
he will be mocked and outraged and spit upon, and they
will flog him and kill him, and on the third day he will
rise. And they understood nothing of all this, and this
saying was hidden from them, and they did not know
what was being said.

And it happened as he drew near Jericho there was a
blind man sitting by the road, begging. And when he
heard the crowd going through he asked what was
going on; and they told him that Jesus of Nazareth was
passing by. And he cried out, saying: Jesus, son of
David, have pity on me. Those who were escorting him
scolded the man, to silence him, but he screamed all the
harder: Son of David, have pity on me. Jesus stopped
and ordered that he be brought before him. And as he
approached he asked him: What do you want me to do
for you? He said: Lord, let me see again. And Jesus
said to him: See again; your faith has saved you. And
immediately he could see again, and he followed him,
glorifying God. And all the people, seeing this, gave
praise to God.

§ And he entered Jericho and was passing through it.
And behold, there was a man called Zacchaeus, and he
was a chief tax collector, and he was rich. And he was
trying to see which one was Jesus and could not see him
from the crowd, because he was short of stature. So he
ran on ahead and climbed a sycamore tree so that he
could see him, because he was going to pass by it. And
as he came to the place Jesus looked up and said to him:
Zacchaeus, hurry and come down, for I must stay in
your house today. And he hastened and came down,

and welcomed him with joy. And when they saw this everybody muttered, saying: He has gone in to stay with a sinful man. But Zacchaeus stood before the Lord and said: See, Lord, I am giving half of my possessions to the poor, and if I have made anything dishonestly at someone's expense, I give it back fourfold. Jesus said to him: Salvation has come to this house today, because this man also is a son of Abraham; for the son of man came to seek out and save the lost.

As they were listening to him, he told an additional parable because he was close to Jerusalem and they thought that the Kingdom of God would appear very soon. So he said: A certain highborn man went on a journey to a far country to get a kingdom for himself and then return. And he summoned ten slaves who belonged to him and gave them ten minas and told them: Engage in business until I come. But his citizens hated him, and they sent an embassy after him, saying: We do not want this man to be king over us. And it happened on his return, after he had got the kingdom, he ordered those slaves to whom he had given the money to be summoned, so that he might learn what business they had got done. And the first appeared, and said: Master, your mina has earned ten more minas. And he said: Well done. Good slave, because in the least matter you were trustworthy, know that you now have power over ten cities. And the second one came and said: Master, your mina has made five minas. And to this one also he said: Know that you are set over five cities. And the other one came and said: Master, here is your mina which I kept hidden away in a napkin. For I was afraid of you because you are a severe man, who pick up what you did not put down and harvest what you did not sow. He said to him: Out of your own mouth I judge you, bad slave. You knew that I am a severe man who pick up what I did not put down and harvest what I did not sow? Then why did you not put out my money to the bankers? Then when I returned I could have taken it out with interest. And to those who were standing by he said: Take his mina away and give it to the one who has ten minas—and they said to him: Master, he has ten minas—I tell you that to everyone who has it shall be given, and from him who does not have even what he has shall be taken away. But those enemies of mine, who did not want me to be king over them, bring them here and slaughter them in my presence.

And when Jesus had said this he went on with his journey up to Jerusalem.

And it happened that when he came near Bethphage and Bethany, near the hill which is called the Mount of Olives, he sent two of his disciples ahead, saying to them: Go into the village that lies before you, and as you go in you will find a colt tethered, on which no man has ever ridden. And when you have untied him bring him. And if anybody asks you: Why are you untying him? answer thus: His master needs him. And those whom he had sent on this errand went and found it as he had said they would. And as they were untying the colt his masters said to them: Why are you untying the colt? And they said: His master needs him. And they brought the colt to Jesus and threw their clothing upon him and mounted Jesus on him; and as he went on they strewed their clothing in the road. And as he approached the descent from the Mount of Olives, all the multitude of his disciples, rejoicing, began to praise God in a great voice for all the powers they had seen displayed, saying: Blessed is he who comes, the King, in the name of the Lord; peace in heaven, and glory in the highest. And some of the Pharisees in the crowd said to him: Master, reprove your disciples. And he answered and said: I tell you, if these are silent, the stones will cry out.

And as he approached and looked at the city he wept over it, saying: If you only knew on this day, even you, what leads to peace! But now it is hidden from your eyes. For the days will come when your enemies will run an entrenchment around you and encircle you and crush you from every side, and they will level you to the ground, and your children in you, and they will not leave stone upon stone in you, because you did not recognize the time of your visitation.

And he went into the temple and began to drive out those who sold there, saying to them: It is written: And my house shall be a house of prayer. But you have made it into a den of robbers.

And he was teaching day by day in the temple. But the high priests and the scribes looked for a way to destroy him, and so also did the leading men among the people, but they could not think of what to do, for all the populace hung on his words.

§ And it happened on one of those days when he was teaching the people in the temple and preaching the gospel, the high priests and the scribes came up to him, along with the elders, and they said to him: Tell us by what authority you do this, or who it is who gave you this authority. He answered and said to them: I too will ask you a question, and you tell me. Was the baptism of John from heaven or from men? They discussed this among themselves, saying: If we say: From heaven, he will say: Why did you not believe him? But if we say: From men, the whole populace will stone us to death, for they are convinced that John was a prophet. And they answered that they did not know whence it came. And Jesus said to them: Neither will I tell you by what authority I do this.

And he began to tell the people this parable: A man planted a vineyard, and let it out to farmers, and left the country for some time. And when the time came he sent his slave to the farmers so that they could give him some of the fruits of the vineyard. But the farmers lashed him and sent him away empty-handed. He sent another slave in addition and they lashed him too and outraged him and sent him away empty-handed. He added still a third and sent him, and they wounded him and threw him out. Then the lord of the vineyard said to himself: What shall I do? I will send them my beloved son; perhaps they will respect him. But when they saw him the farmers discussed it with each other, and they said: This is the heir. Let us kill him, so that the inheritance will be ours. And they threw him out of the vineyard and killed him. What will the lord of the vineyard do to them? He will come and destroy those farmers and give the vineyard to others. When they heard it, they said: May it never happen! But he looked at them and said: What then is this that is written? The stone that the builders rejected has come to be at the head of the corner. And anyone who falls on that stone shall be broken; and he on whom it falls shall be crushed by it. And the scribes and the high priests were looking for a way to lay their hands on him at that very time, and they were afraid of the people, for they knew that he had spoken that parable against them. And they watched their opportunity and sent spies who pretended to be righteous men, so that they could seize on something he said and be able to turn him over to the government and the authority of the governor. And they questioned him, saying: Master, we know that you speak and teach straight, and do not take account of persons, but truthfully teach the way of God. Is it lawful to pay the tax to Caesar or not? But he knew their knavery and said to them: Show me a denarius. Whose is the image and whose name is inscribed? They said: Caesar's. And he said to them: Then give Caesar what is Caesar's and God what is God's. And they could not get a hold on this saying before the people, and they wondered at this answer and were silent.

Then there came to him certain of the Sadducees, who say that there is no resurrection, and they questioned him, saying: Master, Moses wrote for us that if a man's brother dies, married but without children, his brother should take his wife and raise up issue for his brother. Now there were seven brothers; and the first one took a wife and died without children; and the second took her, and the third, and in the same way all seven left no children, and died; and finally the woman died. So in the resurrection, whose wife will the woman be? For all seven had her as wife. Jesus said to them: The sons of this life marry and are given in marriage, but those who have been called worthy to attain that other life, and the resurrection from the dead, neither marry nor are given in marriage. For they can no longer die, for they are like angels, and being sons of the resurrection they are sons of God. But that the dead waken Moses bore witness, at the bush, when he says: The Lord God of Abraham and the God of Isaac and the God of Jacob; for he is not God of the dead but of the living, for all live in him. Then some of the scribes answered and said: Master, you have spoken well; for they no longer dared question him on anything. But he said to them: How do they say that the Christ is the son of David? For David himself says in the Book of Psalms: The Lord said to my Lord: Sit on my right, so that I may put your enemies beneath your feet. So David calls him Lord, and how can he be his son?

And in the hearing of all the people he said to his disciples: Beware of the scribes, who like to walk about in their robes, who love the salutations in the market-places and the first seats in the synagogues and the foremost couches at the dinners, who eat up the houses of the widows and pray long as an excuse. The greater the condemnation these will receive.

§ Then he looked out and saw the people throwing their gifts into the treasury, rich people; and he saw a poor widow tossing in two little coins. And he said: Truly I tell you, this widow who is poor has put in more than all. For they all put in their gifts out of their surplus, but she put in out of her deficit, her whole livelihood.

And when some said concerning the temple that it was made beautiful with fine stones and dedications, he said: There will come days when of all this that you see there will be no stone set on stone that will escape falling to ruin. But they questioned him, saying: Master, when will this be, and what will be the sign when this is about to happen? He said: See to it that you are not led astray. For many will come in my name saying: I am he, and: The time is near. Do not follow them. But when you hear of wars and dissensions, do not be frightened. For all this must come first, but the end will not be soon. Then he said to them: Nation shall rise up against nation and kingdom against kingdom, there will be great earthquakes, and in places there will be pestilences and famines, and horrors and great signs from the sky. But before all these things they will lay their hands on you and persecute you, turning you over to the synagogues and prisons, as you are brought before kings and chiefs because of my name. This will be your time to testify. Then store it in your hearts that you must not study beforehand how you will defend yourselves, for I will give you such lips and such skill that all your antagonists will be unable to stand against you or speak against you. But you will be betrayed even by parents and brothers and kinsmen and friends, and they will put some of you to death, and you will be hated by all because of my name. But not one hair of your head shall be destroyed. Through your endurance you will possess your own souls. But when you see Jerusalem encircled by encampments, then know that her desolation is near. Then let those who are in Judaea flee to the mountains, and those who are in the middle of the city go out, and those who are in the provinces not go into her, because these are the days of her retribution, for all the scriptures to be fulfilled. Woe to the women who are with child in those days and the women who are nursing in those days. For there will be great stress upon the land and anger against this people, and they will fall to the edge of the sword and be led captive into all the nations, and Jerusalem will be trampled by the nations until the times of the nations are fulfilled. And there will be portents in the sun and the moon and stars, and on earth distress of nations in bewilderment of the sound of the sea and its surf, as people faint from fear and expectation of what is advancing upon the world, for the powers of the skies will be shaken. And then they will see the son of man coming upon the cloud with power and great glory. As these things begin to happen, look up and raise your hands, because the time of your deliverance is near.

And he told them a parable: Look at the fig tree and all the trees. When they put forth leaves, you look at them for yourselves and know that the summer is now near; so also when you see these things happening you know that the Kingdom of God is near. Truly I tell you that this generation will not pass by before all these things are done. The sky and the earth will pass away but my words may not pass away. But look to yourselves so that your hearts may not become heavy with surfeit and drunkenness and thoughts of this life, lest that day come upon you suddenly like a trap; for it will come upon all those who are settled upon the face of the whole earth. Be wakeful at every moment, praying for strength to escape all those things that are going to happen, and to stand before the son of man.

And during the days he would teach in the temple, but for the nights he would go out and stay at the Mount of Olives; and all the people would go out at dawn to the temple to hear him.

§ The festival of the unleavened bread drew near, which is called the Passover. And the high priests and the scribes were looking for a way to destroy him, for they were afraid of the people. And Satan entered into

Judas, the one called Iscariot, who was one of the number of the twelve. And he went and talked with the high priests and generals about how to betray him to them. And they were delighted and contracted to give him money. And he agreed, and looked for an opportunity to betray him, when the crowd was not there.

And the day of unleavened bread came, when it was time to sacrifice the paschal lamb. And Jesus sent out Peter and John, saying: Go and make preparations for us to eat the feast of the Passover. And they said to him: Where shall we prepare it? And he said to them: See, as you go into the city, a man carrying a pot of water will meet you. Follow him into whatever house he enters. And say to the master of the house: The master says to you: Where is my guest chamber where I can eat the Passover dinner with my disciples? And he will show you a large upper room, furnished. There prepare it. And they went and found it as he had told them, and made ready the Passover. And when the time came, he took his place, and the apostles with him. And he said to them: I greatly desired to eat this Passover dinner with you, before my suffering; for I tell you that I shall not eat it again until there is fulfillment in the Kingdom of God. And he accepted a cup and gave thanks and said: Take this and divide it among yourselves; for I tell you, I will not drink of the produce of the vine from now until the Kingdom of God arrives. And he took a loaf and gave thanks and broke it and gave it to them, saying: This is my body [which is given for your sake; do this in remembrance of me. And so too with the cup, after dinner, saying: This cup is the new covenant in my blood, which is poured out for your sake]. But see, the hand of the betrayer is with me, on the table. Because the son of man goes the way appointed, but woe to that man through whom he is betrayed. And they began to ask among themselves which of them it could be who was going to do this thing.

And a dispute arose among them over which of them was thought to be the greatest. But he said to them: The kings of the Gentiles are as lords over them, and those who exercise authority are called their benefactors. Not so you; but let the greater among you be as the younger, and let him who leads be as him who serves. For who is greater, he who dines, or he who serves him? Is it not he who dines? Yet I am among you as the one who serves. But you are the ones who have stayed with me in my times of trial; and I appointed for you, as my father appointed a kingdom for me, that you shall eat and drink at my table in my kingdom, and sit upon thrones and judge the twelve tribes of Israel. Simon, Simon, behold, Satan asked for you, to sift you like grain, but I asked for you that your faith should not fail you. So you, one day, turn to your brothers and strengthen them. But he said to him: Lord, with you I am ready to go to prison and to death. But he said: I tell you, Peter, the cock will not crow today until you have denied three times that you knew me.

And he said to them: When I sent you forth without purse or bag or shoes, surely you did not lack for anything? They said: Nothing. But he said to them: But now, let him who has a purse, take it; let him who has a bag, likewise; let him who has no sword sell his coat and buy one. For I tell you, this that has been written must be fulfilled in me: He was even counted among the outlaws. For what is said about me comes to fulfillment. They said: Lord, here are two swords. But he said to them: It is enough.

And he went out and proceeded according to his custom to the Mount of Olives. And when he had reached the place he said to them: Pray that you do not come to the time of trial. And he himself withdrew from them about a stone's throw, and went on his knees and prayed, saying: Father, if you will, take this cup from me; but let, not my will, but yours, be done. And an angel from the sky was seen by him, giving him strength. And as he came into his agony he prayed the more intensely, and his sweat became like drops of blood falling on the ground. And he stood up from his prayer and went to his disciples and found them asleep after their sorrow, and said to them: Why do you sleep? Get up and pray that you do not come to the time of trial.

And while he was still speaking, behold, a crowd came, and the man called Judas, one of the twelve, was leading them, and he came up to Jesus to kiss him. But Jesus said to him: Judas, are you betraying the son of man with a kiss? When his companions saw what was going to happen, they said: Lord, shall we strike with the sword? And one of them struck the slave of the high priest and took off his right ear. But Jesus spoke forth and said: Let that be enough. And he took hold of the man's ear and healed him. But Jesus said to the high priests and generals of the temple and elders who were present: Did you come out with swords and clubs as if I were a highwayman? Day by day I was with you in the temple and you did not put forth your hands against me. But this is your time, and the power of darkness.

They seized him and led him away and took him to the house of the high priest; and Peter followed him at a distance. And when they lit a fire in the middle of the courtyard and sat by it together, Peter sat among them. A serving girl saw him sitting by the fire, and she stared at him and said: This man was with him too. But he denied it, saying: Woman, I do not know him. And after a little while someone else saw him and said: You are one of them too. But Peter said: Man, I am not. But after an interval of about an hour another man insisted on it, saying: Truly this man was with him; he is a Galilaean. But Peter said: Man, I do not know what you are talking about. And at that moment while he was still talking the cock crew. And the Lord turned and looked at Peter, and Peter remembered the Lord's saying, how he had told him: Before the cock crows this

morning you will deny me three times. And he went
outside and wept bitterly.

And the men who had hold of Jesus mocked him,
lashing him and covering his head and asking him:
Which one hit you? Prophesy! And they said many
other things against him, reviling him.

And when it was day, the elders of the people were
assembled, the high priests and the scribes, and they
brought him before their council, saying: If you are the
Christ, tell us. But he said to them: If I tell you, you will
not believe me; and if I ask you you will not answer.
From now on the son of man will be sitting on the right
of the power of God. And they all said: Are you then
the son of God? But he said to them: You are saying
that I am. And they said: Why do we still need
testimony? For we ourselves have heard it from his
mouth.

§ And their whole assemblage rose up and brought
him before Pilate. And they began to accuse him,
saying: We found that this man was corrupting our
people and interfering with the payment of taxes to
Caesar and calling himself the King anointed. Pilate
questioned him, saying: Are you the King of the Jews?
He answered him and said: It is you who say it. And
Pilate said to the high priests and the mob: I find no
guilt in this man. But they insisted, saying: He is
disturbing the people with his teaching throughout
Judaea, all the way from Galilee to here. When Pilate
heard this he asked if the man were a Galilaean, and
understanding that he was from Herod's sphere of
authority, he sent him off to Herod, who was himself in
Jerusalem during these days. Herod was greatly
pleased at seeing Jesus, for he had wished to see him for
some time, because he had heard about him, and he
hoped to see some miracle performed by him. And he
questioned him at considerable length, but Jesus gave

him no answer. And the high priests and the scribes
stood there strenuously accusing him. And Herod
despised him and put shining clothing on him in
mockery and sent him back with his guards to Pilate.
And Herod and Pilate became friends with each other
on that same day, after having been at enmity before.

Now Pilate called together the high priests and the
chief men and the people and said to them: You
brought me this man as one who was corrupting the
people, and look, I have judged him in your presence
and found him not guilty of any of the things you charge
him with. Nor did Herod either, for he sent him back to
us. And see, nothing has been done by him to deserve
death. So I will teach him a lesson and let him go. But
they screamed in full cry, saying: Take him away and let
our Barabbas go. He was a man who had been thrown
into prison on account of an uprising with bloodshed
that had taken place in the city. And again Pilate spoke
to them, wishing to let Jesus go. But they cried out
saying: Crucify, crucify him. A third time he said to
them: But what harm has this man done? I have found
nothing about him to deserve death. I will teach him a
lesson and let him go. But they kept at him, demanding
in loud voices that he be crucified, and their voices
prevailed. And Pilate decided that they should have
what they demanded; and he set free the man they
asked for, who had been thrown into prison for
insurrection and murder, and he gave Jesus up to their
will.

And as they led him away, they seized on a certain
Simon of Cyrene who was on his way in from the
country, and loaded him with the cross to carry behind
Jesus. And a great multitude of the people followed
him and women who mourned and lamented for him.
And Jesus turned to them and said: Daughters of
Jerusalem, do not cry for me, but for yourselves and
your children, because, behold, the days are coming
when they will say: Blessed are the barren, and the

wombs that did not breed and the breasts that did not nurse. Then they will begin to say to the mountains: Fall upon us; and to the hills: Cover us. For if they do these things when the wood is green, what will happen when it is dry?

Two others also, who were malefactors, were led along with him to be put to death. And when they came to the place which is called The Skull, there they crucified him and the malefactors, one on the right and one on the left. And Jesus said: Father, forgive them, for they do not know what they are doing. They divided up his clothing and cast lots for it. And the people stood there watching. But the chief men sneered at him, saying: He saved others, let him save himself, if this is the anointed of God, the chosen one. And also the soldiers came up to him and mocked him, offering him vinegar and saying: If you are the King of the Jews, save yourself. There was also an inscription above him, saying: This is the King of the Jews. And one of the malefactors hanging there reviled him and said: Are you not the Christ? Save yourself and us. But the other answered, reproving him, and said: Do you not fear God because you share his sentence? And we are justly punished, for we are getting what we deserve for what we have done; but he has done nothing out of the way. And he said: Jesus, remember me when you enter upon your kingdom. He said to him: Truly I tell you, this day you will be with me in paradise. And now it was about the sixth hour, and darkness came over the whole earth until the ninth hour, with the sun eclipsed, and the veil of the temple was split down the middle. And Jesus cried out in a great voice and said: Father, into your hands I give my spirit; and when he had said this he breathed his last. And when the company commander saw what happened, he glorified God, saying: Truly this was a righteous man. And all those crowds who had gathered together for this spectacle, when they had watched what happened, beat their breasts and went away. But

those who were known to him stood at a distance, and
also the women who had followed him from Galilee,
watching all this.

And behold, there was a man named Joseph who was
one of the council, a good and righteous man, who had
not agreed with the council and their action. He was
from Arimathaea, a city of the Jews; and he was
expecting the Kingdom of God. He came to Pilate and
asked for the body of Jesus, and he took it down and
wrapped it in fine linen, and laid him in a tomb cut in
the rock, where no one had ever been buried. It had
been the Day of Preparation and the sabbath was
beginning to dawn. And the women who had come with
him from Galilee followed and saw the tomb and how
the body was placed there. Then they returned and
prepared spices and ointments.

§ And for the sabbath they rested, according to the
commandment; but on the first day after the sabbath
just before daylight they came bringing the spices which
they had prepared. And they found the stone rolled
away from the tomb, and they went in but did not find
the body of the Lord Jesus. And it happened that as
they were at a loss about this, behold, two men stood
before them in radiant clothing. And as the women
were full of fear and bowed their faces toward the
ground, the men said: Why do you look for the living
among the dead? He is not here, he has wakened.
Remember how he talked to you when he was still in
Galilee, saying that the son of man must be betrayed
into the hands of sinful men, and be crucified, and rise
again on the third day. And they remembered his
words, and returned from the tomb and reported all
these matters to the eleven and all the others. The
women were Mary the Magdalene and Joanna and
Mary the mother of James; and the other women who
were with them told the apostles the same story. And
to them these words seemed to be madness, and they

did not believe the women. But Peter started up and ran to the tomb, and stooped and saw only the linen bindings, and came back to them marveling over what had happened.

And behold, on the same day, two of them were making their way toward a village named Emmaus sixty furlongs away, and they were talking with each other about all these things that had occurred. And it happened that during their talk and discussion Jesus himself came up and went along with them, but their eyes were prevented from recognizing him. And he said to them: What is this you are talking about, tossing it back and forth as you go? And they stopped, frowning. And one, whose name was Cleopas, answered and said to him: Are you the only visitor to Jerusalem who does not know what happened in it during these days? He said: What things? They said: The story of Jesus of Nazareth, who was a powerful prophet in act and word before God and all the people, and how our high priests and those who rule over us gave him over to the judgment of death and crucified him. We had been hoping that he was the one who was going to liberate Israel. But with all that, this is now the third day since these things happened to him. But also some women of our group astonished us. They went at dawn to the tomb and did not find his body, and came back saying that they had even seen a vision of angels, who say that he is alive. And some of those who were with us went back to the tomb, and found it as the women had said, but did not see him. And he said to them: O mindless and slow in the heart to believe all that the prophets have told you. Did not the Christ have to suffer this and enter into his glory? And beginning from Moses, and through the prophets, he expounded to them all that was in the scriptures concerning himself. And they approached the village they were making for, and he pretended to be going on farther. And they pressed him, saying: Stay with us, because it is nearly night and the sun is already set. And he went in to stay with them.

And it happened that as he took his place to eat with them he took a loaf and blessed it and broke it and gave some to them. And their eyes were opened and they recognized him. But he himself vanished from their sight. And they said to each other: Were our hearts not burning when he talked with us on the road, when he unfolded the scriptures to us? And they rose up in that same hour and returned to Jerusalem, and found the eleven and their companions assembled and saying that truly the Lord had awakened and been seen by Simon. And they described what had happened on the road and how he had been recognized by them in the breaking of the bread. While they were saying these things he himself stood in their midst and said to them: Peace be with you. They were startled and full of fear and thought they were looking at a ghost. And he said to them: Why are you shaken, and why do doubts arise in your hearts? Look at my hands and my feet and see that I am myself. Touch me and see, because a ghost does not have flesh and bones as you see that I have. And as he said s he showed them his hands and his feet. And when they still could not believe for joy, and were full of wonder, he said to them: Do you have anything to eat here? And they gave him a portion of cooked fish; and he took it and ate it in their presence.

And he said to them: These are my words which I spoke to you while I was still with you, that there must be fulfillment of all that was written in the law of Moses and the prophets and the psalms about me. Then he opened their minds to the understanding of the scriptures. And he said to them that thus it was written for the Christ to suffer, and rise from the dead on the third day, and for the preaching in his name of repentance for the forgiveness of sins, to all the nations; beginning from Jerusalem; of these things you are witnesses. And behold, I send forth the promise of my father to you. And do you rest in the city until you are clothed with power from on high.

And he led them out as far as Bethany, and raised his hands and blessed them. And it happened that in the act of blessing he departed from them and was carried up to heaven. And they did obeisance to him and turned back to Jerusalem with great joy, and they were constantly in the temple praising God.

JOHN

John is probably not the apostle, but a follower or disciple of his. The gospel is now generally thought to have been written between A.D. 80 and 120.

§ IN THE BEGINNING WAS THE WORD, and the word was with God, and the word was God. He was in the beginning, with God. Everything came about through him, and without him not one thing came about. What came about in him was life, and the life was the light of mankind; and the light shines in the darkness, and the darkness did not understand it.

There was a man sent from God; his name was John. This man came for testimony, to testify concerning the light, so that all should believe through him. He was not the light, but was to testify concerning the light. The light was the true light, which illuminates every person who comes into the world. He was in the world, and the world came about through him, and the world did not know him. He went to his own and his own people did not accept him. Those who accepted him, he gave them power to become children of God, to those who believed in his name, who were born not from

blood or from the will of the flesh or from the will of
man, but from God.

And the word became flesh and lived among us, and
we have seen his glory, glory as of a single son from his
father, full of grace and truth. John bears witness
concerning him, and he cried out, saying (for it was he
who was speaking): He who is coming after me was
before me, because he was there before I was; because
we have all received from his fullness, and grace for
grace. Because the law was given through Moses; the
grace and the truth came through Jesus Christ. No one
has ever seen God; the only-born God who is in the
bosom of his father, it is he who told of him.

And this is the testimony of John when the Jews sent
priests and Levites from Jerusalem to ask him: Who are
you? And he confessed, and made no denial, but
confessed: I am not the Christ. And they asked him:
What then? Are you Elijah? And he said: I am not.
Are you the prophet? And he answered: No. Then they
said to him: Who are you? So that we can give an
answer to those who sent us. What do you say about
yourself? He said: I am the voice of one crying in the
desert: Make straight the way of the Lord; as Isaiah the
prophet said. Now they had been sent by the Pharisees.
And they questioned him and said to him: Why then do
you baptize, if you are not the Christ, or Elijah or the
prophet? John answered them saying: I baptize with
water; but in your midst stands one whom you do not
know, who is coming after me, and I am not fit to untie
the fastening of his shoe. All this happened in Bethany
beyond the Jordan, where John was baptizing.

The next day he saw Jesus coming toward him and
said: See, the lamb of God who takes away the
sinfulness of the world. This is the one of whom I said:
A man is coming after me who was before me, because
he was there before I was. And I did not know him. But
so that he might be made known to Israel, this was why
I came baptizing with water. And John bore witness,
saying: I have seen the Spirit descending like a dove

from the sky, and it remained upon him; and I did not know him, but the one who sent me to baptize with water was the one who said to me: That one, on whom you see the Spirit descending and remaining upon him, is the one who baptizes with the Holy Spirit. And I have seen, and I have borne witness that this is the son of God.

The next day John was standing with two of his disciples, and he saw Jesus walking about and said: See, the lamb of God. His two disciples heard what he said and followed Jesus. Jesus turned about and saw them following him and said: What are you seeking? They said to him: Rabbi (which translated means master), where are you staying? He said to them: Come and see. So they came, and saw where he was staying, and stayed with him for that day. It was about the tenth hour. Andrew, one of the two who heard Jesus and followed him, was the brother of Simon Peter. He went first and found his brother Simon and said to him: We have found the Messiah (which is, translated, the Christ). He took him to Jesus. Jesus looked at him and said: You are Simon, the son of John. You shall be called Cephas (which means Peter).

The next day Jesus wished to go out to Galilee. And he found Philip and said to him: Follow me. Philip was from Bethsaida, the city of Andrew and Peter. Philip found Nathanael and said to him: We have found the one of whom Moses wrote in the law, and the prophets: Jesus the son of Joseph, from Nazareth. And Nathanael said to him: Can anything good come from Nazareth? Philip said to him: Come and see. Jesus saw Nathanael coming toward him and said of him: See, a true son of Israel, in whom there is no guile. Nathanael said to him: How is it that you know me? Jesus answered and said to him: I saw you when you were under the fig tree, before Philip called you. Nathanael answered: Master, you are the son of God, you are the King of Israel. Jesus answered and said to him: Because I told you I saw you under the fig tree, you believe? You will see greater things than that. And he said to him: Truly truly I tell you, you will see the heaven open and the angels of God ascending and descending to the son of man.

§ And on the third day a wedding took place at Cana, in Galilee, and the mother of Jesus was there; and Jesus also, and his disciples, had been invited to the wedding. And when the wine gave out, Jesus' mother said to him: They have no wine. Jesus said to her: What is that to you and me, madam? My time has not yet come. His mother said to the servants: Do whatever he tells you. Now there were six stone water jars set by for the lustration, which is the custom of the Jews, each holding two or three measures. Jesus said to them: Fill the jars with water. And they filled them to the brim. And he said to them: Now pour it out and take it to the master of the feast. And they took it to him. When the master of the feast tasted the water that had turned into wine—and did not know where it came from, but the servants who had poured it knew—the master of the feast called the bridegroom and said to him: Everybody first puts out the good wine and the poorer wine after they have drunk well; but you kept the good wine until now. This was the first of his miracles Jesus performed, at Cana in Galilee, and displayed his glory, and his disciples believed in him.

After this he went down to Capernaum, himself and his mother and his brothers and disciples, and they stayed there for a few days.

And the Passover of the Jews drew near, and Jesus went up to Jerusalem. And in the temple he found people selling oxen and sheep and doves, and the money changers sitting there; and he made a scourge out of ropes and drove them all out of the temple, and the sheep and the oxen, and he scattered the coins of the money changers and overturned their tables, and to the sellers of doves he said: Take these things out of here; stop making the house of my father a house of business. His disciples remembered that it is written: Jealous concern for your house consumes me. The Jews spoke forth and said to him: What sign do you give us that you can do this? Jesus answered and said to them: Destroy this temple and in three days I will raise it up again. But the Jews said: This temple was built in forty-six years; and you will raise it up in three days? But he had been speaking of the temple of his body. Thus when he rose from the dead, his disciples remembered that he had said this, and believed in the scripture and the word that Jesus had spoken. But when he was in Jerusalem at the Passover, at the festival, many believed in his name, seeing the miracles he performed. But Jesus himself did not entrust himself to them, because he knew them all, and knew that he had no need for anyone to tell him about man, for he himself knew what was in man.

§ There was a man among the Pharisees, Nicodemus by name, a councillor of the Jews. He came to Jesus at night and said to him: Master, we know that you came as a teacher from God; for no one could perform the miracles you perform if God were not with him. Jesus answered and said to him: Truly truly I tell you, if one is not born from above, he cannot see the Kingdom of God. Nicodemus said to him: How can a man be born when he is old? Surely he cannot enter his mother's womb a second time and be born? Jesus answered: Truly truly I tell you, if one is not born from water and spirit, he cannot enter the Kingdom of God. What is born from the flesh is flesh, and what is born from the spirit is spirit. Do not wonder because I told you: You must be born from above. The wind blows where it will, and you hear its sound, but you do not know where it comes from or where it is going. So it is with everyone who is born from the spirit. Nicodemus answered and said to him: How can this happen? Jesus answered and

said to him: You are the teacher of Israel and do not
understand this? Truly truly I tell you that we tell you
what we know, and testify to what we have seen, and
you do not accept our testimony. If I tell you of earthly
matters and you do not believe, how will you believe if
I tell you of heavenly matters? And no one has gone up
to heaven except the one who came down from heaven,
the son of man. And as Moses raised up the snake in
the desert, so must the son of man be raised up, so that
everyone who believes in him may have everlasting life.
For God so loved the world that he gave his only son, so
that everyone who believes in him may not be destroyed but may have everlasting life. For God did not
send his son into the world to judge the world, but so
that the world could be saved through him. He who
believes in him is not judged. He who does not believe
in him has already been judged, because he did not
believe in the name of the only son of God. This is the
judgment, because the light came into the world and
people loved the darkness more than the light because
their actions were wicked. For everyone who does bad
things hates the light and does not come toward the
light, lest his actions be discovered; but he who
accomplishes the truth comes toward the light, so that
it may be made clear that his actions were with God.

After this Jesus and his disciples went into the land of
Judaea, and there he spent some time with them and
baptized. And John also was baptizing at Aenon near
Salim, because there were many waters there, and the
people came to him and were baptized. For John had
not yet been thrown into prison. Now there was a
dispute between the disciples of John and a Jew about
lustration. And they came to John and said to him:
Master, the one who was with you beyond Jordan, to
whom you testified, see, he is baptizing and all come to
him. John answered and said: A man cannot receive
anything unless it is given to him from heaven. You
yourselves bear witness that I said: I am not the Christ.
But I said: I am sent before him. He who has the bride

is the bridegroom; but the friend of the bridegroom, who stands by and listens to him, rejoices with a joy that comes from the voice of the bridegroom. This is my joy which is fulfilled. He must increase, and I must be diminished. He who comes from above is above all. He who comes from the earth is of the earth and speaks from the earth. He who comes from heaven is above all. What he testifies to is what he has seen and heard, and no one accepts his testimony. He who accepts his testimony proves that God is true. For he whom God sent speaks the words of God, for there is no measure to what the spirit gives. The father loves the son and has given all things into his hand. He who believes in the son has everlasting life; but he who disbelieves in the son will not see life, but the anger of God remains upon him.

§ When the Lord realized that the Pharisees had heard that Jesus was making more converts than John and baptizing them (in fact, Jesus himself was not baptizing but his disciples were), he left Judaea and went back to Galilee. He had to pass through Samaria. So he came to the city in Samaria which is called Sychar, near the piece of land which Jacob gave to Joseph his son. There was a well of Jacob there. Now Jesus was tired from his journey and thus sat down by the well. It was about the sixth hour. A woman of Samaria came to draw water. Jesus said to her: Give me a drink. For his disciples had gone off to the city to buy provisions. So the Samaritan woman said to him: How is it that you, a Jew, are asking for a drink from me, a Samaritan woman? [For Jews have no dealings with Samaritans.] Jesus answered and said to her: If you knew the gift of God, and who it is that says to you: Give me a drink; *you* would have asked *him*, and he would have given you living water. She said to him: Lord, you have no bucket to let down, and the well is deep. From where then do you have the living water? Surely you are not greater than Jacob our forefather, who gave us this well, who drank from it himself, as did his sons and his cattle. Jesus answered and said to her: Whoever drinks from this water will be thirsty again; but he who drinks from the water I shall give will not be thirsty forevermore, but the water I shall give him will turn within him into a spring of water jetting up into everlasting life. The woman said to him: Lord, give me this water so I shall not be thirsty or have to come here to draw it up. He said to her: Go and tell your husband and come back. The woman answered and said to him: I have no husband. Jesus said to her: You did well to say: I have no husband. You have had five husbands and the one you have now is not your husband. What you said was true. The woman said to him: Lord, I see that you are a prophet. Our fathers worshipped on this mountain; but you people say that Jerusalem is the place where one should worship. Jesus said to her: Believe me, madam, the time is coming when you will worship the father neither on this mountain nor in Jerusalem. You worship what you do not know; we worship what we do know, because salvation comes from the Jews. But the time is coming and it is now when the true worshippers will worship the Father in the spirit and in truth, for the Father looks for such worshippers. God is spirit and those who worship him must worship in the spirit and in truth. The woman said to him: I know that the Messiah, who is called the Christ, is coming. When he comes, he will tell us all. Jesus said to her: I am he, talking to you.

Thereupon his disciples came and were surprised that he had been talking to a woman, but no one said: What are you looking for? Or: Why are you talking with her? Then the woman left her water jar and went off to the city, and said to the people: Come and see a man who told me everything I have done. Might he not be the Christ? They went forth from the city and came to him. In the meanwhile his disciples questioned him and said to him: Master, eat. But he said to them: I have food to eat which you do not know of. So the disciples said to each other: Could someone have brought him something to eat? Jesus said to them: My food is to do the will of him who sent me and finish his work. Do you not say: There are four more months, and then comes the harvest? But see, I tell you, raise up your eyes and look at the fields, see that they are white for harvesting. And now he who reaps takes his wages and gathers the crop for everlasting life, so that sower and reaper alike can be happy. For in this matter it is true to say that the sower is one person and the reaper another. I sent you to harvest what you never labored on. Others labored, and you came in upon their labor.

And many Samaritans from that city believed in him because of what the woman said when she testified: He told me everything I have done. So when the Samaritans came to him they invited him to stay with them, and he stayed there for two days. And many more believed in him because of what he himself said, and they said to the woman: It is no longer because of your talk that we believe; we ourselves have heard, and we know that this is truly the savior of the world.

At the end of the two days he went from there to Galilee; for Jesus himself had testified that a prophet has no honor in his own country. But when he came to Galilee the Galilaeans welcomed him, for they had seen what he did in Jerusalem at the festival, since they had themselves gone to the festival. So then he returned to Cana in Galilee where he had made the water into wine. And there was a certain prince, whose son was sick, in Capernaum. This man, hearing that Jesus had come from Judaea to Galilee, went to him and asked him to come to his house and heal his son, for he was going to die. Then Jesus said to him: Unless you see miracles and wonders, you will not believe. But the prince said to him: Lord, come to my house before my little boy dies. Jesus said to him: Go on your way; your son lives. The man believed in the word Jesus had spoken to him and went on his way. And just as he was coming home his slaves met him saying that his son was

alive. So he asked them at what hour he had got better;
and they said: Yesterday at the seventh hour the fever
left him. So the father realized that it was at the time
when Jesus had said: Your son lives; and he, with all his
household, believed. This was the second miracle Jesus
performed, when he came from Judaea to Galilee.

§ After that, there was a festival of the Jews, and Jesus
went up to Jerusalem. In Jerusalem by the Sheep Gate
there is a pool for which the name in Hebrew is
Bethzatha. It has five porches. There would lie a crowd
of afflicted people, blind, lame, paralyzed, [waiting for
the water to be disturbed. For an angel of the Lord
would come down to the pool from time to time, and
the water would be disturbed. And whoever was first to
enter the pool after the disturbing of the water would
be healed of the infirmity that afflicted him]. There was
one man there who had had his sickness for thirty-eight
years. And seeing him lying there, and knowing that he
had had it for a long time, Jesus said to him: Do you
wish to be healthy? The sick man answered: Lord, I
have no man to put me into the pool when the water is
disturbed; and while I am on my way someone else gets
there ahead of me. Jesus said to him: Arise, take up
your bed, and walk. And immediately the man was
healthy, and he took up his bed and walked. It was the
sabbath on that day; so the Jews said to the man who
had been healed: It is the sabbath, and it is not lawful
for you to carry your bed. But he answered them: The
man who made me healthy was the one who told me:
Take up your bed and walk. They asked him: Which is
the man who said to you: Take it up and walk? But the
man who had been healed did not know who it was,
since Jesus had disappeared into the crowd that was
there. Afterward Jesus found him in the temple and
said to him: See, you have become healthy. Sin no
more, lest it be the worse for you. The man went away

and told the Jews that it was Jesus who had made him healthy. And that was why the Jews persecuted Jesus, because he did this on the sabbath. But he answered them: Until now my father has been doing his work, and I too am doing my work. For this the Jews sought all the more to kill him, because he not only was breaking the sabbath but even called God his own father, making himself the equal of God. But Jesus answered and told them: Truly truly I tell you, the son cannot do anything by himself unless he sees the father doing it; for what he does the son does likewise. For the father loves the son and shows him everything he himself does, and he will show him greater deeds than these for you to wonder at. For as the father wakes the dead and gives them life, so the son also gives life to whom he will. Nor does the father judge anyone, but he has given all judgment to his son, so that all may honor the son as they honor the father. He who does not honor the son does not honor the father who sent him. Truly truly I tell you that he who listens to my words and believes in him who sent me has life everlasting, and does not come to judgment, but has gone over from death to life. Truly truly I tell you, the time is coming, and it is now, when the dead shall hear the voice of the son of God, and those who have heard shall live. For as the father has life in himself, so he has given the son life to have in himself. And he gave him authority to pass judgment, because he is the son of man. Do not wonder at this, because the hour is coming when those who are in the graves will hear his voice and come out, those who have done good, to the resurrection of life, and those who have done evil to the resurrection of judgment. I cannot do anything by myself. I judge as I hear, and my judgment is just, because I do not seek my own will but the will of him who sent me. If I testify about myself, my testimony is not true; he who testifies about me is someone else, and I know that the testimony he gives about me is true.

You have sent to John and he has testified to the truth; but I do not take my testimony from man, but I say this so that you may be saved. He was the lamp that burns and shines, and you wished to exult for a time in his light; but I have testimony greater than John's, for the works that my father gave me, for me to fulfill them, these same works that I do, testify concerning me that the father sent me, and the father who sent me has testified concerning me. You have never heard his voice or seen his shape, and you do not have his word remaining among you, because you do not believe the one he sent to you. You search the scriptures, because you think they have life everlasting in them; and it is they who testify to me; and you are not willing to come to me and to have life. I do not receive glory from men; but I know you and that you do not have the love of God in you. I came in the name of my father and you do not accept me; if someone else comes in his own name, you will accept him. How can you believe, when you receive your glory from each other, and do not look for the glory that comes from God alone? Do not suppose that I shall accuse you to my father. Your accuser is Moses, in whom you put your hopes. If you believed Moses, you would believe me, for he wrote about me. But if you do not believe his writings, how shall you believe my sayings?

§ After this Jesus went across the Sea of Galilee, that is, Tiberias. And a great crowd was following him, for they saw the miracles he worked for the sick. Jesus went up onto the mountain, and sat there with his disciples. And the Passover, the festival of the Jews, was near. So Jesus lifted up his eyes and saw that a great crowd had come to him, and he said to Philip: Where shall we buy bread so that these can eat? He said this, making trial of him, for he knew what he was going to do. Philip answered: Two hundred denarii worth of bread is not enough for everyone to have a little bit. Andrew, the brother of Simon Peter and one of the disciples, said to him: There is a boy here who has five barley loaves and two little fishes; but what is that for all these people? Jesus said: Have the people take their places on the ground. There was plenty of grass in the place. So the men took their places, to the number of five thousand. Then Jesus took the loaves and gave thanks and passed them out to the people who were lying there, and so too with the fishes, as much as they wanted. And when they were filled, he said to his disciples: Gather up the broken pieces that are left over so that nothing will be lost. So they gathered them up and filled twelve baskets from what was left of the five barley loaves after the people had eaten. When the people saw what miracles he had done, they said: Truly this is the prophet who is coming into the world. Jesus, realizing that they were going to come and carry him off to make him king, withdrew back up the mountain, all by himself. When night came his disciples went down to the sea, and embarking on a ship, they began to cross over the sea to Capernaum. And now it was dark and Jesus had not yet come to them; and the sea was rough from a great wind blowing. When they had rowed about twenty-five or thirty furlongs they saw Jesus walking on the sea and coming close to the ship, and they were frightened. But he said to them: It is I, do not be afraid. They wanted to take him aboard the ship, and immediately it was at the shore for which they were making.

The next day the crowd that was standing on the other side of the sea had seen that there had been no other ship there except the one, and that Jesus had not gone aboard the ship with his disciples, but the disciples had gone away without him. But ships from Tiberias arrived near the place where they had eaten the bread after the Lord had given thanks. So when the crowd saw that neither Jesus nor his disciples were there, they themselves boarded the ships and went to Capernaum

in search of Jesus. And when they found him on the
other side of the sea, they said to him: Master, when
did you reach here? Jesus answered them and said:
Truly truly I tell you, you look for me not because you
saw signs but because you ate the loaves and were fed.
Try to earn, not the food that perishes, but the food
that remains into life everlasting, which the son of man
will give you, for God the Father set his seal upon him.
Then they said to him: What shall we do, to do the
work of God? Jesus answered and said to them: This is
the work of God, to believe in the one he sent. Then
they said to him: What sign are you accomplishing, for
us to see and believe you? What work are you doing?
Our fathers ate the manna in the desert, as it is written:
He gave them bread from heaven to eat. Then Jesus
said to them: Truly truly I tell you, it was not Moses
who gave you bread from heaven, but my father gives
you the true bread from heaven; for the bread of God is
what comes down from heaven and gives life to the
world. Then they said to him: Lord, give us always this
bread. Jesus said to them: I am the bread of life. He
who comes to me will not be hungry, and he who
believes in me will not be thirsty, ever. But I have said
to you that you have seen but do not believe. All that
my father gives me will come to me, and the one who
comes to me I will not drive out, because I have come
down from heaven not to do my own will but the will of
him who sent me; and this is the will of him who sent
me, that I should lose nothing of all he gave me but
raise it up again on the last day. For this is the will of my
father, that everyone who sees the son and believes in
him shall have life everlasting, and I shall raise him up
on the last day.

Now the Jews murmured about him because he had
said: I am the bread which came down from heaven;
and they said: Is not this Jesus the son of Joseph, whose
father and mother we know? How is it that he now
says: I have come down from heaven? Jesus answered

and said to them: Do not murmur among yourselves.
No one can come to me unless the father who sent me
pulls him; and I will raise him up on the last day. It is
written in the prophets: And they shall all be taught
from God. Everyone who has listened and learned
from the father comes to me. Not because anyone has
seen the father, except for the one who is beside God;
he has seen the father. Truly truly I tell you, he who
believes has life everlasting. I am the bread of life. Your
fathers ate the manna in the desert and died. This is the
bread which comes down from heaven so that one may
eat of it and not die. I am the bread which lives, which
came down from heaven. If one eats of this bread he
will live forever, and the bread I will give, for the sake
of the life of the world, is my flesh.

The Jews quarreled with each other, saying: How can
this man give us his flesh to eat? Jesus said to them:
Truly truly I tell you, unless you eat the flesh of the son
of man and drink his blood, you have no life in you. He
who eats my flesh and drinks my blood has life
everlasting, and I will raise him up on the last day. For
my flesh is the true food, and my blood is the true
drink. He who eats my flesh and drinks my blood stays
in me, and I in him. As the living father sent me and I
live through the father, so he who eats me will also live
through me. This is the bread which came down from
heaven; not as our fathers ate and died, he who eats
this bread will live forever.

All this he said as he taught in the synagogue in
Capernaum. Then many of his disciples hearing him
said: This is a hard saying. Who can listen to it? And
Jesus knew in his heart that his disciples were murmuring about this, and said to them: Is this too difficult for
you? What if you were to see the son of man going up
to where he was before? It is the spirit that makes life,
the flesh is no help. The words I have spoken to you are
spirit and life. But there are some of you who do not
believe. For Jesus knew from the beginning who were

the ones who did not believe and who was the one who
would betray him. And he said: This is why I told you
that no one can come to me unless it is given him from
the father. Because of this, many of his disciples left
him thenceforth and no longer went about with him. So
Jesus said to the twelve: You do not wish to go away?
Simon Peter answered him: Lord, to whom shall we
go? You have the words of everlasting life, and we have
believed, and we know that you are the holy one of
God. Jesus answered them: Did I not choose you
twelve? And one of you is an enemy. He meant Judas,
the son of Simon Iscariot; for he, one of the twelve, was
going to betray him.

§ And after that Jesus went about in Galilee; for he did
not wish to go about in Judaea, because the Jews were
seeking to kill him. Now the festival of the Jews which
is the Feast of the Tabernacles was at hand. And his
brothers said to him: Remove from here and go to
Judaea, so that your disciples also can see the works
that you perform; for no one acts in secret and then
hopes to be well known. If you are doing these things,
show yourself to the world. For even his brothers did
not believe in him. And Jesus said to them: My time is
not yet come, but your time is always ready at hand.
The world cannot hate you, but it hates me, because I
testify concerning it that what it does is wicked. You go
up to the festival I will not yet go up to this festival,
because my time is not yet completed. He told them
this and remained in Galilee. But when his brothers
went up to the festival, then he went too, not openly
but in secret. So then the Jews looked for him at the
festival and said: Where is he? And there was much
murmuring about him in the crowds. Some said: He is
good; and others said: No. He leads the people astray.
But none spoke openly about him, through fear of the
Jews.

And now the festival had gone halfway, and Jesus went up to the temple and taught. And the Jews were astonished and said: How does this man have learning when he was never a student? Jesus answered them and said: My teaching is not my own but his who sent me; if anyone wishes to do his will, he will know about the teaching, whether it comes from God or whether I speak on my own account. He who speaks on his own account is looking for his own glory; but he who looks for the glory of him who sent him is the true man, and there is no wrong in him. Did not Moses give you the law? And not one of you obeys the law. Why are you trying to kill me? The crowd answered: You are possessed. Who is trying to kill you? Jesus answered and said to them: I did one thing and you all are astonished. This was why Moses gave you circumcision—not that it comes from Moses but from the fathers—and you circumcise a man on the sabbath. If a man receives circumcision on the sabbath so that the law of Moses may not be broken, are you angry with me because I made a whole man healthy on the sabbath? Do not judge by appearance, but make the judgment that is just. Then some of the people of Jerusalem said: Is not this the man they are trying to kill? And see, he speaks in public and they say nothing to him. Might it be that the authorities have seen that this is the Christ? But we know where this man comes from. But when the Christ comes, no one will know where he comes from. Jesus cried aloud as he taught in the temple: You know me and you know where I come from. But I came not on my own account, but he is the true one who sent me, and you do not know him. I know him, because I am from him and it was he who sent me. Then they sought to seize him, but no one laid a hand on him because his time had not yet come. Many in the crowd believed in him, and they said: When the Christ comes, can he perform more miracles than this one has done?

The Pharisees heard the crowd murmuring thus about him, and the high priests and the Pharisees sent officers to seize him. Then Jesus said: For a little more time I am with you and then I go to him who sent me. You will look for me and you will not find me, and where I am you cannot go. Then the Jews said among themselves: Where does this man mean to go where we shall not find him? He cannot be going to go where we are settled among the Greeks, and teach the Greeks? What is this that he said: You will look for me and you will not find me, and where I am you cannot go?

On the last great day of the festival Jesus stood forth and made a declaration, saying: If anyone is thirsty, let him come to me and drink. For one who believes in me, as the scripture says, streams of living water shall flow from deep within him. This he said concerning the spirit, of which those who had put their faith in him would partake; but the spirit was not yet because Jesus was not yet glorified. And some in the crowd who listened to these words said: This is in truth the prophet. And others said: This is the Christ. But others said: Surely the Christ cannot come out of Galilee? Did not the scripture say that the Christ would be of the seed of David, and from Bethlehem, David's village? So there was division in the multitude over him. And some of them wished to seize him, but no one laid hands on him.

Then the officers came back to the high priests and the Pharisees, who said to them: Why did you not bring him? The officers answered: Never has a man spoken like that. The Pharisees answered: Surely you have not been led astray? Do you think that one of the council or of the Pharisees believes in him? Only this rabble which does not know the law and is accursed. Nicodemus, who had gone to Jesus before, who was one of them, said to them: Surely our law does not judge a man without first giving him a hearing and being told what he does. They answered and said to him: Could it be that you are from Galilee too? Study the matter, and know that no prophet originates in Galilee. [And they went away each to his own house.

§ But Jesus went to the Mount of Olives; but at dawn he came back to the temple, and all the people came to him, and he sat and taught them. And the scribes and the Pharisees brought a woman who had been caught in adultery, and they set her in their midst. And they said to him: Master, this woman was caught in the act of adultery. In the law Moses charged us to stone such women to death. But what do you say? This they said to entrap him, so that they could bring a charge against him. Jesus stooped down and wrote with his finger in the dust. But when they continued to question him he stood up and said: Let the one of you who is without sin be the first to throw a stone at her. And again he stooped and wrote in the dust. And when they heard they went out, one by one, the eldest first, and he was left alone, and the woman who had been in their midst. And Jesus stood up and said to her: Woman, where are they? Has no one condemned you? She said: No one, Lord. And Jesus said: Nor do I condemn you. Go, and from now on sin no more.]

Then Jesus talked with them again and said: I am the light of the world; he who follows me will not walk about in darkness but will have the light of life. Then the Pharisees said to him: You are testifying about yourself; your testimony is not true. Jesus answered and said to them: Even if I am testifying about myself, my testimony is true, because I know where I came from and where I am going. But you do not know where I come from or where I am going. You judge according to the flesh but I judge no one. And if I do judge, my judgment is true, because I am not alone but am I and the one who sent me. And in your law it is written that the testimony of two persons is true. I am he who testifies about myself, and my father who sent me testifies about me. Then they said to him: Where is

your father? Jesus answered: You know neither me nor
my father. If you knew me, you would also know my
father. These words he spoke in the treasury as he
taught in the temple. And no one seized him, because
his time had not yet come.

Then again he said to them: I am going, and you will
look for me, and in your sin you will die. Where I am
going you cannot go. Then the Jews said: Will he kill
himself when he says: Where I am going you cannot
go? And he said to them: You come from things below,
I come from things above. You are of this world, I am
not of this world. I told you that you will die in your
sins; for if you do not believe that I am, you will die in
your sins. Then they said to him: Who are you? Jesus
said to them: What I have been telling you from the
beginning. I have much to say about you and much to
judge. But he who sent me is true, and what I heard
from him is what I speak to the world. They did not
realize it was his father he told them about. Then Jesus
said: When you raise the son of man aloft, then you will
know that I am, and that of myself I do nothing, but
what I say is according to what my father taught me.
And he who sent me is with me. He did not leave me
alone, because what I do is his pleasure, always. When
he said this, many believed in him.

Then Jesus said to the Jews who had believed him: If
you remain with my teaching, then you are truly my
disciples and you will know the truth, and the truth will
set you free. They answered him: We are the seed of
Abraham and have never been enslaved to anyone;
how is it that you say: You will be made free? Jesus
answered them: Truly truly I tell you that everyone
who commits sin is the slave of his sin. But the slave
does not remain in the house forever. The son remains
forever. If then the son sets you free, you will be free in
truth. I know that you are the seed of Abraham. But
you are trying to kill me, because my teaching does not
work in you. What I have seen with my father, I tell
you; do then what you have heard from the father.

They answered and said to him: Our father is Abraham. Jesus said to them: If you are the children of Abraham, then do what Abraham did. But now you are trying to kill me, a man who has told you the truth I heard from God. Abraham did not do that. You are doing what your father did. They said to him: We were not bred from promiscuity. We have one father, God. Jesus said to them: If God were your father, you would love me, since I issued from God and come from God; for I did not come on my own account, but he sent me. Why do you not understand what I say? Because you are not able to listen to my reasoning. The father you come from is the devil and you wish to do your father's will. He has been a man killer from the beginning, and he does not stand upon the truth because there is no truth in him. When he speaks his lie he speaks from what is his own, because he is a liar and so is his father. And because I speak the truth you do not believe me. Which one of you proves me in error? If I speak the truth, why do you not believe me? He who is from God listens to the words of God. That is why you do not listen, because you are not from God. The Jews answered and said to him: Are we not right in saying you are a Samaritan, and possessed? Jesus answered: I am not possessed, but I honor my father, and you dishonor me. I do not seek my own glory. He who seeks it is he who judges. Truly truly I tell you, he who follows my teaching shall not look on death, forever. The Jews said to him: Now we know that you are possessed. Abraham died, and the prophets died, and you say: He who follows my teaching shall not taste of death, forever. Can you be greater than our father Abraham, who died? And the prophets died. Who do you think you are? Jesus answered: If I glorify myself, my glory is nothing. It is my father who glorifies me, whom you call your God; and you do not know about him, but I know him. And if I say that I do not know him, I shall be a liar like you. But I know him and I follow his teaching. Abraham your father was joyful

over seeing my day, and he did see it, and was glad.
Then the Jews said to him: You are not yet fifty years
old; and you have seen Abraham? Jesus said to them:
Truly truly I tell you, I am from before Abraham was
born. Then they picked up stones to throw at him, but
he effaced himself and left the temple.

§ On his way he saw a man who had been blind from
birth. And his disciples questioned him, saying: Master, who sinned, this man or his parents, for him to be
born blind? Jesus answered: Neither he nor his parents
sinned; it was so that the workings of God might be
made manifest in him. We must do the work of him
who sent me while it is day. The night is coming, when
no one can work. While I am in the world, I am the
light of the world. So saying, he spat on the ground and
made mud out of the spittle, and put mud on the man's
eyes, and said to him: Go and wash in the pool of
Siloam (which translated means the one who has been
sent). So he went and washed, and came away seeing.
So his neighbors, and those who had seen him before
when he was a beggar, said: Is not this the man who sat
and begged? Some said: It is he. Others said: No, but it
is someone like him. But he said: It is I. Then they said
to him: How were your eyes opened? He answered:
The man called Jesus made mud and smeared it on my
eyes and said to me: Go to Siloam and wash. So I went
and washed, and I saw. And they said to him: Where is
he? He said: I do not know. Then they took the man
who had once been blind to the Pharisees. The sabbath
was the day on which Jesus had made the mud and
opened the man's eyes. Then the Pharisees in turn
asked him how he had got his sight. And he told them:
He put mud on my eyes, and I washed, and I see. And
some of the Pharisees said: This is no man from God,
since he does not keep the sabbath. But others said:
How can a sinful man work such miracles? And there

was division among them. So they said, once more, to
the blind man: What do you have to say about him,
because he opened your eyes? He said: He is a prophet.
But the Jews did not believe it about him, that he had
been blind and got his sight, until they called in the
parents of the man who had got his sight and questioned them, saying: Is this your son, who, you say, was
born blind? How is it that he can now see? His parents
answered and said: We know that this is our son and
that he was born blind. We do not know how it is that
he now can see, and we do not know who opened his
eyes. Ask him; he is of age and he will tell you about
himself. His parents said this because they were afraid
of the Jews, because the Jews had agreed that anyone
who confessed that he was Christ should be barred
from the synagogue. That is why his parents said: He is
of age, ask him. Thus for the second time they
summoned the man who had been blind, and said to
him: Give glory to God. We know that this man is
sinful. The man answered and said: Whether he is
sinful I do not know. One thing I do know, that I was
blind and now I see. Then they said to him: What did
he do to you? How did he open your eyes? He
answered them: I told you before, and you did not
listen. Why do you want to hear it again? Could it be
that you want to be his disciples? And they reviled him
and said: You are his disciple. We are disciples of
Moses. We know that God talked with Moses; but we
do not know where this man is from. The man
answered and said to them: Here is what is astonishing,
that you do not know where he is from and he opened
my eyes. We know that God does not listen to sinners,
but if someone is pious and does his will, to that man he
listens. From the beginning of time it has never been
heard of that anyone opened the eyes of one born
blind; if this man were not from God, he could not have
done anything. They answered and said to him: You
were born all in sin; and you are teaching us? And they

cast him out. Jesus heard that they had cast him out, and he found him and said: Do you believe in the son of man? The man answered: Who is that, Lord? So that I may believe in him. Jesus said to him: You have seen him; and it is he who is talking with you. And he said: I believe, Lord. And worshipped him. And Jesus said: I have come into this world for judgment, so that those who do not see may see, and those who see may go blind. The Pharisees who were with him heard this, and they said to him: Surely, even we are not blind? Jesus said to them: If you were blind, you would have no sin. But now you say: We see. Your sin remains.

§ Truly truly I tell you, he who does not enter the sheepfold through the gate but climbs into it from another place is a thief and a robber; but he who enters through the gate is the shepherd of the sheep. To him the gatekeeper opens, and the sheep listen to his voice, and he summons his own sheep by name and leads them out. When he has put all of his own outside, he goes ahead of them, and the sheep follow him, because they know his voice. But they will not follow a stranger but run away from him, because they do not know the voice of strangers. This is a parable Jesus told them; but they did not know what he was talking about. Again Jesus said: Truly truly I tell you, I am the gate for the sheep. All those who came before me are thieves and robbers; but the sheep did not listen to them. I am the gate. Whoever enters through me shall be saved and go in and out and find pasturage. The thief does not come except to steal and slaughter and destroy; I came so that they may have life, and have abundance. I am the good shepherd. The good shepherd lays down his life for the sheep. The man who is hired, who is no shepherd, whose sheep are not his own, sees the wolf coming and lets the sheep go and runs away; and the wolf ravages and scatters them; because he is hired and the sheep are of no concern to him. I am the good shepherd, and I know mine and they know me, as the father knows me and I know the father, and I lay down my life for the sheep. And I have other sheep which are not from this fold; and I must bring them, and they will listen to my voice, and they will become one flock, one shepherd. That is why the father loves me, because I lay down my life, so that I may take it back again. No one took it from me, but I lay it down of my own will. I have authority to lay it down and authority to take it back. This is the command I had from my father.

Once more there was division among the Jews because of those words. And many of them said: He is possessed, and raves. Why do you listen to him? Others said: These are not the words of a man possessed. Could a fiend open the eyes of the blind?

Then it was the Feast of Dedication in Jerusalem. It was winter, and Jesus walked about in the temple, in the Porch of Solomon. The Jews surrounded him and said to him: How long will you go on agitating our spirits? If you are the Christ, tell us plainly. Jesus answered them: I told you, and you do not believe. The acts I perform in the name of my father, these bear me witness; but you do not believe, for you are not of my flock. My sheep listen to my voice, and I know them, and they follow me, and I give them life everlasting, and they shall not perish forever, and no one will snatch them out of my hand. What my father gave me is greater than all, and no one can snatch it from the hand of the father. I and the father are one. Then the Jews picked up stones once more, to stone him. Jesus answered them: I have shown you many good acts from my father. For which of these acts do you stone me? The Jews answered him: We stone you not for any good act, but for blasphemy, and because you, who are a man, make yourself God. Jesus answered them: Is it not written in your law: I have said: You are gods? If he called those gods to whom the word of God came, and scripture cannot be voided, then do you say of one whom the father hallowed and sent into the world: You blaspheme; because I said I am the son of God? If I do not do the acts of my father, do not believe me. But if I do them, even if you do not believe me, believe the acts, so that you may see and know that the father is in me and I am in the father. Then once again they tried to seize him; and he passed through their hands.

And he went back beyond Jordan to the place where John had been baptizing before, and remained there. And many came to him and said: John wrought no miracle for us, but all that John said about him was true. And many there believed in him.

§ There was a man who was sick, Lazarus, from Bethany, the village of Mary and Martha her sister. It was Mary who anointed the Lord with ointment and wiped his feet with her hair, and it was her brother Lazarus who was sick. So the sisters sent to him saying: Lord, see, a man you love is sick. When Jesus heard it he said: This sickness is not to the death but is for the glory of God so that the son of God may be glorified through it. And Jesus loved Martha and her sister and Lazarus. Now when he heard that he was sick, he remained in the place where he was for two days, after which he said to his disciples: Let us go back to Judaea. His disciples said to him: Master, just now the Jews were trying to stone you; and will you go back there? Jesus answered: Are there not twelve hours in the day? If a man walks in the daytime, he does not stumble, because he sees the light of this world; but if he walks in the night, he stumbles, because the light is not there. This he said, and after this he said to them: Lazarus our friend has gone to his rest, but I am on my way to waken him. So the disciples said to him: Lord, if he has gone to his rest he will be safe. Jesus had been speaking of his death, but they thought he was talking about the rest which comes from sleep. So then Jesus said to them plainly: Lazarus is dead; and I am glad on your account, so that you may believe, that I was not there. But let us go to him. Then Thomas, called the Twin, said to his fellow disciples: Let us also go, so that we may die with him.

When Jesus arrived he found that he had been four days in the tomb. Now Bethany was near Jerusalem, about twenty-five furlongs off. And many of the Jews had come to Martha and Mary to console them for their brother. When Martha heard that Jesus was coming she went out to meet him; but Mary was sitting in the house. Then Martha said to Jesus: Lord, if you had been here, my brother would not have died; even now I know that all that you ask of God God will give you. Jesus said to her: Your brother will resurrect. Martha said to him: I know that he will resurrect in the resurrection on the last day. Jesus said to her: I am the resurrection and the life. He who believes in me shall live, even if he dies, and everyone who lives and believes in me shall not die, ever. Do you believe this? She said to him: Yes, Lord; I believe that you are the Christ, the son of God, who is coming into this world. So saying, she went back and called Mary her sister, saying to her privately: The master is here and calls for you. When Mary heard this, she rose up quickly and went to him; and Jesus had not yet come into the village but was still in the place where Martha had gone to meet him. So the Jews who had been with her in the house, comforting her, seeing that Mary rose up quickly and went out, followed her, supposing that she was on her way to the tomb to lament there. When Mary came to where Jesus was, and saw him, she fell at his feet, saying to him: Lord, if you had been here, my brother would not have died. When Jesus saw her weeping, and saw the Jews who had come with her weeping, he raged at his own spirit, and harrowed himself, and said: Where have you laid him? They said

to him: Lord, come and see. Jesus wept. Then the Jews
said: See how he loved him. But some of them said:
Could not he, who opened the eyes of the blind man,
make it so that this man also might not die? Jesus once
more was inwardly raging, and went to the tomb. It was
a cave, and a stone was set in front of it. Jesus said:
Take away the stone. Martha, the sister of the dead
man, said to him: Lord, by now he smells, since he has
been there four days. Jesus said to her: Did I not tell
you that if you believe you will see the glory of God? So
they took away the stone. And Jesus lifted up his eyes
and said: Father, I thank you for hearing me, and I
know that you always hear me; but because of the
crowd which surrounds me, I said it so that they should
believe that you sent me. After saying this he cried out
in a great voice: Lazarus, come out here. And the man
who had died came out, with his hands and feet
wrapped in bandages, and his face tied up in cloth.
Jesus said to them: Untie him and let him go.

Then many of the Jews, who had gone to Mary and
seen what he did, believed in him; but some of them
went to the Pharisees and told them what Jesus had
done. So the high priests and the Pharisees called a
council and said: What are we doing about this man
who performs so many miracles? If we let him go on
like this, all will believe in him, and the Romans will
come and take away our country and our nationality.
But one of them, Caiaphas, who was high priest for that
year, said to them: You know nothing: nor do you
understand that it is for your advantage for one man to
die, for the sake of the people, and not have the whole
nation destroyed. This he said not of himself, but as
high priest for that year he prophesied that Jesus would
die for the sake of the nation, and not only for the sake
of the nation, but so that he might bring together the
scattered children of God.

From that day on they plotted to kill him.

But Jesus no longer went about publicly among the

Jews, but he went away from there to a place near the
desert, to a city called Ephraim, and there he stayed,
with his disciples. The Passover of the Jews was
approaching, and many went up from the country to
Jerusalem before the Passover, to purify themselves.
They were looking for Jesus, and they said to each
other as they stood in the temple: What do you think?
That he will not come to the festival? But the high
priests and the Pharisees had given orders that if
anyone knew where he was, he should inform on him,
so that they could seize him.

§ But six days before the Passover Jesus came to
Bethany, where Lazarus was, the one Jesus had raised
from the dead. So they prepared a supper for him
there, and Martha served them, and Lazarus was one
of those who dined with him. And Mary brought a
measure of ointment of nard, pure and precious, and
anointed the feet of Jesus and wiped his feet with her
hair; and the house was full of the fragrance of
ointment. One of his disciples, Judas the Iscariot, who
was about to betray him, said: Why was not this
ointment sold for three hundred denarii and given to
the poor? But he said this not because he cared
anything about the poor but because he was a thief and,
being keeper of the purse, used to make off with what
had been put into it. But Jesus said: Let her be, so that
this can serve for the day of my burial; for the poor you
have always with you, but you do not always have me.

The great populace of the Jews knew that Jesus was
there, and they came, not only because of Jesus, but to
see Lazarus, whom he had raised from the dead. But
the high priests plotted to kill Lazarus also, since many
of the Jews were going away because of him, and
believed in Jesus.

The next day the great crowd which had come to the
festival, hearing that Jesus was coming into Jerusalem,

took palm branches and went out to meet him, and they
cried: Hosanna. Blessed is he who comes in the name
of the Lord, and the King of Israel. And Jesus found a
young donkey and rode on it, as it is written: Do not
fear, daughter of Zion. Behold, your King is coming,
riding on the colt of a donkey. His disciples did not
understand this at first, but after Jesus was glorified
they remembered that these scriptures were for him,
and they had done this for him. And the crowd which
had been with him when he called Lazarus from the
tomb and raised him from the dead bore witness to it.
That was why the crowd went to meet him, because
they heard that he had performed the miracle. So the
Pharisees said to each other: See how little good you
are doing. Look, the world has gone after him.

There were some Greeks among those who had gone
up to worship at the festival. These approached Philip,
from Bethsaida in Galilee, and made a request, saying:
Sir, we wish to see Jesus. Philip went and spoke to
Andrew; Andrew and Philip went and spoke to Jesus.
Jesus answered them, saying: The hour has come for
the son of man to be glorified. Truly truly I tell you,
when the grain of wheat falls to the ground, unless it
dies, it remains only itself, but if it dies it bears a great
crop. He who loves his life loses it, and he who hates his
life in this world shall keep it for the life everlasting. If
one serves me, let him follow me, and wherever I am,
there will my servant also be. If one serves me, my
father will honor him. Now my soul is shaken, and what
shall I say? Father, save me from this hour? But this is
why I came to this hour. Father, glorify your name.
Then a voice came from the sky: I have glorified it, and
I shall glorify it again. The people who were standing
by and heard said it had thundered. Others said: An
angel has talked with him. Jesus answered and said:
This voice came not for my sake but for yours. Now is
the judgment of this world, now the leader of this world
will be cast out; and if I am lifted aloft from the earth, I

will draw all to myself. This he said, signifying the kind
of death he was to die. But the multitude answered
him: We heard from the law that the Christ remains
forever; and how is it that you tell us that the son of
man must be lifted aloft? Who is this son of man? So
Jesus said to them: For a little time yet the light is
among you. Walk about while you have the light, so
that the darkness may not overtake you; and he who
walks in darkness does not know where he is going.
While you have the light, believe in the light, so that
you may be sons of light.

Jesus said this and went away and was hidden from
them. But though he had done all these miracles before
them, they did not believe in him, so that the word
spoken by Isaiah the prophet might be fulfilled: Lord,
who believed in the rumor of us? And to whom was the
arm of the Lord revealed? This is why they could not
believe, because Isaiah said, once more: He has
blinded their eyes and hardened their hearts, so that
they may not see with their eyes or understand with
their hearts and be converted; for me to heal them.
Isaiah said this because he knew his glory, and he was
talking about him. Even so, many of the chief men
believed in him, but they did not admit it because of the
Pharisees and for fear of being denied the synagogue,
for they cared more for the opinion of men than for the
glory of God. But Jesus cried out and said: He who
believes in me believes not in me but in him who sent
me, and he who looks on me looks on him who sent me.
As light I came into the world, so that everyone who
believes in me may not stay in the dark. And if one
hears my words and does not keep them, I will not
judge him, for I did not come to judge the world but to
save the world. He who rejects me and does not accept
my words has his judge. The word I have spoken, that
will judge him on the last day. Because I did not speak
from myself, but the father who sent me himself gave
me his commandment, what to say and how to talk.

And I know that his commandment is life everlasting.
So what I say is said as my father told me to say it.

§ Before the feast of the Passover Jesus knew that the
hour had come for him to pass from this world to his
father. He had loved his own people in the world and
he loved them to the end. And when supper was
served, and the devil had already resolved in his heart
that Judas Iscariot, the son of Simon, should betray
him, Jesus, knowing that his father had put everything
into his hands, and that he had come from God and was
going to God, rose up from the supper and laid aside
his clothing and took a towel and girt himself with it.
Then he poured water into the basin and began to wash
the feet of the disciples and dry them on the towel he
was girt with. So he came to Simon Peter. He said to
him: Lord, are you washing my feet? Jesus answered
and said to him: What I do you do not now know, but
you will know it afterwards. Peter said to him: You
shall never wash my feet. Jesus answered him: Unless I
wash you you have no part in me. Simon Peter said to
him: Lord, not only my feet, but also my hands and my
head. Jesus said to him: He who is bathed has no need
to wash, except for his feet, but is clean all over. And
you are clean; but not all of you. For he knew his
betrayer; that is why he said: Not all of you are clean.
So when he had washed their feet and resumed his
clothing and taken his place at supper, he said to them
again: Do you know what I have done for you? You call
me the master and the lord, and what you say is right,
for I am. If then I, the master and lord, have washed
your feet, you also have the duty of washing each
other's feet; for I have given you an example, for you to
do as I have done to you. Truly truly I tell you, there is
no slave greater than his master or any apostle greater
than him who sent him. If you know these things, you
are blessed if you do them. I am not speaking of all of
you. I know which ones I chose. But so as to fulfill what

is written: He who ate my bread has raised his heel against me. I tell you now before it happens, so that when it happens you will believe that I am *I*. Truly truly I tell you, he who accepts anyone I send accepts me, and he who accepts me accepts him who sent me.

After he had said this, Jesus was shaken in spirit, and bore witness, and said: Truly truly I tell you that one of you will betray me. The disciples looked at each other, wondering which was the one he spoke of. One of the disciples, whom Jesus loved, was lying close beside the breast of Jesus; so Simon Peter nodded to this man and said to him: Tell us which is the one of whom he is speaking. So this man leaned back so that he was close to the breast of Jesus and said to him: Lord, who is it? Jesus answered: It is the one for whom I will dip a crust and give it to him. So he took a crust and dipped it and gave it to Judas the son of Simon Iscariot. Then after the crust Satan entered into him. So then Jesus said to him: Do what you are doing quickly. But no one of those at dinner understood what he meant when he said this to him; for some thought, since Judas kept the purse, that Jesus was saying to him: Buy what we need for the festival; or, something to give the poor. But he took the crust and went out at once. Now it was night.

When he went out, Jesus said: Now the son of man has been glorified, and God has been glorified in him. And God will glorify him in himself, and he will glorify him at once. My children, I am with you still for a little while. You will look for me, and as I said to the Jews, where I go you will not be able to go, so I say it to you now, I give you a new commandment, to love each other, as I have loved you and as you do love each other. By this all will know that you are my disciples; if you have love for each other. Simon Peter said to him: Lord, where are you going? Jesus answered: Where I am going you cannot follow me now, but you will follow me later. Peter said to him: Lord, why can I not follow you now? I will lay down my life for you. Jesus answered: You will lay down your life for me? Truly

truly I tell you, the cock will not crow before you have
disowned me three times.

§ Let your hearts not be disturbed. Believe in God and
believe in me. In my father's house there are many
rooms. Were there not, I would have said to you that I
was going to make ready a place for you. And if I go,
and make ready a place for you, I will come back and
take you to myself, so that where I am you may also be.
And you know the way to where I am going. Thomas
said to him: Lord, we do not know where you are
going. How can we know the way? Jesus said to him: I
am the way and the truth and the life. No one goes to
the father except through me. If you had known me you
would also have known my father. Now you know him
and you have seen him. Philip said to him: Lord, show
us the father, and that is enough for us. Jesus said to
him: All this time I have been with you and you do not
know me, Philip? He who has seen me has seen the
father. How can you say: Show us the father? Do you
not believe that I am in the father and the father is in
me? The words I speak to you I do not say for myself.
But my father remaining in me does his works. Believe
me that I am in my father and my father is in me. And if
not, believe because of the works themselves. Truly
truly I tell you, he who believes in me will do, he also,
the works that I do, and he will do greater ones than I
do, because I am going to my father. And whatever you
ask in my name, this I will do, so that the father may be
glorified in the son. If you ask for something in my
name, I will do it. If you love me, you will keep my
commandments. And I will ask my father, and he will
give you another comforter to be with you forever: The
spirit of truth, which the world cannot accept, because
it does not see it or know it; but you know it, because it
stays with you and is in you. I will not leave you
orphans, I will come to you. A little time and the world
will no longer see me, but you will see me, because I

live and you will live. On that day you will know that I
am in my father and you are in me and I in you. He who
has my commandments and keeps them, this is the one
who loves me; and the one who loves me shall be loved
by my father, and I will love him and show myself to
him. Judas (not the Iscariot) said to him: Lord, what
has happened that you mean to show yourself to us and
not to the world? Jesus answered and said to him: If
anyone loves me, he will do as I say, and my father will
love him, and we will come to him and make our
dwelling place with him. He who does not love me will
not do as I say; and what I say, which you hear, is not
mine, but is from the father who sent me.

This I have said to you while I stay with you. But the
comforter, the Holy Spirit whom the father will send in
my name, he is the one who will teach you all and make
you remember all I have said to you. I leave you peace,
I give you my peace. I give it to you, not as the world
gives it. Let your hearts not be disturbed or afraid. You
have heard me say to you: I am going away and I will
come back to you. If you loved me you would rejoice,
because I am going to my father, because my father is
greater than I. And now I have told you before it
happens so that when it happens you will believe. I will
no longer talk much with you, for the ruler of the world
is coming; and he owns no part of me; but so that the
world may know that I love my father, and as my father
gave me his orders, thus I do. Rise up, let us go from
here.

§ I am the true vine, and my father is the grower.
Every branch which bears no fruit he takes off, and
every one that does bear fruit he keeps clean so that it
may bear more fruit. You are already clean, because of
the word I have spoken to you. Stay with me, as I with
you. As the branch cannot bear fruit by itself, unless it
stays on the vine, so cannot you unless you stay with
me. I am the vine, you are the branches. The one who

stays with me as I with him is the one who bears much fruit, because without me you can do nothing. If one does not stay with me, he is cast out like the branch, and dries up, and they gather these and throw them in the fire, and they burn. If you stay with me, and my sayings stay in you, ask whatever you wish and it will be given you. Herein is my father glorified, so that you may bear much fruit and be my disciples. As my father loves me, and I love you, stay in my love. If you keep my commandments, you will stay in my love, as I have kept the commandments of the father and stay in his love. This I have said to you so that my joy may be in you and your joy may be full. This is my commandment, that you love each other as I loved you. No one has greater love than this, to lay down his life for his friends. You are my friends if you do what I tell you to. No longer do I call you slaves, because the slave does not know what his master is doing; but I call you friends, because I made known to you all that I heard from my father. You did not choose me, but I chose you, and I placed you where you may go and bear fruit, and your fruit may last, so that whatever you ask of the father in my name he may give you. This is my commandment to you, to love each other.

If the world hates you, you know that is has hated me before you. If you were of the world, the world would love its own, but because you are not of the world, but I chose you out of the world, therefore the world hates you. Remember the saying I gave you: The slave is not greater than his master. If they persecuted me, they will persecute you also. If they hold to my word, they will hold to yours also. But all this they will do to you because of my name, because they do not know him who sent me. If I had not come and spoken to them, they would have no guilt; but now they have no excuse for their guiltiness. He who hates me hates my father also. If I had not done among them things that no one else has done, they would have no guilt; but now they

have seen, and they have conceived hate both for me
and for my father. But, to fulfill the word that is written
in their law: They hated me, gratuitously. When the
comforter comes, whom I will send you from my
father, the spirit of truth who comes from my father, he
will bear witness concerning me. Do you also bear
witness, since you have been with me from the beginning.

§ I have told you this so that you may not be driven
astray. They will put you out of the synagogue. But the
time is coming when anyone who kills you will be
thought to be doing a service to God. And they will do
this because they know neither my father nor me. But I
have told you these things so that when their time
comes you may remember that I told you about them. I
did not tell you these things from the beginning because
I was with you. But now I am going to him who sent
me, and not one of you asks me: Where are you going?
But because I have told you these things grief has filled
your hearts. But I am telling you the truth; it is to your
advantage for me to go away. If I do not go, the
comforter cannot come to you, but if I go, I will send
him to you. And when he comes he will confute the
world concerning error and righteousness and judgment: error, because they do not believe in me;
righteousness, because I am going away to my father
and you will see me no more; and judgment, because
the ruler of this world has been judged. I have much
else to tell you, but you cannot handle it now; but when
he, the spirit of truth, comes, he will be your guide to
the whole truth, for he will speak, not on his own
authority, but will tell you what he hears, and will
report to you of what is to come. He will glorify me,
because he will take from what is mine and report it to
you. All that the father has is mine; that is why I said
that he takes from me and will report to you.

A little while and you will look on me no longer; and again a little while, and you will see me. So some of his disciples said to each other: What is this that he is telling us? A little while and you will not look on me, and again a little while and you will see me? And: Because I am going to my father? So they said: What is this little while he is talking about? We do not know what he means. Jesus perceived that they wished to question him, and said to them: Is this what you are seeking together to understand, what I meant by: A little while and you will not look upon me; and again a little while and you will see me? Truly truly I tell you that you will weep and mourn, but the world will rejoice. You will have pain, but your pain will turn to joy. A woman has pain when she is giving birth, when her time has come, but when she has borne her child she no longer remembers her affliction, through joy that a human being has been born into the world. So now you also feel pain; but I will see you again, and your hearts will rejoice, and no one will take that joy away from you. And on that day you will not ask me anything. Truly truly I tell you, if you ask the father for anything he will give it to you in my name. Until now you asked for nothing in my name. Ask and you will receive, so that your joy may be complete.

I have told you this in riddles; but the time is coming when I shall speak in riddles no longer but will tell you in plain language about the father. On that day you will ask in my name, and I say that I will not ask my father on your behalf, for the father himself loves you because you have loved me and believed that I came from the father. I came from my father and went into the world. I leave the world again and go back to my father. His disciples said: See, now you are talking in plain language and tell us no more riddles. Now we know that you know all and have no need for anyone to ask you. By this we believe that you came from God. Jesus answered them: Now you believe? The time is coming, and it has come, for you to be scattered each to his own place and leave me alone. And I am not alone, because my father is with me. These things I have told you so that you may have peace in me. In the world you will have affliction; but do not fear, I have defeated the world.

§ Jesus spoke thus, then lifted his eyes to heaven and said: Father, the hour has come. Glorify your son, so that your son may glorify you; as you gave him authority over all flesh, so that he will give life everlasting to all you have given him. And this is the life everlasting, that they know you, the only true God, and Jesus Christ, whom you sent. I have glorified you on earth by completing the work you gave me to do; and now, father, glorify me, in your own presence, with the glory I had with you before the world began. I made your name known to the people you gave me from the world. They were yours and you gave them to me, and they have kept your word. Now they have recognized that all that you gave me was from you; because I gave them the sayings that you gave me, and they accepted them and recognized rightly that I came from you, and believed that you sent me. I ask for their sake; I ask not for the sake of the world but for the sake of those you gave me, because they are yours, and all that is mine is yours and all that is yours is mine, and I am glorified in them. And I am no longer in the world, but they are in the world, and I am going to you. Holy father, keep them by your name, which you gave me, so that they may be one as we are. When I was with them I kept them, by the name which you gave me, and I protected them, and not one of them was lost except the son of perdition, so that the scripture might be fulfilled. But now I am going to you, and I say this in the world so that they may have my joy fulfilled in themselves. I gave them your word, and the world

hated them, because they are not of the world, as I am
not of the world. I do not ask you to take them from the
world, but to keep them from evil. They are not of the
world, as I am not of the world. Consecrate them in
the truth. Your word is truth. As you sent me into the
world, so I sent them into the world; and for their sake
I consecrate myself, so that they also may be consecrat-
ed in the truth.

I ask not for the sake of these only, but also for the
sake of those who believe in me because of the word of
these, so that all may be one, as you, father, are in me
and I in you, so that they also may be in us, so that the
world may believe that you sent me. And I have given
them the glory that you gave me, so that they may be
one as we are one, I in them and you in me, so that they
may be made perfect as one, so that the world may
learn that you sent me and loved them as you loved me.
Father, I wish that wherever I am, those whom you
gave me may be with me also, so that they may look
upon my glory which you gave me, because you loved
me before the establishment of the world. Righteous
father, even the world did not recognize you, but I
recognized you, and these realized that you sent me,
and I made your name known to them and will make it
known, so that the love you had for me may be in them,
and I may be in them.

§ After this prayer Jesus went with his disciples out
beyond the brook Cedron to where there was a garden,
and he and his disciples went into it. And Judas, who
had betrayed him, knew this place, since Jesus had
often gone there with his disciples. So Judas got the
guard, and the servingmen from the high priests and
the Pharisees, and went there with lights and torches
and weapons. Then Jesus, who knew everything that
was in store for him, went out and said to them: Whom
do you seek? They answered him: Jesus of Nazareth.

He said to them: I am he. And Judas, who betrayed him, was standing with them. When he said to them: I am he, they drew back and fell to the ground. Again he asked them: Whom do you seek? And they said: Jesus of Nazareth. Jesus answered: I told you that I am he. So if you are looking for me, let these go. To fulfill what he had said: I have not lost one of those whom you gave me. Now Simon Peter had a sword, and he drew it and struck the slave of the high priest and cut off his right ear. The slave's name was Malchus. But Jesus said to Peter: Put away your sword in its sheath. Shall I not drink the cup which my father gave me?

The guard and its commander and the servingmen of the Jews seized Jesus and bound him and took him first to Annas; for he was the father-in-law of Caiaphas, who was the high priest that year. And it was Caiaphas who had advised the Jews that it was better for one man to die for the sake of the people. And Simon Peter and another disciple followed Jesus. And that disciple was an acquaintance of the high priest, and he went with Jesus into the high priest's court, but Peter stood outside by the door. Then the other disciple, the acquaintance of the high priest, went out and spoke to the doorkeeper and brought Peter inside. Then the girl who was at the door said to Peter: Are you not one also of that man's disciples? He said: I am not. The slaves and the servingmen had made a charcoal fire, because it was cold, and stood by it and warmed themselves; and Peter was standing with them and warming himself.

So then the high priest questioned Jesus about his disciples and about his teaching. Jesus answered him: I have spoken openly to the world. I have taught always in the synagogue and the temple, where all the Jews come together, and I have said nothing in secret. Why do you ask me? Ask my listeners what I said to them. See, they know what I said. When he said this, one of the servingmen standing there gave Jesus a slap, saying: Is this how you answer the high priest? Jesus answered him: If I spoke evil, specify what the evil was. But if I spoke well, why strike me? So then Annas sent him in in bonds to Caiaphas the high priest.

Simon Peter was standing and warming himself. So they said to him: Are you not also one of his disciples? He denied it and said: I am not. One of the high priest's slaves, who was related to the one whose ear Peter had cut off, said: Did I not see you with him in the garden? Once again Peter denied it; and immediately the cock crew.

Now they took Jesus from the house of Caiaphas to the residence. It was early morning. And they themselves did not enter the residence, so as to keep from defilement and be able to eat the Passover. So Pilate came out to them and said: What charge do you bring against this man? They answered and said to him: If he had not been doing evil, we should not have turned him over to you. Pilate said to them: You take him, and judge him according to your law. The Jews said to him: It is not lawful for us to put anyone to death. This was to fulfill the word of Jesus when he foretold the kind of death he was going to die.

Then Pilate went back into the residence and called Jesus in and said to him: Are you the King of the Jews? Jesus answered: Are you speaking for yourself, or did others tell you about me? Pilate answered: I am not a Jew, am I? Your own people and the high priests turned you over to me. What had you done? Jesus answered: My kingdom is not of this world. If my kingdom were of this world, my servingmen would fight to keep me from being turned over to the Jews. But as it is, my kingdom is not here. So Pilate said to him: Then you are a king? Jesus answered: It is you who are saying that I am a king. For this I was born and for this I came into the world, to testify to the truth. For everyone who is on the side of truth listens to my voice. Pilate said to him: What is truth?

And so saying he went back out to the Jews and said to them: I find no fault in him. But you have this

custom, that I should release one man for you at the
Passover. Do you want me to release the King of the
Jews? They shouted back saying: Not this man, but
Barabbas. Barabbas was a robber.

§ Then Pilate took Jesus and had him scourged. And
the soldiers wove a crown of thorns and put it on his
head, and they put a purple cloak about him, and came
before him and said: Hail, King of the Jews. And they
slapped him. And Pilate came out again and said to
them: See, I am bringing him out to you, so that you
may know that I find no fault in him. So Jesus came out,
wearing the crown of thorns and the purple cloak. And
Pilate said to them: Behold the man. When the high
priests and their servingmen saw him they shouted:
Crucify crucify. Pilate said to them: Take him yourselves and crucify him, since I find no fault in him. The
Jews answered: We have a law, and by that law he must
die, because he made himself out to be the son of God.
When Pilate heard them say this, he was more frightened, and he went back into the residence and said to
him: Where do you come from? But Jesus did not give
him an answer. So Pilate said to him: Do you say
nothing to me? Do you not know that I have authority
to let you go, and authority to crucify you? Jesus
answered him: You would not have had any authority
whatever over me, if it had not been given you from
above. Therefore, he who betrayed me to you has the
greater guilt. Thereupon Pilate sought to release him;
but the Jews cried aloud and said: If you let him go, you
are no friend of Caesar's; anyone who makes himself
out to be a king is challenging Caesar. When Pilate
heard these words, he brought Jesus outside and sat
down on the judgment seat at a place called the Stone
Pavement, in Hebrew Gabatha. It was the Day of
Preparation for the Passover, at about the sixth hour.
And he said to the Jews: Behold your king. They
shouted: Off with him, off with him, crucify him. Pilate

said to them: Shall I crucify your king? The high priests answered: We have no king except Caesar. So then he gave him to them to be crucified.

So they took Jesus. And carrying his own cross he went out to what was called the Place of the Skull, which is called in Hebrew Golgotha, where they crucified him, and with him two others, on this side and on that, with Jesus in the middle. And Pilate wrote a label and put it on the cross: and what was written was: Jesus of Nazareth, the King of the Jews. Many of the Jews read this inscription, because the place where Jesus was crucified was near the city; and it was written in Hebrew and Latin and Greek. So the high priests of the Jews said to Pilate: Do not write: the King of the Jews; but write that he said: I am the King of the Jews. Pilate answered: What I have written, I have written.

Then, when they had crucified Jesus, the soldiers took his clothes and divided them into four parts, one for each soldier; and took also his tunic. But the tunic was without a seam, woven in one piece from the top down; so they said to each other: Let us not split it, but draw lots for it, to see whose it shall be. So as to fulfill the scripture: They divided my clothes among themselves, and they threw lots for my apparel.

This is what the soldiers did. But by the cross of Jesus stood his mother; and his mother's sister, Mary the wife of Clopas; and Mary the Magdalene. So Jesus, seeing his mother with the disciple whom he loved standing beside her, said to his mother: Mother, here is your son. Then he said to the disciple: Here is your mother. And from that moment the disciple took her into his own household.

After this Jesus, knowing that all was completed for the fulfillment of the scripture, said: I am thirsty. A bowl full of vinegar was lying by; so they put a sponge soaked with the vinegar on hyssop and held it up to his mouth. So when he received the vinegar, Jesus said: It is ended; and bowing his head he gave up his life.

Now since it was the Day of Preparation the Jews

asked Pilate to have the legs of the crucified men broken and the men taken off, so that the bodies would not still be on the cross on the sabbath, since that sabbath day was an important day. So the soldiers came and broke the legs of the first man, and then of the other man who had been crucified with him; but when they came to Jesus, and saw that he was already dead, they did not break his legs, but one of the soldiers stabbed him in the side with his spear, and at once blood and water came out. And he who saw it has testified to it, and his testimony is true, and he knows that he is speaking the truth, so that you also may believe. For all this took place to fulfill the scripture: They shall not break any bone in him. And again another scripture says: They shall look upon him whom they stabbed.

After that, Joseph of Arimathaea, who was a disciple of Jesus, but secretly, for fear of the Jews, asked Pilate if he could take off the body of Jesus. And Pilate gave permission. So he came and took off his body. And Nicodemus, who had gone to him first by night, also arrived, bringing a mixture of aloes and myrrh, about a hundred pounds weight. Then they took the body of Jesus and wrapped it in strips of linen along with the perfumes, as it is customary for the Jews to prepare bodies for burial. And in the region where he was crucified there was a garden, and in the garden a new tomb where no one had ever been buried. There they placed Jesus, because of the Day of Preparation of the Jews, since the tomb was nearby.

§ Early on the first day of the week, when it was still dark, Mary the Magdalene came to the tomb and saw that the stone had been removed from it. So she ran back until she came to Simon Peter and the other disciple, whom Jesus loved, and said to them: They have taken our Lord from the tomb, and we do not know where they have put him. So Peter and the other disciple came out, and went to the tomb. The two ran together, but the other disciple ran faster than Peter and reached the tomb first, and stooped and looked in and saw the wrappings lying there, but he did not go inside. Then Simon Peter came, following him, and he went into the tomb; and he saw the wrappings lying there, and the napkin, which had been on his head, lying not with the wrappings but away from them and rolled up in a ball. And then the other disciple, who had reached the tomb first, also entered it, and he saw, and believed; for they had never yet known of the scripture, that he was to rise from the dead. Then the disciples went back to where they were staying.

But Mary stood by the tomb, lamenting. And as she lamented, she stooped and looked inside the tomb, and she saw two angels, in white, sitting where the body of Jesus had been lying; one at the head and one at the feet. And they said to her: Lady, why are you lamenting? She said to them: Because they have taken my Lord away, and I do not know where they have put him. So speaking, she turned about, and she saw Jesus standing there and did not know that it was Jesus. Jesus said to her: Lady, why are you lamenting? Whom do you seek? She thought he was the gardener and said to him: Sir, if you took him away, tell me where you put him, and I will take him. Jesus said to her: Mary. Then she turned and said to him, in Hebrew: Rabbuni (which means master). Jesus said to her: Do not hold me, since I have not yet gone up to my father. Go to my brothers and tell them I am going up to my father, and your father, and my God and your God. Mary the Magdalene went and announced to the disciples: I have seen the Lord. And that he had said these things to her.

When it was evening on that day, the first of the week, and the doors of the place where the disciples were staying were locked, through fear of the Jews, Jesus came and stood in their midst and said: Peace be with you. And when he had said this, he showed them his hands and his side. And the disciples were joyful at seeing the Lord. So he said to them once more: Peace be with you. As the father sent me forth, so I also send you. And so saying he breathed his spirit into them, and said to them: Receive the Holy Spirit. For any whose sins you forgive, their sins are forgiven. For any whose sins you keep fast, they are kept fast.

One of the twelve, Thomas, called the Twin, was not with them when Jesus came. So the other disciples said to him: We have seen the Lord. But he said to them: Unless I see the holes from the nails, and put my finger into the holes from the nails, and put my hand into his side, I will not believe. And eight days later the disciples were in the house once again, and Thomas was with them. Jesus came, though the doors were locked, and stood in their midst and said: Peace be with you. Then he said to Thomas: Put your finger here, and examine my hands, and take your hand and put it into my side, and be not an unbeliever but a believer. Thomas answered and said to him: My Lord and my God. Jesus said to him: You have believed me because you have seen me? Blessed are they who have not seen, and believe.

Jesus performed many other such miracles, in the presence of the disciples, which have not been written down in this book; but these have been written down, so that you may believe that Jesus is the Christ, the son of God, and so that, believing, you may have life in his name.

§ After this, Jesus again showed himself to his disciples, by the Sea of Tiberias. And this is how he showed himself. There together were Simon Peter and Thomas called the Twin and Nathanael from Cana in Galilee and the sons of Zebedee and two others of the disciples. Simon Peter said to them: I am going fishing. They said to him: And we are going with you. So they went and manned the ship, and that night they caught nothing. Early in the morning Jesus was standing on the beach, but the disciples did not know that it was Jesus. Jesus then said to them: Children, have you caught anything to eat? They answered him: No. And he said to them: Cast your net in the waters to the right of the ship, and you will find some. So they cast, and they could no longer pull it in because of the quantity of fish. Then that disciple whom Jesus loved said to Peter: It is the Lord. So Simon Peter, when he heard that it was the Lord, put on his outer clothes, for he had been stripped down, and threw himself into the sea. And the other disciples came with the boat, for they were not far from the land but about three hundred feet off, dragging the net full of fish. When they came out on the shore they saw a charcoal fire laid, and a small fish placed on it, and bread. Jesus said to them: Bring some of the fish that you caught just now. So Simon Peter went aboard and hauled ashore the net full of big fish, a hundred and fifty-three of them; and though there were so many, the net did not break. Jesus said to them: Come to breakfast. Not one of the disciples dared ask him: Who are you? For they knew that it was the Lord. Jesus came and took the bread and gave it to them, and the fish likewise.

This was now the third time since he had risen from the dead that Jesus showed himself to the disciples.

When they had breakfasted Jesus said to Simon Peter: Simon son of John, do you love me more than these? He said to him: Yes, Lord, you know that I love you. He said to him: Feed my lambs. He said to him a second time: Simon son of John, do you love me? He said to him: Yes, Lord, you know that I love you. He said to him: Take care of my little sheep. He said to him for the third time: Simon son of John, do you love me? Peter was hurt because he had asked him for the third time: Do you love me? And he said to him: Lord, you know all things, you know that I love you. Jesus said to him: Feed my little sheep. Truly truly I tell you, when you were younger, you girded yourself up and walked about wherever you wished; but when you are old, you will stretch out your hands, and another will gird you and carry you where you do not wish to go. This he said, indicating the kind of death by which he was to glorify God. And when he had said this, he told him: Follow me.

Peter turned about and saw following them the disciple whom Jesus loved, the very one who at the dinner had leaned back close to the breast of Jesus and said: Lord, which one is your betrayer? So seeing this man, Peter said to Jesus: Lord, what of him? Jesus said to him: If I wish him to remain until I come, what is that to you? You, follow me. Therefore the story went out among the brothers that that one was not to die. But Jesus did not tell him that he was not to die, but: If I wish him to remain until I come, what is that to you?

This is the disciple who testifies to these things, and who wrote this, and we know that his testimony is true.

And there are many other things which Jesus did. If they were written down one by one, I do not think the very world could hold all the books that would be written.

THE
REVELATION
OF JOHN

It is now widely believed that the *Revelation* was written not by the author of the gospel, but by another John, of whom tradition speaks as living in Ephesus toward the end of the first and the beginning of the second century.

§ THE REVELATION OF JESUS CHRIST, WHICH
God gave him, to show to his slaves what must happen soon, and he indicated it by sending it through his angel to John, his slave, who bore witness to the word of God and the testimony of Jesus Christ, the things that he saw. Blessed is he who reads and blessed are they who listen to the words of the prophecy and who keep what is written in it. For the time is near.

John to the seven churches which are in Asia: grace be with you, and peace, from him who is, and who was, and who is to come, and from the seven spirits which are in the presence of his throne, and from Jesus Christ, the witness who is to be believed, the first-born among the dead and the leader of the Kings of the earth. To him who loves us and by his own blood set us free from our sins, who made us a Kingdom and made us priests to his God and father, to him the glory and the power forever and ever. Amen. Behold, he will come with the clouds, and every eye shall see him, even they who transfixed him, and all the tribes of the earth shall beat their breasts at the sight of him. Yes. Amen.

I am alpha and omega, says the Lord God, who is, who was, who is to come, the almighty.

I, John, your brother and companion in affliction and in the kingdom and in the endurance which is in Jesus, I was in the island which is called Patmos because of the word of God and the witnessing to Jesus. I was in the spirit on the Lord's day, and I heard behind me a great voice as of a trumpet, saying: Write down what you see into a book and send it to the seven churches, to Ephesus and to Smyrna and to Pergamum and to Thyatira and to Sardis and to Philadelphia and to Laodicea. And I turned to see what voice was speaking with me, and when I turned I saw seven lamps of gold, and in the midst of the lamps one who was like the son of man, wearing a robe that came to his feet and girt beneath the arms with a belt of gold. His head and his hair were white as white wool, as snow, and his eyes were like the flame of fire, and his feet were like fine bronze, as if fired in the furnace, and his voice was like the voice of many waters, and he held in his right hand seven stars, and from his mouth projected a sword, two-edged and sharp, and the sight of him was as the sun shines in its power. When I saw him I fell at his feet like a dead man; and he set his hand upon me and said:

Do not fear. I am the first and the last, I am he who lives, I have been dead, and see, I am alive forever and ever, and I hold the keys of death and Hades. Write, then, what you have seen, and what is and what is to be after this. The mystery of the seven stars which you saw in my right hand, and the seven lamps of gold: the seven stars are the angels of the seven churches, and the seven lamps are the seven churches.

§ To the angel of the church in Ephesus, write: Thus speaks he who holds the seven stars in his right hand, who walks in the midst of the lamps of gold: I know your works, and your toil and your endurance, and that you are not able to endure evil men, and that you have tried those who call themselves apostles and are not, and found them false; you have endurance, and have borne a burden for the sake of my name, and have not grown weary. But I hold it against you that you have lost the love you had at first. Remember whence you have fallen, and repent, and do the works which you did at first; if not, I shall come to you and remove your lamp from its place; unless you repent. But this you have in your favor, that you hate the works of the followers of Nicolaus, which I also hate. He who has ears, let him listen to what the Spirit says to the churches. To the victor, I shall give to eat of the tree of life, which is in the garden of God.

And to the angel of the church in Smyrna, write:

Thus speaks he who is the first and the last, who was dead and came to life: I know your affliction and your poverty, yet you are rich, and I know the blasphemy of those who call themselves Jews and are not, but a congregation of Satan. Do not fear what you are to suffer. See, the devil will throw some of you into prison so that you may be tested, and you will be afflicted for ten days. Be faithful even to the point of death, and I will give you the crown of life. He who has ears, let him listen to what the Spirit says to the churches. The victor shall not be hurt by the second death.

And to the angel of the church in Pergamum, write:

Thus speaks he who holds the sharp two-edged sword: I know where you live. It is where the throne of Satan is. And you keep my name and did not deny your faith in me even in the days of Antipas, who testified to me and was faithful and was put to death in the place where you are and where Satan dwells. But I hold against you a few things; that you have there some who hold with the teaching of Balaam, who taught Balak to set a trap in the way of the sons of Israel so they should eat what was sacrificed to idols, and commit fornica-

tion. So too you have those who hold with the teaching
of the followers of Nicolaus. Repent then, or else I shall
come to you speedily and fight with them with the
sword of my mouth. He who has ears, let him listen to
what the Spirit says to the churches. To the victor I will
give of the manna that is hidden, and I will give him a
white stone, and upon the stone will be written his new
name, which no one knows, only he who receives it.

And to the angel of the church in Thyatira, write:

Thus speaks he who is the son of God, who has eyes
like the flame of fire and his feet are like bronze: I know
your works, your love and faith and service and
endurance, and that your last works are more than your
first. But I hold it against you that you have forgiven
the woman Jezebel, who calls herself a prophetess, and
teaches my slaves and leads them astray into fornication and the eating of what was sacrificed to idols. And
I have given her time in which to repent, and she will
not repent of her fornication. Behold, I will cast her
upon a bed, and will cast her adulterers into great
affliction, if they do not repent of their acts, and I will
strike down her children in death; and all the churches
shall learn that I am he who examines the vitals and the
hearts, and I will give to each of you according to his
acts. I say to the rest of you in Thyatira, who do not
hold this teaching, who have not known the depths of
Satan, as they say: I shall not put another burden upon
you, but that which you have, keep it until I come. And
the victor and he who keeps my works to the end, I
shall give him power over the nations, and he shall
shepherd them with a staff of iron, breaking them as
pottery is broken, as I too have been given by my
father; and I will give him the morning star. He who has
ears, let him listen to what the Spirit says to the
churches.

§ And to the angel of the church in Sardis, write:

Thus speaks he who holds the seven Spirits of God

and the seven stars: I know your works, that you have the name of being alive, and are dead. Be wakeful, and strengthen what is left, which was on the point of death; for I have not found that your tasks were carried out in the sight of my God. Remember then what you have been given to do, and have been told, and observe this, and repent. If you are not wakeful, I shall come to you like a thief, and you cannot tell at what hour I shall come to you. But you have the names of a few in Sardis who have not soiled their clothes, and they shall walk with me in white, because they are worthy. And he who is thus victorious shall be clothed in robes of white, and I shall not obliterate his name from the book of life, and I shall acknowledge his name in the presence of my father and in the presence of the angels. He who has ears, let him listen to what the Spirit says to the churches.

And to the angel of the church in Philadelphia, write: Thus speaks he who is holy, who is true, who holds the key to David, who opens and none shall close, who closes and none shall open: I know your works. See, I have given you an open door which is before you, and none shall be able to close it; because you have little power, and you have kept my word and have not denied my name. Behold, I deliver to you those of the congregation of Satan, those who call themselves Jews, and they are not, but are lying; behold, I shall make them come and worship before your feet, and know that I have given you my love. Because you have kept the word, which was that you should wait for me, I too shall keep you from the time of trial which will come upon the whole inhabited world, to try those who live on earth. I shall come soon. Keep what you have, so that none may take away your crown. The victor, I shall make him a pillar in the temple of my God, and he shall never go forth from it again; and I shall write upon him the name of my God and the name of the city of my God, the new Jerusalem which will come down from heaven from my God; and also my new name. He who has ears, let him listen to what the Spirit says to the churches.

And to the angel of the church in Laodicea, write: Thus speaks he who is Amen, the faithful and true witness, the beginning of the creation of God: I know your works, that you are neither cold nor hot. You should be cold or hot. Thus because you are lukewarm and neither cold nor hot, I will spew you out of my mouth. Because you say, I am rich, and have grown rich, and have no need; and you do not know that you are the wretched one, the pitiful, the poor, the blind, the naked; I advise you to buy of me gold that has been refined in the fire, so that you may be rich; and white clothes to put upon you so that the shame of your nakedness may not be seen; and collyrium to salve your eyes with so that you may see. And those I love, I reprove and admonish. Be eager, then, and repent. See, I stand at the door and knock. If one hears my voice and opens the door, I shall come in to him, and dine with him, and he with me. The victor, I will grant him to sit with me on my throne, as I too have been victorious and sat with my father on his throne. He who has ears, let him listen to what the Spirit says to the churches.

§ After that, I looked, and behold, a door opened in the sky, and the first voice I heard as the voice of trumpet talking to me, saying: Come up here, and I will show you what must happen after this. And at once I was possessed by the Spirit; and behold, a throne was set in the sky, and there was one sitting upon the throne, and he who was sitting was like stone of jasper and cornelian to see, and a rainbow in a circle around the throne, like emerald to see. And in a circle about the throne were twenty-four thrones, and on the thrones were twenty-four elders seated, in white clothing, and crowns of gold upon their heads. And from the throne issue lightning flashes and voices and thunders;

and seven lamps of fire burn before the throne, which
are the seven spirits of God; and before the throne it is
like a sea of glass, like crystal; and in the presence of
the throne and in a circle about the throne are four
animals, teeming with eyes, both before and behind.
And the first animal is like a lion, and the second
animal is like a calf, and the third animal has a face like
a man's, and the fourth animal is like an eagle flying.
And the four animals, each by each of them, have six
wings, and round about and within they are full of eyes;
and they take no rest, day and night, from saying: Holy
holy holy, the Lord God, the almighty, who was and is
and is to come. And when the animals give glory and
honor and thanks to him who sits upon the throne, who
lives forever and ever, the twenty-four elders shall fall
down before him who sits upon the throne, and shall
worship him who lives forever and ever, and they shall
cast down their crowns before the throne, saying: You
are worthy, our lord and our God, to receive the glory
and the honor and the power, because you created all
things, and through your will they were, and were
created.

§ And I saw, in the right hand of him who was sitting
on the throne, a book-roll written on the inside and on
the back, sealed with seven seals. And I saw a strong
angel who cried in a great voice: Who is worthy to open
the book and break the seals on it? And no one in
heaven or on the earth or below the earth was able to
open the book, or to look at it. And I wept much,
because no one was found worthy to open the book and
look at it. And one of the elders said to me: Weep no
more. See, the lion from the tribe of Judah, the scion of
David, has prevailed to open the book and the seven
seals upon it. And I saw, in the space between the
throne and the four animals and the elders, in their
midst, a Lamb standing, like one that has been
slaughtered, with seven horns and seven eyes, which

are the seven Spirits of God sent about to all the earth.
And he came and took it from the right hand of him
who sat upon the throne. And when he had taken the
book, the four animals and the twenty-four elders fell
down before the Lamb, having each one a harp and
golden bowls filled with incense, which are the prayers
of the saints. And they sang a new song, saying: You
are worthy to take the book and open the seals upon it,
because you were sacrificed and you bought for God by
your own blood people from every tribe and tongue
and people and nation, and for our God you made
them be a kingdom, and priests, and they shall be kings
upon the earth.

And I looked, and I heard the voice of many angels
in a circle about the throne and the animals and the
elders, and the number of them was myriads of myriads and thousands of thousands, saying in a great
voice: The Lamb who has been sacrificed is worthy to
receive the power and the riches and the wisdom
and the strength and the honor and the glory and the
blessing.

And I heard all creation, whatever is in the sky and
on the earth and beneath the earth and in the sea, and
everything which is within these, I heard them saying:
To him who sits upon the throne, and to the Lamb,
blessing and honor and glory and power forever and
ever.

And the four animals said: Amen; and the elders fell
down and worshipped.

§ And I saw when the Lamb opened one of the seven
seals, and I heard one of the four animals saying in a
voice as of thunder: Come. And I looked, and behold,
a white horse, and the rider upon it holding a bow, and
he was given a crown, and he came forth a conqueror
and to conquer. And when he opened the second seal, I
heard the second animal saying: Come. And there

came forth another horse, red, and to the rider upon him it was granted to take peace out of the world, so that they shall kill each other, and he was given a great sword. And when he opened the third seal, I heard the third animal saying: Come. And I looked, and behold, a black horse, and the rider upon him holding a balance in his hand. And I heard as it were a voice in the midst of the four animals, saying: A measure of grain for a denarius, and three measures of barley for a denarius, and do not damage the oil and the wine. And when he opened the fourth seal, I heard the voice of the fourth animal saying: Come. And I looked, and behold, a pale horse, and the rider upon it, his name is Death, and Hades came following him, and he was given power over one quarter of the earth to kill by the sword and hunger and death, and by the wild beasts of the earth.

And when he opened the fifth seal, I saw beneath the altar the souls of those who have been slaughtered because of the word of God and the testimony they maintained. And they cried out in a great voice, saying: How long, O Lord holy and true, will you wait to judge and to avenge our blood from those who live upon the earth? And each of them was given a white robe, and it was said to them that they must rest yet a little time until the number is filled of their fellow slaves and their brothers who are to be killed as they were. And I looked when he opened the sixth seal, and there came a great earthquake, and the sun turned black like cloth of hair, and all the moon became as blood, and the stars of the sky dropped upon the earth as the fig tree casts its unripe figs shaken by a great wind, and the sky shrank upon itself like a scroll curling, and every mountain and island was shaken from its place. And the kings of the earth and the great men and the commanders of thousands and the rich and the strong, all, slave and free, hid themselves in the caves and the rocks of the mountains, and said to the mountains and the rocks:

Fall upon us and hide us from the face of him who sits upon the throne and the anger of the Lamb, because the great day of their anger has come, and who can stand?

§ After that I saw four angels standing upon the four corners of the earth, holding the four winds of the world, so that no wind might blow upon the earth or upon the sea or upon any tree. And I saw another angel going up from the rising place of the sun, carrying the seal of the living God, and he cried in a great voice to the four angels, to whom it was granted that they should devastate the earth and the sea, saying: Do not devastate the earth, or the sea, or the trees, until we mark with the seal the slaves of our God, upon their foreheads. And I heard the number of those who were marked, a hundred and forty-four thousand were marked, from every tribe of the sons of Israel:

From the tribe of Judah twelve thousand marked
   with the seal;
from the tribe of Reuben, twelve thousand;
from the tribe of Gad, twelve thousand;
from the tribe of Asher, twelve thousand;
from the tribe of Naphthali, twelve thousand;
from the tribe of Manassah, twelve thousand;
from the tribe of Simeon, twelve thousand;
from the tribe of Levi, twelve thousand;
from the tribe of Issachar, twelve thousand;
from the tribe of Zebulon, twelve thousand;
from the tribe of Joseph, twelve thousand;
from the tribe of Benjamin, twelve thousand
   marked with the seal.

After that I looked, and behold, a great multitude whose number none could count, from every nation and tribe and people and language, standing before the throne and before the Lamb, wearing white clothing, and palms in their hands; and they cry out in a great voice, saying: Salvation to our God who sits upon the throne, and to the Lamb. And all the angels stood in a circle about the throne and the elders and the four animals, and threw themselves down on their faces before the throne and worshipped God, saying: Amen, blessing and glory and wisdom and thanksgiving and honor and power and strength to our God forever and ever. Amen.

Then one of the elders spoke to me and said: Who are these who have white robes put upon them, and where have they come from? And I said to him: My Lord, you know. And he said to me: These are they who have come out of the great persecution, and washed their robes and made them white in the blood of the Lamb. Therefore these are before the throne of God, and they serve him day and night in his temple, and he who sits upon the throne will spread his tabernacle over them. They will not be hungry or thirsty any more, nor shall the sun strike upon them, nor any burning heat, because the Lamb who is in the place before the throne will be their shepherd and guide them to the springs of the waters of life; and God shall wipe every tear from their eyes.

§ And when he opened the seventh seal there was silence in heaven for about half an hour. And I saw the seven angels who stood before God, and there were given to them seven trumpets. And another angel came and stood at the altar holding a golden censer, and there was given to him much incense, for him to place it with the prayers of all the saints in the golden censer which is before the throne. And the smoke went up from the incense, by the prayers of the saints, from the hand of the angel before God. And the angel took the censer and filled it with fire and from the altar and cast it upon the earth, and there came thunders and voices and lightnings and earthquake; and the seven angels who held the seven trumpets made themselves ready to blow.

The first angel blew his trumpet; and there came hail and fire mixed with blood and it was cast upon the earth, and a third of the earth burned up, and a third of the trees burned up, and all the green grass burned up. And the second angel blew his trumpet; and something like a great mountain burning with fire was cast into the sea, and a third of the sea was turned to blood, and there died a third of the creatures of the sea, those which were alive, and a third of the boats were destroyed. And the third angel blew his trumpet: and there fell from the sky a great star burning like a torch, and it dropped upon a third of the rivers and upon the springs of the waters. The name of this star is called Wormwood. And a third of the waters became wormwood, and many of the people died from the waters because they were made bitter. And the fourth angel blew his trumpet; and a third of the sun was struck, and a third of the moon, and a third of the stars, so that a third of them was darkened, and the day lost a third of its shining, and the night likewise.

And I looked, and I heard an eagle flying in the middle of the sky, saying in a great voice: Woe woe woe to those who live upon the earth from the voices of the trumpet still to come, from the three angels who will blow their trumpets.

§ And the fifth angel blew his trumpet; and I saw a star fallen from the sky upon the earth, and there was given to him the key to the well of the bottomless pit. And he opened the well of the bottomless pit; and there came up smoke from the well like the smoke of a great furnace, and the sun was darkened and the air was darkened from the smoke of the well. And out of the smoke came locusts upon the earth, and power was given them, such power as the scorpions of the earth have. And it was said to them that they must not hurt the grass of the land, or any green thing, or any tree, but only those people who do not wear the mark of the seal of God upon their foreheads. And it was granted to them not that they should kill them but that they should torture them five months; and their torture is like the torture of the scorpion, when he strikes a man. And in those days men shall look for death but not find it, and they shall desire death but death shall escape them. And the appearance of the locusts was like that of horses armed for battle, and upon their heads crowns like gold, and their faces like the faces of men, and they had hair like the hair of women, and their teeth were like those of lions, and they had breastplates like breastplates of iron, and the noise of their wings was as the noise of the chariots of many horses galloping into battle. And they have tails like scorpions, and stings, and in their tails is the power to hurt men for five months. They have as king over them the angel of the bottomless pit, whose name in Hebrew is Abaddon, and in Greek he has the name Apollyon. One woe has come and gone; see, there are still two more woes to come after this.

The sixth angel blew his trumpet; and I heard a single voice from the horns of the altar of gold which is before God, saying to the sixth angel, who held the trumpet: Set free the four angels who are bound, by the great river Euphrates. And the four angels were set free, they who were made ready for the hour and the day and the month and the year, to kill a third part of mankind. And the number of the cavalry of their armies is twenty thousand ten thousands; I heard their number. And thus I saw the horses in my vision and the riders upon them, wearing breastplates colored as fire and hyacinth and sulphur, and the heads of the horses are like the heads of lions, and from their mouths issue fire and smoke and sulphur. From these three afflictions a third of the people were killed, from the fire and smoke and sulphur that came out of their mouths. For the power of the horses is in their mouths and in their tails; for their tails are like snakes with heads, and with these they do harm. And the rest of the people, who had not been killed in these afflictions, did not repent of the works of their hands, so as to stop their worshipping of demons and idols of gold and silver and bronze and stone and wood, which can neither see nor hear nor walk; nor did they repent of their murders or their magic-making or their fornication or their thieving.

§ I saw another strong angel coming down from the sky, clothed in cloud, and the rainbow was on his head, and his face was like the sun, and his feet like pillars of fire, holding in his hand an opened book-roll. He planted his right foot upon the sea, and his left foot upon the land, and cried out in a great voice, as a lion roars. And when he cried, the seven thunders spoke in their own voices. And when the seven thunders spoke, I was about to write, and I heard a voice out of the sky, saying: Seal up what the seven thunders have spoken, and do not write it down. Then the angel whom I saw standing on the sea and the land lifted his right hand into the sky, and swore by him who lives forever and ever, who created the sky and what is in it, and the earth and what is in it, and the sea and what is in it, that there shall be no more time; but in the days of the voice of the seventh angel, when he shall blow his trumpet, the mystery of God shall be accomplished, as he announced to his slaves the prophets. The voice which I heard out of the sky, I heard it again speaking to me, saying: Go, take the open book-roll in the hand of the angel who stands upon the sea and the land. I went toward the angel, bidding him give me the book. And he said to me: Take it, and eat it, and it will make your stomach bitter, but in your mouth it will be sweet as honey. And I took the book from the hand of the angel, and ate it, and in my mouth it was like sweet honey; and when I had eaten it, my stomach was bitter. Then they said to me: You must prophesy again concerning the peoples and the nations and the languages, and many kings.

§ He gave me a reed that was like a staff, saying: Rise up, and measure the temple of God and the altar and those who are worshipping there. But leave out the courtyard which is outside the temple and do not measure it, for it has been given to the Gentiles, and they shall walk the holy city forty-two months. I shall give power to my two witnesses, and they shall prophesy for a thousand two hundred and sixty days, wearing sackcloth.

These are the two olive trees and the two lamps that stand before the Lord of the world. And if anyone tries to injure them, fire comes out of their mouth and eats up their enemies; and if anyone tries to injure them, so must he be killed. These have the power to close the sky, so that no rain may drench the days of their prophesying, and they have power over the waters to turn them into blood, and to strike the earth with every plague, as many times as they wish.

And when they finish their testimony, the beast that comes up from the bottomless pit will do battle with them and defeat them and kill them. Their bodies will lie in the square of the great city, which is called in the way of the spirit Sodom and Egypt, where also their Lord was crucified. Those of the peoples and the tribes and the tongues and the nations shall look upon their bodies three days and a half, and they shall not give up their bodies to be laid away in the tomb. And those who dwell on the earth shall rejoice over them and be happy, and send each other gifts, because these two prophets tormented the dwellers upon the earth.

But after three days and a half the breath of life from God went into them, and they stood upon their feet, and great fear fell upon those who were watching them.

And they heard a great voice out of heaven saying: Come up here. And they went up into heaven in the cloud, and their enemies beheld them. In that hour there was a great earthquake, and a tenth part of the city fell down, and in the earthquake seven thousand names of men were killed, and the rest were full of fear and gave glory to the God of heaven. The second woe has come and gone; behold, the third woe comes soon.

The seventh angel blew his trumpet, and there were great voices in the sky, saying: The kingdom of the world has become the kingdom of our Lord, and of his Christ, and he shall be king forever and ever. Then the twenty-four elders who were seated before God on their thrones fell down upon their faces and worshipped God, saying: We thank you, Lord God almighty, who are and who were, because you have taken your great power and become King. The nations were angry, and your anger came, and the time for the judging of the dead, and for the giving of their wages to your slaves, the prophets and the saints and those who fear your name, the small and the great; and the time to destroy the destroyers of the earth.

Then the temple of God in the sky was opened, and the ark of his covenant was seen in his temple, and there came lightning flashes and voices and thunders and earthquake and much hail.

§ Then there was seen a great portent in the sky, a woman clothed in the sun, and the moon beneath her feet, and upon her head a crown of twelve stars, and she was great with child, and cried out in her travail and the pain of birth. And there was seen another portent in the sky, behold, a dragon ruddy and great, with seven heads and ten horns, and upon his heads seven diadems, and his tail swept a third of the stars from the sky and threw them upon the earth. The dragon stood before the woman who was about to give birth, so that when she bore her child he might devour it. And she bore a son, a male, who will shepherd all the nations with a staff of iron; and her child was snatched away to God and to his throne. Then the woman fled away into the desert, where she has her place made ready for her from God, to be nourished there for a thousand two hundred and sixty days. And there was a battle in the sky, Michael and his angels fighting with the dragon. The dragon and his angels fought, but they did not have the power, and there was no more place found for them in heaven, but he was thrown out, the great dragon, the ancient snake, who is called the Devil and Satan, who leads astray the whole inhabited earth, he was flung to the earth and his angels were flung with him. Then I heard a great voice in the sky, saying: Now is come the salvation and the power and the kingdom of our God and the authority of his Christ, because the prosecutor of our brothers has been cast down, who accused them before our God, day and night. And they defeated him through the blood of the Lamb and the word to which they testified, and they did not love their life; even to the point of death. Therefore, be glad, heavens and those who pitch their tents there. Woe to you, earth and the sea, because the devil has gone down to you, in great anger, knowing that he has little time.

After the dragon saw that he had been flung down upon the earth, he pursued the woman who had borne the male child. There were given to the woman the two wings of the great eagle, so that she might fly into the desert to her place, where she is kept time and times and half a time away from the face of the snake. But the snake cast from his mouth behind the woman water like a river, so that he might have her swept away on the river. But earth helped the woman, and earth opened her mouth and drank down the river which the dragon had cast out of his mouth. Then the dragon was angry because of the woman, and went away to do battle with the rest of her seed, those who keep the commands of

God and hold the testimony of Jesus. And he stood on the sand of the sea.

§ Then I saw a beast coming up from the sea, with ten horns and seven heads, and upon his horns ten diadems, and upon his heads the names of blasphemy. The beast I saw was like a leopard, and his feet as those of a bear, and his mouth as the mouth of a lion. And the dragon gave him his power and his throne and great authority. And one of his heads was as if stricken to death, and his death blow had been healed. Then the whole earth went in wonder after the beast, and they worshipped the dragon because he had given authority to the beast, and they worshipped the beast, saying: Who is like the beast, and who can fight with him? And there was given to him a mouth to speak great things and blasphemies, and he was given authority to act for forty-two months. Then he opened his mouth to blasphemies against God, blaspheming his name and his habitation, those who inhabit the sky. [And it was given to him to do battle against the saints, and defeat them,] and he was given authority over every tribe and people and language and nation.

And all who dwell upon the earth shall worship him, each one whose name is not written in the book of life of the slaughtered Lamb from the establishment of the world. He who has ears, let him listen. He who leads into captivity, into captivity he goes. He who kills with the sword must himself be killed by the sword. Such is the endurance and the faith of the saints.

Then I saw another beast coming up out of the ground, and he had two horns like a lamb, and spoke like a dragon. He exercises all the authority of the first beast in the sight of the first beast; and he causes the earth and all who dwell upon it to worship the first beast, whose death blow was healed. He makes great portents, so that he even makes fire come down from the sky to the earth in the sight of men. And he leads astray the inhabitants of the earth, because of the portents it has been given him to make before the beast, telling the inhabitants of the earth to make an image to the beast, who took the blow of the sword and lived. And it was granted to him to give life to the image of the beast, so that the image of the beast may even speak, and cause those who will not worship the image of the beast to be killed. And he causes all, the small and the great, the rich and the poor, the free and the slaves, he causes the giving of his mark to them upon their right hand or upon their forehead, so that none can buy or sell unless he has the mark, the name of the beast or the number of his name. The secret meaning is read thus. He who has a mind, let him compute the number of the beast; for it is the number of a man. And his number is six hundred and sixty-six.

§ Then I looked, and behold, the Lamb standing on Mount Zion, and with him a hundred and forty-four thousand with his name and the name of his father written on their foreheads. And I heard a voice out of the sky like the voice of many waters and like the voice of great thunder, and the voice which I heard was like the voice of lyre players who play upon their lyres. They sing a new song before the throne and before the four animals and the elders; and none could understand the song except only the hundred and forty-four thousand who have been bought from the earth. These are they who have not been soiled with women; for they are virgin. These are they who follow the Lamb wherever he leads. These were bought from men as a first fruit for God and the Lamb, and in their mouth was found no lie. They are blameless.

Then I saw another angel flying in the middle of the sky, with an everlasting message of good news to announce to those who sit upon the earth and to every nation and tribe and language and people, saying in a great voice: Fear God, and give glory to him, because the hour of his judgment is come, and worship him who made the sky and the earth and the sea and the springs of waters. And another second angel followed him saying: Babylon the great is fallen, is fallen, she who from the wine of the fury of her lust has drunk up all the nations. And another third angel followed them saying in a great voice: If anyone worships the beast and his image, and takes the mark upon his forehead or his hand, he himself also shall drink of the wine of the fury of God, which has been poured of unmixed wine in the cup of his anger, and he shall be tortured with fire and sulphur before the holy angels and before the Lamb. And the smoke of their torture shall go up forever and ever, and they shall not rest, day and night, they who worship the beast and his image, and any who takes the mark of his name.

Such is the endurance of the saints, who keep the commands of God and the faith of Jesus.

And I heard a voice out of the sky saying: Write. Blessed are the dead who die in the Lord henceforth. Yes, says the Spirit, so that they may rest from their labors; for what they have done goes with them.

Then I looked, and behold, a white cloud, and sitting upon the cloud one who was like the son of man, wearing upon his head a crown of gold and in his hand a sharp sickle. And another angel came out of the temple, crying in a great voice to him who sat upon the cloud: Put forth your sickle and reap, for the time to reap has come, because the harvest of the earth is ripe. And he who was sitting upon the cloud put forth his sickle upon the earth, and the earth was harvested. And another angel came out of the temple in the sky, he also having a sharp sickle. And another angel came from the altar, he who has charge of the fire, and spoke in a great voice to the holder of the sharp sickle, saying: Put forth your sharp sickle and cut the clusters on the vine of the earth, because its grapes are ripe. And the angel put forth his sickle on the earth, and gathered from the vine of the earth and put the grapes in the great press of the anger of God. And the press was trampled outside the city, and the blood from the press came up to the bridles of the horses, for sixteen hundred furlongs.

§ Then I saw another portent in the sky, great and wonderful, seven angels who have seven plagues which are the last, because the anger of God is fulfilled in them. And I saw what was like a sea of glass mixed with fire, and those who had come triumphant from the beast and his image and the number of his name standing by the sea of glass, with the lyres of God. They sang the song of Moses the slave of God and the song of the Lamb, saying: Great and wonderful are your works, Lord God almighty; just and true your ways, King of the nations; who shall not fear you, Lord, and glorify your name? Because you alone are holy, because all the nations will come and worship before you, because your judgments are made manifest.

After this I looked, and the temple of the pavilion of testimony was opened in heaven, and the seven angels with the seven plagues came out of the temple wearing clean bright linen and girt beneath the arms with belts of gold. And one of the four animals gave to the seven angels seven bowls full of the anger of the God who lives forever and ever. And the temple was full of the smoke of the glory of God, and of his power, and no one was able to go into the temple, until the seven plagues of the seven angels are done with.

§ Then I heard a great voice from the temple saying to the seven angels: Go and pour out the seven bowls of the anger of God upon the earth. And the first went forth and poured out his bowl upon the earth, and there was a sad sore wound inflicted upon the men who have the mark of the beast and worship his image. Then the second poured out his bowl upon the sea; and there was blood as from a dead man, and every living thing died which was in the sea. And the third poured out his bowl into the rivers and the springs of the waters; and they turned to blood. I heard the angel of the waters saying: You are just, you who are and were, the holy one, because you made these judgments, because they poured out the blood of the saints and the prophets, and you have given them blood to drink. They are worthy of this. And I heard from the altar a voice saying: Yes, Lord God almighty, true and just are your judgments. Then the fourth poured out his bowl upon the sun; and it was granted to it to burn men in fire. And men were burned in a great blaze, and they blasphemed the name of God who holds authority over these plagues, and did not repent so as to give him glory. The fifth poured out his bowl upon the throne of the beast; and his kingdom turned dark, and they chewed their tongues from pain, and blasphemed the God of heaven because of their pain and their wounds, and did not repent of their works. And the sixth poured out his bowl upon the great river Euphrates; and its water was dried, so as to make ready the way of the kings from the rising of the sun. And I saw from the mouth of the dragon and from the mouth of the beast and from the mouth of the false prophet three unclean breaths, like frogs; for these are breaths of spirits, making portents, which go out to the kings of all the world, to gather them for the battle of the great day of almighty God.

Behold, I come like a thief; blessed is he who is watchful and keeps care of his clothes, so that he does not walk about naked and people see his disorderliness.

And he brought them together in the place which is called in Hebrew Armageddon.

Then the seventh poured out his bowl upon the air; and a great voice came out of the temple from the throne, saying: It is done. And there were lightning flashes and voices and thunders, and there was a great earthquake, such as there has not been since man has been upon the earth, so great was this earthquake. And the great city was made into three parts, and the cities of the nations fell down. Then Babylon the great was remembered before God, to give her the cup of the wine of the fury of his anger. And every island fled, and the mountains were not found. And hail heavy as talents' weight came down from the sky upon men; and the men blasphemed God from the affliction of the hail, for its affliction is very great.

§ Then there came one of the seven angels who held the bowls and talked with me, saying: Come here, I will show you the judgment upon the great harlot who sits upon many waters, with whom the kings of the earth have made free, and the inhabitants of the earth have been made drunk on the wine of her lechery. He took me away in the spirit to a deserted place. And I saw a woman sitting on a scarlet beast, full of the names of blasphemy, with seven heads and ten horns. The woman was wearing purple and scarlet, and gilded with gold and precious stone and pearls, with a golden cup in her hand, full of the abomination and filthiness of her harlotry, and on her forehead a name written, a mystery, Babylon the Great, the Mother of Harlots and of the Abominations of the Earth. And I saw the woman drunk from the blood of the saints and the blood of the martyrs of Jesus. And I wondered, seeing her, with a great wonder. Then the angel said to me: Why did you wonder? I will tell you the mystery of the woman and of the beast who carries her, who has the seven heads and the ten horns. The beast you saw was and is not, and will come up out of the bottomless pit and go to destruction; and the inhabitants of the earth will admire him, they whose names have not been written in the book of life from the establishment of the world, when they see the beast and that he was and is not and is to be. Thus interprets the mind which has wisdom. The seven heads are seven hills, where the

woman sits upon them. And there are seven kings.
Five have fallen, one is, the other has not come yet, and
when he comes, short is the time he is to stay. And the
beast who was and is not, he too is the eighth and
comes from the seven, and he goes to destruction. And
the ten horns you saw are ten kings, who have not yet
taken their kingdom, but take their authority as kings
for one season together with the beast. These have a
single will, and they give their power and authority to
the beast. These shall fight with the Lamb and the
Lamb shall defeat them, because he is the Lord of
Lords and the King of Kings, and those on his side are
called and chosen and faithful. Then he said to me: The
waters you saw, on whom the harlot is sitting, are
peoples and multitudes and nations and tongues. And
the ten horns you saw, and the beast, they shall hate the
harlot and make her desolate and naked, and eat her
flesh, and burn her with fire; for God has given it into
their hearts to do his will, and make one purpose and
give their kingship to the beast, until the words of God
are fulfilled. And the woman you saw is the great city
who holds kingship over the kings of the earth.

§ After that I saw another angel coming down from the
sky, having great authority, and the earth was lit with
his glory. And he cried out in a strong voice, saying:
Babylon the great is fallen, is fallen, and has become
the habitation of demons and the prison of every
unclean spirit and the prison of every bird that is
unclean and detested, because all the nations have
drunk of the wine of the fury of her lechery, and the
kings of the earth have made free with her, and the
merchants of the earth have become rich from the
power of her luxury.

And I heard another voice out of the sky saying:
Come out of her, my people, so that you may not have
any part in her sins, and may not share any of her
afflictions; because her sins are stuck fast, and reach the

sky, and God has remembered her wrongdoings. Give to her duly as she has given, and double what is double according to her acts; in the cup where she has mixed mix double for her; as much as she has glorified herself and taken her delight, give her in like measure torment and sorrow; since in her heart she says: I sit as a queen, and I am not widowed, and I cannot look upon sorrow. Because of this in one day her afflictions will come, death and sorrow and hunger, and she shall be burned in the fire; because God who has judged her is a strong master. And the kings of the earth, who reveled with her and took their delight with her, shall weep and beat themselves over her when they see the smoke of her burning, standing far off for fear of her torment, saying: Woe woe for you, the great city, Babylon the city, the strong city, because in a single hour your judgment came. And the merchants of the earth shall weep and mourn over her, because no one buys their cargo any more, their cargo of gold and silver and precious stone and pearls and linen and purple and silk and scarlet, and every aromatic wood and every article of ivory and every article of most precious wood and bronze and iron and marble, and cinnamon and cardamon and incense and perfume and frankincense and wine and oil and fine flour and wheat and cattle and sheep, their cargo of horses and chariots and bodies, and the souls of men. And the harvest of the desire of your soul is gone from you, and all that was fat and bright is perished from you, and they shall never find it again. The dealers in these things, who grew rich from her, shall stand far off for fear of her torment weeping and mourning, saying: Woe woe for the great city, who was clothed in linen and purple and scarlet, and gilded in gold and precious stone and pearl, because in a single hour all these riches were made desolate.

And every shipmaster and every navigator of the coast and the sailors and they who work on the sea stood far off and cried out as they saw the smoke of her burning, saying: Who is like the great city? And they threw dust on their heads and cried out in tears and lamentations: Woe woe for the city, the great city, from whom all who have ships on the sea grew rich, from her prosperity; because in a single hour she is made desolate.

Rejoice over her, heaven and saints and apostles and prophets, because God has judged her with your judgment.

Then one strong angel lifted up a stone like a great millstone and threw it into the sea, saying: With such a stroke Babylon the great city shall be stricken and shall not be found any more. And the voice of lyre players and singers and flute players and trumpeters shall not be heard in you any more, and every craftsman of every craft shall not be found in you any more, and the voice of the mill shall not be heard in you any more, and the light of the lamp shall not shine in you any more, and the voice of the groom and the bride shall not be heard in you any more; because your merchants were the great men of the earth, because in your witchery all the nations wandered astray. And in her was found the blood of the prophets and the saints and all who were slaughtered upon the earth.

§ After this I heard a great voice as of a great multitude in heaven, saying: Alleluia: the salvation and the glory and the power of our God, because his judgments are true and just; because he judged the great harlot who spoiled the earth with her harlotry, and he avenged the blood of his slaves shed by her hand. And they said again: Alleluia. And the smoke of her goes up forever and ever. Then the twenty-four elders fell down, and the four animals, and worshipped the God who sits upon the throne, saying: Amen, alleluia. And a voice came from the throne, saying: Praise our God, all you his slaves, who fear him, the small and the great. And I heard a voice as of a great multitude and as the voice of many waters and as the voice of strong thunders, saying: Alleluia: because the Lord our God the almighty is king. Let us rejoice and be glad, and we shall give glory to him, because the marriage of the Lamb has come, and his wife has made herself ready, and it has been given to her to clothe herself in bright clean linen; for the linen is the righteousness of the saints. And he said to me: Write: Blessed are they who have been called to the feast of the marriage of the Lamb. And he said to me: These are the true words of God. And I fell down before his feet to worship him. But he said to me: See that you do not. I am your fellow slave and the fellow slave of your brothers who keep the testimony of Jesus. Give your worship to God. For the testimony of Jesus is the spirit of prophecy.

Then I saw the sky open, and behold, a white horse, and the rider upon him called faithful and true, and in righteousness he judges and does battle. His eyes are flame of fire, and on his head are many diadems, inscribed with the name which no one knows except himself, and he wears a mantle dyed in blood, and his name is called the Word of God. And the armies which are in heaven followed him on white horses, wearing linen white and clean. And from his mouth projects a sharp sword, so that he may strike the nations; he will shepherd them with a staff of iron; and he will trample the press of the wine of the fury of the anger of God almighty. He wears upon his mantle and upon his thigh the name written: King of Kings and Lord of Lords.

Then I saw an angel standing in the sun, and he cried out in a great voice saying to all the birds that fly in the middle air: Come, gather here to the great feast of God, so that you may eat the flesh of kings and the flesh of captains of thousands and the flesh of the strong and the flesh of horses and of their riders, and the flesh of all the free and the slaves and the small and the great. And I saw the beast and the kings of the earth and their armies gathered to do battle with him who sits upon the horse and with his army. Then the beast was captured, and with him the false prophet, who made the portents in his presence, by which he led astray those who took the mark of the beast and worshipped his image. The two of them were cast alive into the lake of the fire that burns with sulphur. And the rest were killed by the sword of the rider on the horse, the sword which projects from his mouth, and all the birds fed upon their flesh.

§ Then I saw an angel coming down from the sky, holding the key to the bottomless pit and a great chain in his hand. And he seized the dragon, the ancient snake, who is the Devil and the Satan, and bound him for a thousand years, and cast him into the bottomless pit, and locked it and sealed it over him, so that he may lead the nations astray no longer, not until the thousand years are ended. After that he must be set free for a little time.

And I saw thrones, and there were some seated upon them, and judgment was given by them; and I saw the souls of those killed with the ax for the testimony of Jesus and the word of God, and who did not worship the beast or his image or take his mark upon their forehead and their hand. And they came to life and were kings with Christ for a thousand years. The rest of the dead did not come to life until the thousand years were ended.

This is the first resurrection. Blessed and holy is any of those who have part in the first resurrection. Over them the second death has no power, but they shall be priests of God and Christ, and be kings with him for the thousand years.

And when the thousand years are ended, Satan shall be set free from his prison, and will go out to lead astray the nations also who are in the four corners of the earth, Gog and Magog, to lead them into battle, and their number is as the sand of the sea.

And they went up across the width of the earth, and

encircled the encampment of the saints and the beloved city; and fire came down from heaven and ate them up; and the devil, who led them astray, was cast into the lake of fire and sulphur, where is also the beast, and the false prophet, and they shall be tortured day and night forever and ever.

And I saw a throne, great, white, and sitting upon it was he from whose face the earth and the sky fled, and no place was found for them. And I saw the dead, the great and the small, standing before the throne, and books were opened. And another book was opened, which is the book of life. And the dead were judged from what was written in the books, each according to his works. And the sea gave up the dead that were in her, and Death and Hades gave up the dead that were in them, and each was judged according to his works. And Death and Hades were cast into the lake of fire. This is the second death, the lake of the fire. And if anyone was not found written in the book of life, he was cast into the lake of fire.

§ I saw a new heaven and a new earth; for the first heaven and the first earth are gone, and the sea is no more. And I saw the holy city, the new Jerusalem, coming down out of heaven from God, and made ready as a bride is arrayed for her husband. And I heard a great voice from the throne saying: Behold, the tabernacle of God among men, and he shall dwell with them, and they shall be his people, and God himself shall be among them and shall wipe every tear from their eyes, and death shall not be any more, nor shall sorrow nor lamentation nor pain be any more, because the first things have gone. And he who sat upon the throne said: Behold, I make all new. And he said: Write, because these words are trustworthy and true. And he said to me: They have come to pass. I am alpha and omega, the beginning and the end. I shall give to him who is thirsty from the spring of the water of life, a free gift.

The victor will inherit these things, and I shall be his God, and he will be my son. To the cowards and the unbelievers and the corrupt and the murderers and the fornicators and the wizards and the idolaters and all who are false, their portion shall be in the lake that burns with fire and sulphur, which is the second death.

Then there came one of the seven angels who held the seven bowls full of the seven last plagues, and he talked with me, saying: Come here, I will show you the bride, the wife of the Lamb. And he took me away, in the spirit, to a mountain great and high, and showed me the holy city Jerusalem coming down out of heaven from God, wearing the glory of God. Her radiance is like most precious stone, like stone of jasper that shines as crystal. She has a wall great and high, with twelve gates, and on the gates twelve angels, and names inscribed, which are of the twelve tribes of the sons of Israel. On the east three gates, and on the north three gates, and on the south three gates, and on the west three gates. And the wall of the city has twelve lower courses, and on them the twelve names of the twelve apostles of the Lamb.

And he who was talking with me had a measuring rod of gold, to measure the city and its gates and its wall. The city is set foursquare and its length is as much as its width. And he measured the city with his rod at twelve thousand furlongs; the length and the width and the height of it are equal. And he measured the wall at a hundred and forty-four cubits, according to the measurement of man, which is that of an angel. The material of the wall is jasper, and the city is gold clear like clear glass. The lower courses of the wall of the city are adorned with every precious stone. The first course is jasper; the second sapphire; the third chalcedony; the fourth emerald; the fifth sardonyx; the sixth cornelian; the seventh chrysolite; the eighth beryl; the ninth topaz; the tenth chrysoprase; the eleventh hyacinth; the twelfth amethyst. And the twelve gates were twelve pearls; gate by gate each was a single pearl. The great street of the city is gold clear as translucent glass. I saw no temple in it; for the Lord God almighty is its temple; and the Lamb. And the city has no need of the sun or the moon, to shine on it, for the glory of God illuminates it, and its lamp is the Lamb. And the nations shall walk about through its light, and the kings of the earth bring their glory into it; and its gates shall never be closed for the day, for there will be no night there; and they shall bring the glory and honor of the nations into it. Nor shall anything that is profane enter into it, nor anyone who practices foulness and lying, but only they who are written in the book of life of the Lamb.

§ And he showed me the river of the water of life shining like crystal and issuing from the throne of God and the Lamb. Between the great street of the city and the river which were on one side and the other was the tree of life, bearing twelve fruits, yielding its fruit month by month, and the leaves of the tree for the healing of the nations. Everything accursed shall be gone henceforth. And the throne of God and the Lamb shall be in it, and his slaves shall serve him, and they shall see his face, and his name shall be upon their foreheads. And there will be no night any more, nor shall they have any need of the light of the lamp and the light of the sun, because the Lord God will illuminate them, and they shall be kings forever and ever.

Then he said to me: These words are trustworthy and true, and the Lord God of the spirits of the prophets sent his angel to show his slaves what must happen soon. Behold, I shall come soon. Blessed is he who keeps the words of the prophecy of this book.

And I, John, am he who heard and saw these things. And when I heard and saw, I fell down to worship before the feet of the angel who showed me these things. But he said to me: See that you do not. I am your fellow slave and the fellow slave of your brothers the prophets and those who keep the words of this book. Give your worship to God.

And he said to me: Do not seal up the words of the prophecy of this book, for the time is near. Let the wrongdoer do wrong still, let the foul man be foul still, let the righteous man do right still, let the saint be saintly still. Behold, I shall come soon, and my repayment comes with me, to give to each according to his work. I am alpha and omega, the first and the last, the beginning and the end. Blessed are they who wash their robes, so that they shall have access to the tree of life and may enter by the gates into the city. Outside shall be the dogs and the wizards and the fornicators and the idolaters and all who love and do falsehood.

I Jesus sent my angel to bear witness to these things for you to the churches. I am the scion and generation of David, the shining star, the morning star.

And the Spirit and the bride say: Come. Let him who hears say: Come. Let him who is thirsty come, let him who wishes take the water of life, a free gift.

For all who hear, I bear witness to the words of the prophecy of this book. If anyone adds to them, God will inflict upon him the punishments that have been written in this book; and if anyone takes away from the words of the book of this prophecy, God will take away his share of the tree of life and the holy city, which have been written in this book.

And he who bears witness to these things says: Yes, I come soon. Amen, come, Lord Jesus.

May the grace of the Lord Jesus be with all.

NOTES

MARK

1.14 "After John was betrayed." John was turned in or handed over *(paradidōmi)* to the authorities, but the word frequently implies treachery, as in Judas's betrayal, 3.19, 14.18, etc.

3.12 "not to divulge what he was doing." Literally, "not to make him known."

3.18 "Cananaean." Or "the zealot," see Matthew 10.4 and Luke 6.15. Cananaean does not refer to a place.

6.3 "made it difficult for him." *Eskandalizonto.* See the note on Matthew 5.29. Here we are to understand that the disbelief of his own people actually impeded Jesus in the exercise of his powers. In Matthew 13.58 it merely made him unwilling.

6.22 "the daughter of Herodias." Some manuscripts would make this girl "his daughter Herodias."

6.52   "their hearts had become impenetrable." More literally, "their hearts were hardened" (perfect passive participle of *pōreō);* but the sense is not that they were hardhearted or pitiless, but that meaning and message did not get through to them. Compare Matthew 13.15.

7.3   "elders"; or "ancestors."

8.24   Here, as in 16.4, the word is *anablepō.* In neither place does the usual sense, "look up," seem to have any point. Here, possibly, the meaning is that the man recovered some sight. The prefix *ana* frequently indicates that something is done again.

9.43   "Gehenna." Here I cannot do better than quote Nineham's note in full: *"hell:* A word with so many irrelevant associations that it is probably better to keep to the original word, *Gehenna.* This was a valley west of Jerusalem where at one time children were sacrificed to the god Moloch (2 Kings 23.10, Jer. 7.31, 19.5f, 32.35); after being desecrated by Josiah it came to be used as a refuse dump for Jerusalem, a fact which explains the imagery of worm and fire borrowed from Isaiah 66.24 in v. 48. The suggestion is of maggots preying on offal and fires perpetually smoldering for the destruction of refuse. Because of all its bad associations, the Jewish imagination had come to picture *Gehenna* as the place of future torment for the wicked cf. e.g. 2 Esdras 7.36."

10.30   "now in this time . . . persecutions." I follow Nineham in thinking these words are probably spurious.

14.3   "Simon the leper." In Matthew 26.6, this

scene of anointing also takes place in the house of Simon the leper. But it remains inconceivable that in this time and place any leper could have had his own house and entertained guests at dinner. This Simon remains a mystery. Note, however, that in John 12.1–3, the anointing takes place in the house of Lazarus; and though this Lazarus was surely no leper, his name has in later times been constantly associated with leprosy in such terms as "lazaretto" and "lazarhouse." This may be through confusion with Lazarus the beggar of Luke 16.20–21, who, though not described as a leper, was covered with sores. But there is no explanation of how the confusion could have existed *before* Mark's composition.

14.34 "keep watch." Or "stay awake." So too in 14.37.

14.46 "bound him." A little free, perhaps, but the normal sense of the word *krateō*, "seized him," as in 49 below, would be tautologous here. "Overpowered" would imply a struggle. What the verb really means is that they prevailed over him, got him into their power or under their control.

14.72 "threw himself down." Meaning uncertain, variously translated.

16.4 "looking again." See 8.24 and note.

16.8 In many manuscripts the Gospel of Mark ends here.

16.20 The following two sentences constitute an alternative ending to follow on 16.8.

1.1 "origin" is *genesis,* that is, "birth," but also "genealogy." "son," that is, "descendant."

1.2 "was the father of." Literally (throughout 2–16) "begot."

1.16 "the Christ." Greek *christos,* "the anointed," "the Messiah."

1.18 "engaged." The engagement is regarded as a marriage except that it has not been consummated. So Joseph is called her husband, Mary is called his wife, and the word translated "put away" is the same as that used elsewhere for "divorce."

2.1 "Magians." *Magoi.* In Classical Greek, *Magos* denotes: 1. a member of one of the tribes of the Medes; 2. a priest or seer, within the Medo-Persian empire, who must belong to this tribe. This may be the sense here, but it is not certain, and I have thought it best to leave the term as a proper name. Though *Magos* gives us "magic," these Magi were not necessarily magicians, and though they may well have been astrologers, to translate "astrologers" is to say more (despite the star) than the Greek does.

2.13 "Awake." Or, "when you awake." So also in verse 20.

3.1 "preaching." Here and elsewhere the word *kēryssō* has been translated, according to convention, "preach." Literally, it denotes the activity of a herald (*kēryx*), the announcing or proclamation of a message; in this case, the gospel or the good news. It is thus to be distinguished from "teaching" (*didaskō*), for which see 4.23 and note.

4.1 "tested." The word *peirazō* may be translated "test" or "make trial of" (the basic meaning) or "tempt." In this case the testing is done by means of temptation.

4.12 "betrayed." See the note on Mark 1.14.

4.15 "Gentiles." The plural of *ethnos*, which means a nation or tribe. In the Gospels, this plural usually, but not always, signifies all who are not Jews.

4.23 "teaching." The word is *didaskō*, to be clearly distinguished from *kēryssō*, "preach," see note on 3.1. "Teaching" covers not only such extended discourses as the "Sermon on the Mount" but also the expounding of the scriptures, the parables, and other sayings of Jesus, and answers to questions and challenges.

5.22 "fool." Greek *raka;* but the exact meaning is not known.
"sinner." Greek *mōros*, regularly "fool." But this second insult is obviously worse than the other, and I think it may not here mean "fool" but denote immorality or lewdness, a sense found several times in Euripides.
"Gehenna." See Mark 9.43.

5.29 "makes you go amiss." The Greek verb is *skandalizō*. The basic concept is that of a physical block (*skandalon*) which impedes right progress or understanding and causes diversion into wrong courses, sin, or error, or at least causes difficulty. There is no one English word which will translate *skandalon* or *skandalizō*. For other notes on the term, see on Matthew 13.21, 15.12, 16.23, 17.27, 26.31; Mark 6.3.

5.47 "pagans." *Ethnikoi*, found here and at 6.7

and 18.17, is perhaps to be distinguished from *ethnē* (see note on 4.15) as being more a term of reproach.

6.2   "hypocrites." *Hypokritēs* means "actor." The people in question are here not so much dissemblers as those who put on an act, or make a big production of their good works.

6.11   "sufficient." A guess. *Epiousios* is rare and of uncertain meaning. Enough for the day, day by day? see below, 34.

6.13   "temptation." Or "do not bring us to the time of trial." *Periasmos*, from *peirazō;* see on 4.1, and see Luke 22.40.
      "from evil." Or "from the evil one."

6:24   "mammōn." That is, money.

8.6   "son." Greek *pais*. This means "child" but, like Latin *puer*, can also mean "servant," here and elsewhere. Luke (7.2), telling the same story, definitely calls the sufferer a slave *(doulos)*, whereas John (4.46) calls him the man's son.

9.18   "Official." *Archōn*. This may mean no more here than "leading citizen" or "important man." Mark (5.22) calls him Jairus, one of the leaders of the synagogue.

10.2   "apostles." The noun *apostolos* is formed from the verb *apostellō*, "send forth," which appears below (5).

11.5   "are told good news." Or "have the gospel preached to them." These phrases, in fact, mean the same thing. See above, 3.1, and note.

13.15   "stiffened." Matthew uses the word *pachynō* in much the same sense as Mark's *pōreō*, see Mark 6.52 and note.

13.21   "does not stand fast." Or "is driven from his course"; *skandalizetai*, see on 5.29.

14.1 "children." Or "servants." Plural of *pais*.
See 8.6 and note.

15.2 "elders." Or "ancestors," see note on
Mark 7.3.

15.12. "objected." The Greek is *skandalizō*, on
which see 5.29 and note. The sense here is
unusual. One is tempted to translate
"were scandalized," which would fit the
sense, and "scandal," like "slander," does
derive from *skandalon*. But in view of the
basic sense, it is more likely that the
Pharisees were "put off."

16.19 "close . . . open." Perhaps, more literally,
"bind . . . loose."

16.23 "you would put me off." Literally, "you
are my *skandalon*," that is, my misleader,
thus like the arch-misleader, Satan.

17.27 "cause . . . trouble." *Skandalizō* again.
The use of the term here introduces a
commentary on it in chapter 18, where it
appears as "leads astray" (6), "troubles
which shall be caused" (7), "makes you go
amiss" (8,9).

18.24 "ten thousand talents." A fantastic sum,
amounting to millions. The denarius, mentioned below (28) is a day's wage for a
laborer, 20.2. "stater." This coin was
worth four drachmas, that is, twice two.

19.12 "sexless men." The Greek word used
here is *eunouchos*, but I have refrained
from "eunuch" because only those "made
sexless by other men" are commonly so
called in English (I do not believe that
"have made themselves sexless" denotes
self-castration). *Eunouchos* means "bed-
keeper." It first appears in Herodotus
and applies particularly to the King of
Persia's castrated harem guards, who also,
as the only males admitted to the bed-

chamber, were his trusted confidential agents.

21.3 "their master." Or "the Lord."

21.35 "one they stoned." I think the sense intended may well be: "One they beat to death, and one they killed with weapons, and one they stoned to death."

23.12 "He who is greater than you." So I read it. But the meaning may be "he who is greatest (the greater) among you."

25.21 "come in and share your master's festivities." Literally, "enter into the joy *(chara)* of your master." But as the word *euphrosynē* can mean either a state of happiness or a joyous occasion, a banquet, so I think *chara* is here similarly extended. Here and in other passages, the chosen come inside (enter) to the feast, and those not chosen are shut out in the dark.

26.7 "reclined." The custom at dinner was to recline, not sit, at table. See note on Luke 7.38.

26.31 "made to fail me." From *skandalizō* again.

26.38 "keep watch." That is, or implies, "stay awake."

26.50 See note on Mark 14.46.

27.16 In a number of manuscripts of Matthew the man is called *Jesus* Barabbas. Bar-Abbas means simply the son of the father.

28.2 In view of the Greek preference for the simple past tense (aorist) where a pluperfect is really meant, I believe it is possible to translate the first part of this sentence: "And behold, there *had been* a great earthquake, for the angel of the Lord *had come* down."

1.35 "man." Or "husband."

2.14 Or (variant reading) "good will to men."

2.26 "Anointed." That is, the Christ, or Messiah.

2.37 Or possibly "a widow eighty-four years old."

3.14 "No extortion." The word practically translates into "shakedown."

3.16 "spoke forth." The word *apokrinomai* is usually translated "answer," but in the Gospels is frequently used where no question is indicated; but in this particular case "answer" would be acceptable.

3.23–38 For this list, as for that in Matthew 1.2–16, I have done my best to be reasonably consistent. No two translations that I have consulted agree exactly on spellings. Also, some names appear in both Greek and Hebrew forms. For "Old Testament characters" I have generally preferred the Hebrew forms (written for our texts, of course, in Greek letters). But Judah of the Old Testament really has the same name as Judas of the New, and Jacob is the same as James; and Jesus is the Greek form of Joshua.

4.43 "bring the good news." That is, preach the gospel.

7.38 "stood behind by his feet." Jesus, in accordance with the custom of the time and place, was not sitting at a table, but reclining on a couch with his head toward the table and his feet away from it.

11.3 "sufficient." See Matthew 6.11 and note.

11.51 "the temple." Strictly, "the house," but

where the stoning of Zachariah is mentioned in 2 Chronicles 24 it is "the house of God."

12.20 "that soul." That is, "that life," since *psychē* means both "soul" and "life."

16.22 "to recline close by Abraham." Literally, "to Abraham's bosom," but what this seems to mean is reclining close by him at a feast. See also John 13.23, and for feasting with Abraham, Isaac and Jacob, Matthew 8.11.

21.19 "possess your own souls." Or "win your lives."

21.25 "nations." Or "Gentiles."

22.19–20 The words enclosed in square brackets are not found in all manuscripts, and are thought by many, if not most, scholars to be a later addition.

23.16 "teach him a lesson." The word *paideuō* properly means "educate," but in Biblical Greek it seems to have the special sense "chastise," that is, have someone whipped.

JOHN

1.1 "the word was God." Or, more literally, "God was the word."

1.15 "he cried out, saying." Or "saying: This is he of whom I said."

1.38 "master." That is, "teacher."

1.41 "Messiah." See Matthew 1.16 and note.

1.42 "Cephas" and "Peter" both mean "rock." See Matthew 16.18.

2.4 "madam." Greek *gynai,* that is, the form of direct address, or vocative, of *gyne.*

Gyne translates into "woman," "lady," and "wife." Here "woman" in English is merely rude, and in tragedy *gynai* is, or may be, a term of respect, used by messengers and slaves in addressing queens and great ladies. For the vocative there is *no* good English equivalent, and in translating I have used various words. Here, perhaps, "mother"?

3.3 "from above." Or "again."

3.5 "spirit." The word *pneuma* means both "spirit" and "wind" as in verse 8 below.

4.9 "Jew." John uses the term Jew, usually in the plural, *Ioudaioi,* far more frequently than the other three evangelists put together. Here the use seems to be straightforward and clear. Elsewhere, as in 5.10, 16, 18, "Jews" means the religious authorities who appear in the other gospels, and sometimes in John, as any or all of "high priests, scribes and Pharisees." Still another usage is exemplified in 11.19 where, from the sequence of thought, "Jews" plainly means "the people of Jerusalem."

4.9 "have no dealings with." Greek *ou gar synchrōntai,* more literally, "do not share what they use," that is, do not eat and drink from the same vessels. See Marsh, p. 210.

5.2 For the Sheep Gate, see Nehemiah 3.1. The pool is evidently a swimming pool. The better-known form for the name Bethzatha is Bethesda.

5.3–4 The bracketed words are missing from many manuscripts and are deleted by many editors and translators; but without context the reply of the paralytic to Jesus is incomprehensible.

5.41 I have translated *doxa* as "glory" because
that is its regular meaning in the New
Testament. But in Classical Greek *doxa*
also means "opinion," and it goes with the
verb *dokeō*, "think," "suppose," which
appears in this very passage: "because you
think they have life everlasting" (verse 39
just above; so also verse 45 below). So
verse 41 could also read either "I do not
derive my opinion from men" or "I do not
accept the opinion of men." Contrast
verse 42, "I know" *(egnōka)*. Then in
verse 44 the opinion, not glory, which men
take from each other is contrasted with the
true thought which comes from God
alone. See 12.43.

6.26 "signs." The word is *sēmeia*, sometimes
translated "miracles" or "portents."

6.66 "because of this." Or "from this time on,"
but then "thenceforth" would be repeti-
tious.

6.70 "an enemy." The Greek is *diabolos;* "a
devil"? I prefer "an enemy" or "my
enemy."

7.53– The material here enclosed in square
8.11 brackets is missing entirely from some
manuscripts, and placed elsewhere in others. Most modern editors and commenta-
tors reject it as spurious.

8.28 "when you raise the son of man aloft."
The allusion is probably to his crucifixion,
but may also hint at his ultimate exalta-
tion.

8.45 "and so is his father." Or "and the father
of it (that is, the lie, or falsehood)."

10.24 "agitating our spirits." Or "keeping us in
suspense."

11.19 "Jews." In the context, this plainly means

"the people of Jerusalem." See the note on 4.9.

11.33 "raged at his own spirit." Very difficult. The word *embrimaomai* seems to mean, originally, "be angry with" (Mark 14.5) or "enjoin sternly" (Matthew 9.30; Mark 1.43). Here the object of the verb is plainly his own spirit; the idiom in verse 38 below shows inward disturbance. I had thought at first that the meaning would be that Jesus was angry with himself, and the words could easily bear that meaning. And he has been told twice that he has failed his friend. But self-reproach is not to the point; self-incitement is. I take it that not in anger but something close to it, furious urgency, Jesus is nerving himself to an extraordinary act. "Sternly enjoined" is not strong enough; therefore, "raged at."

12.11 "going away." That is, leaving the flock, deserting, defecting.

12.34 "remains." That is, here or *with us*.
"must be lifted aloft." That is, taken away *from us*. See also 8.28.

12.43 "glory of God." The word *doxa,* used here twice, can mean both "opinion" and "glory." See the note on 5.41.

13.2 "betray him." This I take to be the meaning of the Greek, rather than "the devil had already put it into the heart of Judas . . . to betray him."

13.19 "I am I." Or, simply, "I am."

15.27 "Do you also bear witness." Or "You also are my witnesses."

16.2 "will be thought to be doing a service to God." Or "will think he is doing a service to God."

17.15 "evil." Or "the evil one."

19.20 "Jews." That is, the people of Jerusalem, see the notes on 4.9 and 11.18.

THE REVELATION OF JOHN

22.21 Or "with his saints."